The Ulster Defence Regiment

by the same author

The RUC: A Force Under Fire

CHRIS RYDER

The Ulster Defence Regiment

AN INSTRUMENT OF PEACE?

Methuen

First published in Great Britain 1991
by Methuen London
Michelin House, 81 Fulham Road, London SW3 6RB

Copyright © 1991 Chris Ryder

The author has asserted his moral rights

The copyright in extracts quoted in this book is as follows:
p. 59 © 1972 *Belfast Telegraph*
p. 66 © 1974 *Defence*
p. 181 © 1990 the UDR
p. 186 © 1980 HMSG (Crown)
p. 198 © 1980 Michael Canavan/SDLP
p. 207 © 1990 *Independent*

A CIP catalogue record for this book
is available from the British Library
ISBN 0 413 64800 1

Photoset by Deltatype Ltd, Ellesmere Port, Cheshire
Printed in Great Britain by Mackays of Chatham PLC

For my parents

Contents

List of Illustrations

Acknowledgements and thanks for permission to reproduce photographs are due as follows: to the *Belfast Telegraph* for plates 1a and b; to the Army Information Service Northern Ireland for plate 2b (Crown Copyright); to Pacemaker Press for plates 2a,4b,6a,6b,6c,7a,7b and 8b.

Abbreviations

CID	Criminal Investigation Department
DPP	Department of Public Prosecutions
DUP	Democratic Unionist Party
GOC	General Officer Commanding
INLA	Irish National Liberation Army
IRA	Irish Republican Army
IRB	Irish Republican Brotherhood
IRSP	Irish Republican Socialist Party
PIRA	Provisional Irish Republican Army
RIC	Royal Irish Constabulary
RUC	Royal Ulster Constabulary
RUCR	Royal Ulster Constabulary Reserve
SDLP	Social Democratic and Labour Party
SPG	Special Patrol Group
UDR	Ulster Defence Regiment
UFF	Ulster Freedom Fighters
USC	Ulster Special Constabulary
UUAC	United Ulster Action Council
UVF	Ulster Volunteer Force
UWC	Ulster Workers' Council

Preface

'The eleventh night' of July, the eve of the Orange marches to commemorate the Battle of the Boyne in 1690, is traditionally the festive night of the year for the majority Protestant community in Northern Ireland. The images of their vividly remembered history are as immediate and relevant as those on last night's television news.

All over the province, huge bonfires, piled high with old furniture, tyres and wood, collected for weeks in advance, blaze fiercely through the night. Firemen hose the surrounding houses to keep them cool as the Lambeg drums thunder and the drink flows in gargantuan Ulster measures. With throats well lubricated and passions fired by the 'electric soup' and the 'lunatic's broth', the entire repertoire of partisan songs, glorifying the Protestant King William's victory over the Catholic King James at the Boyne, are raucously sung, again and again, to the point of hoarseness. Young men and women swagger and dance around the fires, in a tribal ritual of unusual intensity.

On a recent eleventh night, it was no surprise to the residents of a leafy South Belfast mews when a pounding disco got under way in the Ulster Defence Regiment's barracks at Malone Road, adjacent to their homes. The revelry continued into the small hours of the next morning, so it was with relief at the promise of some sleep that they eventually welcomed the unmistakeable strains of 'God Save the Queen'.

That night, however, Britain's national anthem, which usually marks the end of a public function in Northern Ireland, was capped by a full-blooded rendition of 'The sash my father wore', one of the most rousing Orange songs. By itself this was an insignificant episode but, in the light of the controversial reputation of the almost totally Protestant UDR, it was an important symptom. Supporters would obviously dismiss it as a bit of harmless holiday revelry, but to many it would tend to justify the widespread and worrying doubts about the impartiality and integrity of the Regiment and where its true loyalty ultimately lay.

The role and future of the controversial UDR, raised in 1970 as a fully-fledged regiment of the British army to replace the notorious auxiliary police, the B Specials, is now one of the central issues in the efforts by the British and Irish governments to bring peace, reconciliation and stability to divided Northern Ireland.

Every year, save one, since the end of the Second World War in 1945, a British service man or woman has been killed on active service. The exception was the year of 1968, coincidentally the same year that the Troubles in Northern Ireland began. Since then, the British army has been deployed there on continuous, active service, supporting the local police force, the Royal Ulster Constabulary, in keeping the peace between Republican and Loyalist terrorists waging a campaign that has so far cost the lives of almost 3,000 people. On average, someone – policeman, soldier, terrorist or civilian – has been killed every two-and-a-half days; or injured every five-and-a-half hours, a total of 31,000 victims.

In the same period the cancer of Irish terrorism has spread beyond the island, indiscriminately killing and threatening not only those connected with Irish affairs but others uninvolved, as far away as the United States, in several European countries and on the British mainland itself.

Twice, in little over five years, the Irish Republican Army has come within a hair's breadth of wiping out a British prime minister and a cadre of the most senior members of government. At Brighton, in the early hours of 12 October 1984, five people were killed and many more, including several members of the government were injured, when a bomb exploded inside the Grand Hotel. Among those who escaped unhurt was the then prime minister, Margaret Thatcher.

On 7 February 1991, in London at the height of the Gulf war against Iraq, prime minister John Major and his war cabinet were shaken, but uninjured, when an IRA mortar bomb, fired over adjoining rooftops from a van abandoned in Whitehall, landed in the back gardens of the houses in Downing Street, causing extensive damage where the very heart of British government beats.

Earlier, in 1979, Irish terrorists even managed to penetrate the precincts of the British parliament itself and murder Airey Neave, MP, the then Conservative opposition spokesman on Northern Ireland, by booby-trapping his car.

There are other milestones of bloody massacre along the way, so numerous that they are now involuntarily forgotten by all but the nearest and dearest of the victims, or those who still bear the mental and physical scars and are forced to live the rest of a life blighted by their experience or grief. But the conflict in Northern Ireland has not only been costly in terms of human suffering. The damage and destruction has totalled more than £700m, the equivalent of £3,800 paid out every hour in compensation for death, injury and damage to property. A survey carried out in 1990 for the Bank of Ireland, by the economic consultants, Davy Kelleher McCarthy, calculated that the negative impact of the Troubles on the Northern Ireland economy was £286m, a loss for every man, woman and child living there of some £190 a year. Maintaining law and order there will cost £762m in the fiscal year 1991/92. In Great Britain itself, a security review after the attack on Downing Street led to an enhancement of protective measures for those facing the risk of terrorist attack which will cost at least another £100m a year.

The effect of the Northern Ireland Troubles has also led to a corrosion of human rights and civil liberty in Britain. The balance of the scales of justice has been called into question by now notorious miscarriages of justice like the cases of the Guildford Four, the Maguire family, Judith Ward, the so-called

M62 bomber, and the Birmingham Six. Emergency legislation, like the Prevention of Terrorism Act, has become semi-permanent. The friendly British policeman, 'Dixon of Dock Green', now frequently carries a gun or riot shield and cannot even bid 'Evening all' from behind the perspex visor of his protective helmet. All these effects are to an overwhelming extent, due to the Northern Ireland problem.

This problem basically arises from the mutually contradictory objectives of the two communities who live there. In general, Catholics who are either Nationalist or Republican want to see a united Ireland. Some are fanatical and believe that it can only be achieved by violence. Others want to see a peaceful convergence, which would eventually eliminate the border. Unionists, or Loyalists, as the name implies, want Northern Ireland to remain part of the United Kingdom. They see themselves as British and oppose what they fear would be a united Ireland dominated by Catholic values which they do not share. Extremists believe that the IRA enjoys tacit support from the Irish government for its terrorist activities and they think that violence is necessary to defend their link with Britain. Many of them also fear that Britain is far from committed to maintaining Northern Ireland's position in the United Kingdom in the long term.

Against this background the brunt of the resulting Troubles has been borne by the locally recruited security forces, the Royal Ulster Constabulary, and the Ulster Defence Regiment (UDR), who face the threat of terrorist attack constantly, both on duty and off. In an earlier book, *The RUC: A Force Under Fire* (Methuen 1989), I told the story of the police, an account, in the words of former Chief Constable, Sir John Hermon, of 'extraordinary men and women doing an extraordinary job'. His words could equally apply to the UDR. With a strength of 6,300, they are the largest infantry regiment in the British army, and they have now been on unbroken active service for a longer period than any unit since Napoleonic times.

This book traces their story, for much of the way along a parallel path to the RUC. Both forces share equally controversial origins; for historical reasons membership of both is overwhelmingly Protestant; and, in the divided society which they risk their lives and limbs to protect, both have exhibited unrivalled dedication and courage. Both also provoke strong feelings amongst the differing shades of opinion in both the Protestant/Unionist/Loyalist majority and the Catholic/Nationalist/Republican minority.

There, in my view, their histories diverge. The RUC, through its ever increasing professionalism and impartiality, still enjoys the confidence of the majority and is steadily shaking off the bonds of its history, breaking down minority distrust and earning widespread, if sometimes grudging, acceptance and respect.

The UDR, by contrast, draws uncritically fierce support from the majority Protestant community, who sees it as the last dependable bastion against betrayal by the British government. At the same time, it does not command the full confidence of the minority community and is even feared and hated by many members, whose traditional distrust is fostered by the involvement of some UDR soldiers in terrorist incidents.

In telling the UDR story, I know that however I strive to reflect these conflicting points of view, I too will come in for criticism from both sides. The UDR has long been inward looking and notoriously sensitive to outsiders analysing its affairs. Its opponents have all too often exploited events to discredit the UDR. It is important, therefore, that I explain my standpoint in writing this book. Without reservation, I condemn the use of violence. The merciless, brutal activities of the Provisional IRA and those on the Loyalist side who resort to violence have long exceeded the force of every adjective of condemnation. I fully support the RUC in its efforts to be impartial, accountable, professional and effective. I admire the courage, commitment and sacrifice of the UDR and recognise the contribution it has made to protecting the entire community. I can find no shred of justification or sense in the murder offensive pursued so relentlessly against the UDR by the IRA and its fellow-travellers. That said, however, I have formed certain impressions about the Regiment from my work as a journalist in Northern Ireland over the last two decades and in researching and writing this book. So, while I have attempted to explain the UDR story from the differing points of view, my own conclusions have influenced the tone of the book and are outlined in the closing chapter.

Over the years, many people have helped me in reporting on Northern Ireland and with this book. They are too numerous to mention individually, but it has been of inestimable benefit to have had the time of not only the great, the good and the involved, but of many others caught up in events. Many of them would not want me to name them, but I thank them all for their unstinting assistance.

In singling out others for particular mention, I run the risk of offending by omission. If so, I apologise, but for their help while I was writing this book I have especially to thank: David Pipe, Harry Stevenson, Roy Hattersley, Linda Faith, Rory McShane, Lord Fitt, Paddy Devlin, Ken Maginnis and his staff, especially June, Michael Canavan, Jonathan Stephenson, Jeffrey Donaldson, Dick O'Brien, Michael Collins, Richard Ford, Kevin McNamara, Frank King and Dr Garrett FitzGerald.

My thanks are also due to the brave UDR family near Lisnaskea, for their frankness, and to Mrs Norma Johnston, at Kilkeel, who bears her loss with such courage and compassion for other mothers and widows.

Regrettably, the UDR decided not to cooperate with me, but I want to thank those involved, especially Lieutenant-General Sir John Waters, for fully considering my request. As ever, the staff at AIS Lisburn were helpful, within the prescribed limits. I want to record my sincere gratitude to Stuart Reed, but especially to Carolyn Arnold and Brad Fleming. None of those mentioned here, of course, bear any responsibility for my independent conclusions. Some of them, I know, disagree with me, but I hope that they will nevertheless accept my sincerity.

Other people who facilitated me in differing ways, for which I am appropriately grateful, were Max Hastings, the Editor-in-

Chief of the *Daily Telegraph* and *Sunday Telegraph*, Tom Pride, the News Editor, John Harrison, Marty Wright and all at Pacemaker, the encyclopaedic Walter Macauley, David Hooper of Biddle & Co and Anthony Goff, my agent.

Ann Mansbridge and Sarah Hannigan patiently mid-wifed my extended labours and led all those at Methuen who have so speedily produced this book.

Finally, I want to thank my wife Anne, and our family, Michelle, Paul, Declan and Edward, for their support and encouragement.

Chris Ryder
Belfast
April 1991

As poppy petals gently fall
Remember us who gave our all
Not in the mud of foreign lands
Nor buried in the desert sands

In Ulster field and farm and town
Fermanagh lanes and drumlin'd Down
We died that violent death should cease
And Ulstermen might live in peace

UDR Soldier

1 The B Specials

The lineage of the Ulster Defence Regiment can be traced back to the early years of this century, through the B Specials, Northern Ireland's all-Protestant auxiliary police, to the Ulster Volunteer Force, an unofficial Protestant militia, raised to resist, by armed force, the repeated will of the British parliament that Ireland should have Home Rule.

It is now clear that from the outset this image of the UDR permanently blighted the British government's idealistic hopes that the Regiment could shed the sectarian straitjacket it had inherited and become an impartial, non-sectarian force, drawn proportionately from both Protestant and Catholic communities, to help the Royal Ulster Constabulary maintain law and order. Its unfortunate parentage and subsequent British security policy in Northern Ireland, often implemented for pragmatic, short-term reasons, have therefore condemned the UDR to notoriety and led to it being widely regarded, by Protestants and Catholics alike, as the ultimate guarantor of the Protestant/Unionist/Loyalist cause in Northern Ireland.

The roots of this controversial reputation, unwillingly inherited by the UDR, lie in the turbulent events of just over a hundred years ago. As the campaign for Irish Home Rule from Britain gathered force in the 1880s and 90s and the early years of the present century, the Unionists in the north of Ireland became more and more determined in their opposition. 'Home Rule means Rome Rule,' they said, summing up their unwillingness to become a Protestant minority in what they feared would be an all-Ireland Catholic state run from Dublin.

The backbone of their resistance became the Ulster Volunteer Force, an unauthorised 100,000-strong militia formed by the leaders of the Unionist cause and financed by the landed gentry and business community. It was raised from 'reliable men' among the 218,206 who had signed the Ulster Covenant in September 1912, many with their own blood, as a sign of their opposition to severing their umbilical cord with Britain. The UVF was designed to demonstrate that the Protestants in the north of Ireland would resist Home Rule with force and in April 1914, with the connivance of Unionist political leaders, they defiantly imported 30,000 rifles and 3 million rounds of ammunition to underscore their determination not to be coerced into any links with Dublin.

The introduction of Home Rule was postponed with the outbreak of the First World War in 1914. Many members of the UVF then enlisted in the British forces where they formed the 36th Ulster Division. During the Battle of the Somme, fought across the poppy fields of northern France in the early days of July 1916, 5,522 of them perished in a single day, during which they took more than 500 prisoners and won four Victoria Crosses, Britain's highest gallantry award, made only in wartime. Unionists regarded the sacrifice as the most telling demonstration there could be of their loyalty to Ulster, Empire and the British Crown. But their hopes that it would quench the Home Rule cause were in vain.

Many of those who fought and died at the Somme were volunteers from the southern counties of Ireland, but there were other nationally-minded Irishmen who judged that 'England's difficulty was Ireland's opportunity' and used the nation's preoccupation with the World War as a diversion for their own plans.

A few months before the Somme on Easter Sunday, 23 April 1916, in Dublin, a group of armed Irish Nationalists took over the main post office and displayed a proclamation declaring the formation of an independent Irish Republic. The Rising attracted little public support and was easily put down within a few days by the British army. Indeed its leaders were jeered as they were arrested and taken away to prison, but their speedy execution was deeply resented and the anti-British feeling this stimulated was soon transformed into popular support for the new Irish Republican Army and Sinn Fein (Ourselves Alone), its political wing.

By 19 January 1919, when there was an election to the British parliament, Sinn Fein had become a major political force, winning 73 of the 103 Irish seats. Instead of taking their seats in London, the members announced the setting up of a new Irish parliament in Dublin. The same day, at Soloheadbag, a remote corner of County Tipperary, an eight-strong IRA 'flying column' ambushed two members of the all-Ireland police force, the Royal Irish Constabulary, who were escorting a horse- drawn cart delivering gelignite to a quarry. The constables were killed and their weapons and the explosives captured. The attack marked the beginning of what is now called Ireland's War of Independence.

At first the RIC, the eyes and ears of British power in turbulent Ireland, bore the brunt of the IRA violence. The guerrilla leaders calculated that if they could undermine the police they could easily take command of the administrative sinews of the country and, ultimately, full control. For in those days the police were not only concerned with maintaining law and order; they also performed a wide range of important regulatory duties which included, for example, checking weights and measures. In a poorly educated society they were often called on to fill in forms and read or write letters, a service that contributed to their unrivalled intimate knowledge of the community they served. This produced high grade raw intelligence which was filtered up the RIC organisation all the way back to the authorities at Dublin Castle, providing a clearly focused snapshot of the public mood.

The initial shock of the IRA assault on the RIC was so effective that before long the police were on the run. The well organised campaign against them of intimidation and assassination was given credence by the support of Dail Eireann, the rebel parliament now firmly established in Dublin. Members of the RIC and all too often their wives and children, who had been respected pillars of their communities, were boycotted and harassed. They often had to acquire their basic needs by forcibly serving themselves in the local shops and leaving the money on the counter. In the teeth of ever more vicious attacks, they were driven from their network of small barracks in villages and towns and forced to regroup in heavily guarded installations in the larger towns. Many were killed or wounded, morale collapsed and there was a flood of resignations.

In October 1919, an increasingly worried government in London posted General Sir Nevil Macready, the Commissioner of the Metropolitan Police and a veteran of the Boer War, to Dublin to direct a campaign of repression against the IRA uprising and stabilise the situation.

With the RIC demoralised and in disarray, the cutting edge of his force became 7,000 ex-soldiers, veterans of the war, recruited in 1920, who became known as the Black and Tans because of the khaki army trousers they wore with dark green police jackets, a consequence of uniform shortages. Together with 1,400 auxiliaries, ex-officers formed into 100-strong companies and, paid the then astronomical bounty of £1 a day, they imposed a reign of terror and reprisal throughout the country, but without significant success. The IRA campaign was unstoppable and steadily undermined British authority in Ireland.

By the end of 1920, against this violent background, parliament in London had passed the Government of Ireland Act; but although it conceded partition, which satisfied the Unionists in the North by allowing them to remain under Britain's wing, its provisions for limited devolution to the new Dail in Dublin fell far short of the full-blooded independence for the whole of Ireland demanded by Sinn Fein and the IRA.

The Act failed to halt the violence, which intensified into a cycle of bloody reprisal and counter-reprisal. By the time a truce was agreed, with some difficulty, in July 1921, there had been 418 RIC members and 146 British soldiers killed, as well as at least eighty civilians, men, women and children. The British government moved to resolve the worsening situation by underlining its commitment to partitioning the North, and offering an improved, but still limited form of self-government to the South.

The Dail unanimously rejected the British offer but agreed to negotiate. This triggered a major split within the IRA and when a treaty was finalised in December 1921, recognising the partition settlement, a cruel civil war erupted. Hardliners, led by Eamon de Valera, rejected the partition treaty and insisted on an all-Ireland settlement, but were eventually crushed by the new government, led by Michael Collins, which took office in Dublin. It was bedevilled by widespread bitterness and political recrimination over the merits of the settlement, an issue that scarred and still divides the country's political system today.

Throughout this period the violence was mainly confined to the southern and western counties of the island but the Unionists in the North were deeply alarmed. Their earlier belligerence had persuaded the British government to abandon Home Rule and concede their demand for partition, but they feared that if the IRA secured power they would eventually overwhelm the North and there were fears that the British government might not come to their assistance. Furthermore, the extent of partition and the exact line of the new North-South border had still not been finalised. Once again the Unionists of Ulster decided to look to their own security. To the British government, preoccupied with containing the situation in Ireland and finding it hard to obtain the manpower to do so, the Unionists' offer of help was most welcome.

There were already vigilante groups in existence in some areas, a response to the general disorder and lawlessness. In East Belfast, in July 1920, soldiers demobbed after the war went on the rampage when they found that their jobs had been filled in their absence. The Reverend John Redmond, a local clergyman, was able to calm them after a spirit grocery store was ransacked but the next day they looted thirty-two public houses and were only prevented from pillaging C. E. Bourke's draper's shop by a man with a revolver standing on a chair in the doorway.

Other shopkeepers were forced to close for business and defend their premises by issuing staff with pokers, chair-legs and other similar weapons. Local clergymen and Orangemen, clad in their regalia, had limited success in calming the mob, so a public meeting was called at St Patrick's School, Ballymacarett, which agreed that a force of volunteer police should be formed to protect property. There was a flood of volunteers but many promptly withdrew when they found they were not to be armed. Eventually thirty-two men were sworn in as Special Constables and unarmed, distinguished only by coloured armbands, they patrolled East Belfast, under the command of a clergyman, the Reverend Major Chestnutt Chesney, who had wartime military experience.

Elsewhere similar bands of vigilantes were recruited in a bid to contain the growing violence in the North, which was dominated by increasingly ugly sectarian clashes. In Banbridge, County Down, that same summer, mobs of Protestants led by a band drove Catholic workers from local linen factories in the aftermath of the funeral of Lieutenant-Colonel Gerald Smyth, a local man serving as an RIC officer, who had been murdered by the IRA in County Cork.

During this same period, in Lisburn, County Antrim the murder of another senior RIC officer, District-Inspector Oswald Swanzy, pursued because he was reputed to have participated in the earlier shooting of the Lord Mayor of Cork, sparked off such serious sectarian disturbances that a curfew was imposed from 10.30 pm to 5.30 am.

An act, dating back to 1832, was invoked to swear in about 700 Special Constables to aid the RIC, but after some were prosecuted for looting almost half of them resigned.

Along the border, in County Fermanagh, another unofficial vigilante group had driven an IRA raiding party away from Lisbellaw the same July. The activities of such groups, largely drawn from the remnants of the old UVF formations, were condoned by the hard-pressed British army and RIC who turned a blind eye on the basis that they were on the same side.

The Unionists had long lobbied the British authorities in Belfast and Dublin for the formation of a Special Constabulary, which was important to them because it would draw their sympathisers into the fabric of the legitimate security forces. They were also most anxious to have a well equipped security force which they could trust and control in the event of any British retreat from the promise of partition, or if the British would not come to their aid to withstand an IRA attempt at taking the North. Although many of the officer class in the RIC had Unionist sympathies, the rank and file, in Unionist eyes, comprised predominantly southern Catholics; at best sitting on the fence to see which way things would go; at worst IRA sympathisers and no friends of Unionism.

In the autumn of 1920, therefore, a new committee of officials set up in Belfast to maintain law and order in the North, was given approval by the Cabinet in London to raise a force of Special Constables for use only in the North. It was a highly significant decision for it was the first act of British policy to recognise the partition of Ireland.

The plan, which mirrored the earlier Unionist proposals, provided for a 2,000-strong force of full-timers to be known as A Specials. Organised on a county basis, under the command of the RIC, ex-servicemen were to be given priority in joining up. The pay, at £3 17s 6d a week, with free uniform and quarters and a discharge bounty, was well above the military wages and generous by the civilian pay scales at the time, even for highly skilled tradesmen.

They were to be supported by a force of B Specials, voluntary part-timers who would do duty one night in ten in their local area. Wearing caps and armbands for identification, it was envisaged that they would perform duty in the company of an RIC officer, although not in Nationalist areas. The force was to be unpaid save for a half-yearly allowance of £5 to pay for tram fares and wear and tear of clothing. Those with a bicycle would get another shilling allowance and there would be a hot-meal payment of 2s 6d for additional duties. Belfast alone was to have 4,000 B Specials, with more in the rural areas. The plan also provided for the registration of a force of C Specials, a 6,000-strong general reserve to be called out in an emergency. There would be no uniform or allowances and they would be armed from police stations if the need arose.

The RIC was to issue and control the enrolment forms and those enlisted were to be chosen by a panel of specially appointed magistrates; but the Unionist establishment and the UVF moved instantly to bypass RIC involvement and dominate the creation of the new force. Even before the official recruiting advertisements were published in the Belfast newspapers on 1 November 1920, the UVF was being mobilised to join up. Ten days earlier its commanding officer, Lieutenant-Colonel Wilfred Spender, issued an internal memorandum from Unionist headquarters in Belfast Town Hall stating there was no reason why the UVF should not furnish the numbers required for the new forces. To ensure that they did, the UVF obtained and submitted enrolment forms in bulk. The selection committees were later criticised by a British army officer in a report to London. He accused them of 'a want of moral courage . . . in excluding undesirables,' which resulted in the B Specials having 'a large leaven of a bad type'.

Within a year of their formation the force levels had risen to 8,000 A and 25,000 B Specials with a further 405 officers and 10,500 men registered as C Specials. The deployment of the Specials stoked up the intensity of the serious sectarian conflict in the North and before long they had achieved as notorious a reputation as the Black and Tans and the auxiliaries.

The July truce in 1921 had little effect in the North where serious trouble and killings continued, providing a lawless and uncertain background when the new Northern Ireland government assumed responsibility for security on 22 November, shortly before the conclusion of treaty talks in London, which led to the partition settlement. Such was the new government's uncertainty about the future and their ability to defend partition that almost at once they demanded an arsenal of 26,200 rifles and 5,240,000 rounds of ammunition be shipped to Carrickfergus by the British government. Senior Unionists and UVF leaders were actually talking of raising a force of 150,000 men. There was also talk of disbanding the RIC and Specials and creating a new military force incorporating 20,000 UVF men for whom there was no official security role at that stage.

Lieutenant-Colonel Charles Wickham, the RIC Commissioner for police in Belfast, who was in charge of the Specials and struggling in vain to assert control, was so alarmed by these proposals that he submitted a memorandum to the British government suggesting an expansion of the C Specials to bring these proposed irregular militias under some measure of restraint. His paper was leaked and reached the Irish negotiators in London, already alarmed at the plight of the Nationalist minority soon to be isolated in the North at the mercy of the Specials, whose undisciplined behaviour was a matter of serious concern.

A contemporary report by a police officer at the Belfast headquarters summed up the concerns:

> There can never be any possibility of establishing confidence and security so long as the B force, the ordinary Protestant countryman and, in many cases, the corner boy, is supplied with arms and clothing by his government and authorised to 'get on top', as it were, of his neighbour.

The report continued:

> In my own district there are B men who have confessed they committed a certain murder but evidence could not be gathered from the victim's relations or from the witnesses since all had been intimidated and warned that if they identified the B men, they would 'go down' next.

The influential *Manchester Guardian* communicated the fears about the Specials to a wider audience in March 1921 in a critical editorial.

> The Special Constabulary, drawn almost exclusively from the ranks of the Orange Lodges and the Unionist 'Volunteers', was nominally raised to protect life and property and to maintain order, not to become a force of terrorists exercising powers of death over their Catholic neighbours, for in the Ulster Unionist mind Catholic and Sinn Feiner are synonymous. Ulster's case against a single

parliament for Ireland has always rested on its alleged fear of persecution. It will be a bad beginning for the Ulster parliament if its establishment coincides with the dragooning of the Catholic minority in the six counties by an armed Protestant force administering a sort of lynch law.

The British government, embarrassed already by such widespread criticism in parliament and the press of the now notorious Specials, hastily disowned the Wickham plan but, because of the serious situation, did allow the new Northern Ireland government to recruit a further 700 A and 5,000 B Specials.

Early in 1922, as the civil war in the South raged, it was agreed between the British government and representatives of the new administration in Dublin and Belfast that the RIC would be speedily disbanded and replaced by two new police forces, one in each jurisdiction.

The new Irish government, in a brave bid to put law and order on a new footing, decided that the southern police force was to be a civil unarmed organisation called the Garda Siochana, (Civil Guards – Guardians of the Peace), which came into existence after the RIC was formally disbanded on 4 April 1922.

In the North, the 2,000 remaining RIC members were reprieved until a parliamentary committee had considered the policing question. It began work in January and reported in March, recommending a 3,000-strong force, with one-third of the places reserved for Catholics, the remainder to be recruited from the former members of the RIC and Specials. It was to be called the Ulster Constabulary. By the time it came into official existence on 1 June, Buckingham Palace had been prevailed upon to allow the force to be called the Royal Ulster Constabulary. At the same time, the Specials were formally named the Ulster Special Constabulary.

Sectarian trouble was worse than ever. In one three-week period there were 138 killings: 96 Catholics and 42 Protestants. With the RUC in its infancy, the Specials were required to bear the brunt of the disturbances. Of the 2,000 RIC officers in and around Belfast who were paid off as the RUC came into existence, only 250 enlisted in the new force, a development that decreased the already limited supervision of the Specials.

There seemed to be little urgency in getting the RUC operational. After three months in existence, only one-third of its complement had been recruited. The RUC was actually built from the top down, with priority being given to the command structure and the recruitment of 'suitable' officers, in Unionist eyes. This was a most important investment, for compliant officers were essential to political control of the force, which the Unionists forged from the beginning.

Unionist insecurity knew no limits during this period. A boundary commission was studying the fixing of the border between North and South. At first the proposal was to isolate the nine counties of the old province of Ulster but, after the Unionists had done their sums, they pushed, successfully, for a more favourable split, taking only six counties into the North, which gave them a safe two-to-one majority over the Catholics.

The worsening violence in Northern Ireland deeply concerned the new government in Dublin, who were being put under pressure by the Catholic Church and other representatives of the abandoned northern Catholics after a series of grim murders and outrages, many of which continued to be carried out by the Specials. In one chilling incident eight members of a Catholic family were murdered in their Belfast home by five armed men, generally believed to be Specials, although this has never been proved.

London was terrified that the pro-settlement government in Dublin would collapse and be replaced by IRA hardliners who would overthrow the precarious deal and perhaps even march on the North, so it resisted Unionist belligerence for action against the IRA in the aftermath of a number of serious clashes in the contentious border area.

Instead it pushed representatives from both sides into discussions about ways to break the spiral of tension and violence. The result was a pact, agreed between leaders of the new administrations in the North and South, designed with

London's prodding to create a working relationship between them and draw the Catholics in the North more wholeheartedly into the workings of the new government in Belfast. Winning their confidence in the forces of law and order was the priority, and a new advisory committee was set up to oversee Catholic recruitment to fill the one-third quota reserved for them in the new RUC. Further confidence-building measures included a £500,000 relief scheme to aid the 10,000 workers and 23,000 homeless displaced during the recent sectarian pogroms.

In a bid to defuse the potentially explosive situation, it was also agreed that police detachments in Nationalist areas and search parties looking for arms would consist of both Protestant and Catholic officers.

Unionists, defying the Government of Ireland Act, which provided for a Council of Ireland, did not really want a relationship with the South or more than nominal Catholic involvement in the running of the North. The hollowness of their commitment to the pact was exposed within a few days. After an RIC officer had been shot and murdered in Belfast, a party of Specials entered Arnon Street, on the northern fringe of the city centre, and shot two men dead in their homes. A third was beaten to death with a sledgehammer and his 7-year-old son was shot in the head and died a day later.

These reprisals created further panic among Catholics and, under the terms of the pact, Dublin asked for more information about the incident. Repeated requests were ignored in Belfast, effectively ending the pact and breaking off the slim hope of formal relations between the two parts of Ireland. There was no substantial political dialogue between them again for forty years.

The last vestige of the pact was the police advisory committee which was urged into life by London, beginning to baulk at the cost of massaging Unionist insecurity by maintaining nearly 50,000 men at arms.

The committee met only three times, never with its full complement of twelve present. The Belfast government had no desire to make it work, preferring instead to see as many of the 'loyal' Specials as possible fill the quota reserved for Catholics and thus maintain control of the RUC. The Catholic members of the committee were equally half-hearted about their task, succumbing to intimidation and the mood of sullen non-cooperation with the Unionist government that was to dominate Nationalist and Catholic attitudes for the next four decades.

Turning a blind eye to Unionist packing of the Specials, the wave of reprisals and sectarian intimidation by the force and backing down on the enforcement of the Catholic quota in the RUC was an inexcusable abdication of responsibility by the British government which was to have far reaching consequences. Permitting the fledgling Unionist administration to gain control of the state security force and fill it with its own supporters was akin to letting them raise a private army. The neglect condemned Northern Ireland to deep-seated law and order problems, with which it is still plagued, and prevented the RUC from being regarded as anything other than the armed wing of Unionism.

If the potentially far-reaching provisions of the pact had been acted on, events in Northern Ireland might have developed quite differently and the resentments which later repeatedly exploded into violence might have been avoided. Furthermore, the concept of policing a community might have been distinguished from the role of defending the state, to the long term benefit of the law-abiding majority from both communities.

With the collapse of the pact, the Unionists stepped up their policy of repressing the Catholic minority to assert their own authority. Ignoring advice from sympathisers in London about antagonising the government, they passed the Special Powers Act in April 1922. This draconian piece of legislation enabled the authorities to detain and intern suspects without trial. Prisoners could be flogged or executed; coroners' inquests could be dispensed with; land and property could be commandeered for security purposes; organisations, meetings, publications and gatherings could be prohibited by simple ministerial order. If any unforeseen security problem developed, the minister was empowered to take all such steps and issue all such orders as might be necessary to preserve the peace.

The Act was put into action within a month. As a result, over the weekend of 20–22 May, several houses belonging to the Unionist gentry, including the O'Neills and the Londonderrys, were put to the torch. On the Monday morning, W. J. Twaddell, a Unionist member of the northern parliament, was shot dead in the city centre of Belfast as he arrived at his place of business.

A crisis Cabinet meeting later in the day decided to outlaw the IRA and other Republican groupings under the new Act and implement internment without trial. In the early hours of the next day some 300 suspects were rounded up by Specials and the army in dawn swoops and before long 400 were in indefinite custody. Not a single Unionist supporter was interned despite the fact that the violence was clearly being carried out by armed gangs in both communities.

Soon afterwards the Lord Mayor of Belfast succeeded in negotiating a ten-day truce which brought the shooting and killing to a halt. In 1922 the partitioned province of Northern Ireland had a violent birth with 295 murders, all but 64 of them in Belfast. The following two years were, by stark contrast, models of public tranquillity, with only four murders and, as the curfew was lifted and the internees released, the new province settled down to a precarious peace.

But the fear and bitterness among the Nationalist minority, repressed by Unionism and abandoned to their fate by the Nationalists on the rest of the island, was to simmer away dangerously. Stamped indelibly on their political consciousness was the anti-minority ferocity of the forces of law and order; the one-sided application of internment at a time when twice as many Catholics as Protestants were being murdered; and the fact that they were now subject to Unionist law and order not by the police but by the security forces, which they regarded as partial.

Although the violence had subsided and the Northern Ireland parliament had got down to work, the final agreement that the border would enclose the six northern counties, Londonderry, Tyrone, Fermanagh, Armagh, Down and Antrim, was not reached until December 1925.

Within a week of the settlement the Ulster prime minister, James Craig, announced the disbandment of the 3,500-strong force of A Specials and the standing down of some 200 C Specials, who had been mobilised for duty. It was a reluctant decision on the part of the Ulster government but London was pressing for a reduction in the 'swollen police force' which had at one time reached a strength of some 42,000 Specials on top of the considerable army garrison in Ulster. Each year there had been a battle with Belfast over the financing. The five-year bill for keeping the Specials under arms had reached a total of £7,426,000, of which London had contributed £6,780,000.

Previous pressure from London to stand down some men had been avoided by pressing for a reduction of pay, from 10s to 7s a day, on the A Specials. This time, the financial constraints imposed by London left the Ulster government no option but to impose cuts. Faced with a bleak future in the dole queues, the Specials rebelled for better terms.

In Londonderry and several other locations the men seized their barracks and placed the officers under open arrest to seek an improvement on the disbandment terms – two months' pay. The detachment at Prince's Dock in Belfast said they had enough food to last for a month and that no arms, ammunition, equipment or barracks would be surrendered unless an additional tax-free bounty of £200 per man was paid out.

The protest was not total but nevertheless represented a serious challenge to the authority of the government, who simply could not afford the demand. It blamed ex-service members from outside Northern Ireland for fomenting discontent and issued an ultimatum saying that if the protest did not end, the force would be disbanded forthwith and the men would forfeit all claims to discharge pay and allowances. At the same time it called on employers to recognise their moral responsibilities by absorbing the men into their workforces. The threat worked. After a meeting, organised by the authors of the revolt from Londonderry, it quietly collapsed and the A Specials were wound up before the end of December 1925.

Prime responsibility for law and order then resided in the RUC, backed up by the B Specials, whose strength was fixed at a maximum of 20,000. The cost of maintaining them was in future to be met from the block sum voted from London to Northern Ireland for its internal government.

Organised on county lines, the B Specials had become increasingly professional. Their standard of firearms training was high and contingency plans had been laid and rehearsed as to how they could be mobilised at short notice to defend the border and strategic installations. Members of the force were required to perform a certain number of patrols every three months in their local area to qualify for the small annual bounty payment of between £3 and £10, depending on how often they were called out. When they were mobilised for full-time duty they were entitled to the old A Special rate of 7s a day.

With the border question resolved, Northern Ireland settled down to a period of comparative tranquillity. So, over the next few years, as financial pressures forced the government into economies, the B Specials became a candidate for cutbacks.

By the start of the 1930s the Ulster Special Constabulary had been whittled down to a strength of only 12,150 and in 1931 it was all but disbanded, again to save money, when the Ministry of Finance ordered its budget to be cut by more than half, to just £20,000. The entire force was put on a reserve footing, with members required to parade only once a year with their equipment, for a bounty of 5s. But it was decided to permit the B men to engage in unlimited, but voluntary, shooting practice and some of the considerable stocks of ammunition were earmarked for this purpose. The vast majority were permitted to hold officially issued weapons at their homes in order that they could respond quickly to any emergency call-out.

So, for a time, the B Specials became virtually a camaraderie of shooting clubs, competing against each other in crackshot competitions, with revolver and rifle, at a whole network of indoor and outdoor shooting ranges throughout Northern Ireland. This activity was perceived by Catholics as the maintenance of an armed Unionist army to keep them in their place, for the B force remained entirely Protestant.

In 1932 the role of the B Specials was in the melting pot again after fresh rioting erupted in Belfast. The initial cause of the trouble was joint protests by Catholic and Protestant workers over the low rates of relief paid to the unemployed, in comparison with cities in Britain. This unique display of working-class unity dismayed the Unionist government who kept their people under control by stifling any discussion of social and economic issues in favour of frequently restating the IRA threat to their well-being and the need for solidarity to defeat it.

The RUC alone were grossly incapable of dealing with the demonstrations. They were untrained for the task and seriously undermanned, an uncomfortable analysis presented to the government by worried police commanders. The political answer was to invoke the Special Powers Act, introducing a curfew and a ban on any public marches or rallies. At the same time the spectre of the IRA exploiting the situation to stage a rebellion was deliberately raised, easily rekindling the old sectarian divisions.

With so many people on the streets, the inevitable serious rioting developed. The RUC, it was said, were only able to bring the trouble under control by shooting two men dead and wounding another fifteen. The dead men were both Catholics shot in Catholic areas. By contrast, the fifteen Protestant casualties only suffered fractures, leg, head and scalp injuries, clearly implying that there was a biased police approach.

The crisis caused the government to reconsider the need to increase the size and capability of the police force, but the emphasis of the ensuing reorganisation was to bolster the readiness of the Specials designated to guard the border. It was felt that any need for them elsewhere to support the police could be anticipated. Such a situation actually arose in 1935 when the Orange marches in Belfast on 12 July were fired on, resulting in more sectarian disturbances. As the trouble escalated through the summer months, the entire complement of Specials in Belfast was mobilised to reinforce the RUC. By taking over police duties in quieter areas and guarding stations, they freed RUC men for use in the flashpoint areas, and also played a part in enforcing a curfew in parts of the city. Altogether 11 people lost their lives and 574 were injured before peace was restored.

The real value of the B Specials, as a home-based quick reaction reserve force, was graphically illustrated in July 1938 when a mob of IRA gunmen and sympathisers swooped on Maghera, tore down and burnt the Orange decorations and opened fire on the local RUC station, overwhelming the handful of RUC officers based there.

Local B men were quickly on the scene, rescued the outnumbered RUC men who were under attack and restored order even before police reinforcements arrived from nearby Magherafelt.

In the early months of 1939, after a resurgence of IRA activity, internment without trial was once more introduced and the B Specials were mobilised to provide intensive patrolling as a deterrent against IRA attacks. Their zeal backfired with some embarrassment, however, when it was discovered that a car which was fired on in County Tyrone, after ignoring a red light to stop, was being driven by cousins of the local commandant.

Later in the year, when war was declared by Britain on Germany, fears of a link-up between the IRA and the Germans added a new edge to the situation in Northern Ireland. Irish neutrality, although benevolent to Britain and the United States, was much resented among the Unionists in the North. They wanted to impress the government once again with their 'loyalty' and pressed for conscription to be applied to Northern Ireland.

After police advice against it, on the grounds that it could never be enforced against the eligible Catholic minority,

London decided it would not be worth the trouble, although it extended open arms to the thousands of volunteers who flocked to the colours from both Northern and Southern Ireland.

As war precautions and preparations were stepped up and a military Home Guard was formed throughout Britain, Northern Ireland was asked to follow suit. However, it was decided there were constitutional difficulties in placing Ulstermen under direct military command, so it was agreed that a new category of Specials would provide the Home Guard for Northern Ireland. In the event of an invasion by sea or air it would be expected to fight. In the meantime it was to be on the lookout for enemy parachutists and fifth columnists, as well as the more routine IRA subversives.

To cope with the task, authorisation was given to expand the USC and so another 11,500 men joined up, followed soon after by another 7,000. The new Specials, designated the Ulster Home Guard, were kitted out with military khaki, unlike their colleagues, who wore police-style uniforms.

By February 1942 the whole force, totalling 38,000 men, was organised into 29 battalions, and drilled on military lines, ready to form part of the military response to any invasion. This threat did not materialise and at the end of 1944, with the war in its final phase, the Ulster Home Guard was stood down. It was disbanded the next year and, with financial stringency again the order of the day, the B force was reorganised into two categories – Patrol and Non-patrol. The bounties were £10 and £6 a year respectively; but when mobilised for full-time duty the members were to be paid the equivalent to the RUC. Another reform, of more significance, was that the B force were made subject to the same regulations and discipline as the RUC itself.

The IRA was demoralised by its ineffectiveness during the war, thanks to tough action in the Irish Republic and the North, with many interned for the duration, so the years immediately after the war were trouble free. Nevertheless, Unionist paranoia about the IRA threat continued and for a year the government toyed with the idea of recreating a 1,000-strong force of A Specials. They finally opted instead to form a three-platoon paramilitary Reserve Force within the RUC, equipped with armoured patrol vehicles and heavy automatic weapons. To plug the gap in the RUC ranks 170 men from the B Specials were mobilised for full-time duty.

Throughout the early 1950s it was clear that the IRA was regrouping and planning a renewed campaign of violence. There were a number of arms raids on military installations in Britain and Northern Ireland, the latter provoking several skirmishes with Special patrols along the border.

The well signalled campaign eventually got under way in November 1956 when a series of bombs exploded at a court-house, territorial army barracks, a BBC relay station and bridges throughout Northern Ireland. Several devices failed to go off and a raiding party, heading for an RAF installation on the northern Antrim coast, was intercepted by an RUC platoon acting on information received. Two IRA men were also captured by B Specials operating a vehicle checkpoint in Armagh. The well practiced drill for calling out the B Specials was quickly operated and intensive patrolling, especially in the border areas, was soon in force. The sporadic attacks continued for several months, with police stations, customs posts, drill halls and telephone exchanges being regular targets.

Internment was reintroduced and, for the first time, heli-copters and tracker dogs were deployed by the army to help the RUC and Specials. On the border, 122 roads were closed with spikes and another thirty-six were cratered, leaving only seventeen heavily guarded crossing points. After an RUC constable was killed at Forkhill, County Armagh in July 1958, the third fatal police casualty of the campaign, the Irish government interned a number of people.

The IRA campaign, 605 incidents in all, which claimed six RUC and six IRA lives, attracted no popular support and the vulnerable peace between Catholics and Protestants in Belfast remained. Long before it was formally called off in 1962, the campaign had fizzled out and the humiliated IRA was forced to rethink its strategy.

The B Specials, who suffered twelve wounded, had played an important and effective role in the emergency, with several earning awards for bravery. At the peak 1,600 of them were mobilised for full-time duty in support of the RUC. The strengthened RUC Reserve, the spearhead of the anti-IRA operations, contained 272 Specials, about one-third of the strength. Quite often the local readiness of the men, with their equipment and weapons at home, enabled them to turn out after hearing an explosion and intercept the IRA men, who often made back to the sanctuary of the border.

Many of the part-timers, who were the backbone of the deterrent patrolling and guarding, used their own cars to carry out their tasks, which often gave them the advantage of surprise and led to IRA operations being upset. There was, however, some discontent that while the government grudgingly paid a small mileage allowance, it would not cover insurance premiums against a private vehicle being damaged or destroyed in action.

Predictably, the end of the IRA campaign provoked another review of the Specials, with financial pressures once more dictating penny-pinching austerity where the police force was concerned. It was decided to maintain about 300 mobilised Specials in the RUC to keep the force up to strength and to maintain about 12,000 Specials as an emergency back-up force for the police. The organisation of civil defence precautions against nuclear attack led to a new role for the Specials with training in the operation of geiger counters to detect radiation levels after nuclear explosions. At the same time they were re-equipped with more modern weapons.

In 1966, the fiftieth anniversary of the Easter Rising, the Specials were mobilised again, this time alerted to guard against any activity by their traditional enemy, the IRA. The alert was something of a false alarm and the Easter period passed off without major confrontation or incident. Two years later, again as a cost-cutting exercise, the strength of the force was slashed by one-third with talk of the remaining members being given more thorough training to enable them to act as auxiliary police. This decision cut the USC's strength to 8,285 and a training syllabus outlined that in Belfast and Londonderry the retained Specials would learn routine police duties, including station administration, beat patrols and law lectures, as well as civil defence work incorporating radio procedures and first aid. The whole force was instructed in arms proficiency, laying emphasis on care, safety, accuracy and fire control. The function of the force was laid down as acting in support of the RUC in the protection of life and property and the maintenance of law and order by carrying out patrols of a varying nature, protecting vulnerable points and relieving the regular RUC from routine station duties.

Ultimate command of the USC was exercised by the RUC Inspector-General working through a staff officer who liaised with the six county and two city commandants of the Specials. Local command was in the hands of the county commandants through district and sub-district commandants. Each man was required to carry out four training periods a year and patrols, as required, for which he received an annual bounty of £15, and 9s per hour.

The 1960s had ushered in a period of prosperity and stability previously unknown in Northern Ireland. Internal investment created new jobs in modern industries and unemployment reached record lows. There were even signs of non-sectarian issue politics with the development of a Northern Ireland Labour Party, which drew members from both religious denominations. The collapse of the IRA campaign pushed partition off the active agenda and for the first time liberal Unionists talked of admitting Catholics to the party. Nationalists too exuded a whiff of compromise and began to play a part in public life for the first time.

The emergence of the liberal Unionist, Captain Terence O'Neill, as prime minister, stimulated the mood of change, especially when he brought the Irish prime minister, Sean Lemass, for talks at Stormont, the first such contact for forty years.

The time was ripe for fundamental reform and change, but on both sides the dark forces of extremism were already deployed to undermine it. The IRA, now embarked on a course of subversive political action through front groups campaigning on social and economic issues, had infiltrated and was heavily influencing a new civil rights movement, inspired by the activities of the blacks in the United States, to press for reform in Northern Ireland.

Unionist extremists were simultaneously undermining the standing of O'Neill, thwarting his efforts to achieve equality between Catholics and Protestants, improve relations with the South and generally modernise Northern Ireland. Gunmen, from an organisation styling itself the Ulster Volunteer Force, had carried out several acts of anti-Catholic violence, including the brutal murder of a young Catholic barman, forcing O'Neill to outlaw them. Street disorder over the flying of the Irish tricolour had taken place during an election campaign, marking a slide towards confrontation and a resurgence of the old religious tensions.

The precarious stability and fragile law and order framework finally collapsed in Londonderry on 5 October 1968 when the RUC were ordered by the government to halt a civil rights march. The ensuing disturbances were flashed on to television screens throughout Britain and Ireland, forcing the state of affairs in Northern Ireland into the national spotlight for the first time ever.

Ever since 1925, when the partition settlement had been finalised, successive governments in London had turned a blind eye to the conduct of affairs in Belfast. By convention, they were never raised at Westminster, but Gerry Fitt, the West Belfast MP, who was vigorously batoned by the RUC at the forefront of the Londonderry march, led the cry for the government in London to force O'Neill to carry through the reforms which he admitted were necessary.

The civil rights demands were six-fold: the introduction of a universal franchise – one man, one vote; a redrawing of electoral boundaries to provide a more balanced public representation; the outlawing of religious discrimination; fairer housing allocation between Catholics and Protestants; the repeal of the Special Powers Act; and the disbandment of the B Specials.

Between October and the summer of 1969 the RUC fought vainly to control the rising tide of public disorder. Civil rights marches were invariably met by a counter-march of extreme Unionists, normally led by the voluble Ian Paisley, a fiery fundamentalist preacher who rapidly emerged as a street leader.

The RUC was unprepared for the onslaught. Manpower was inadequate to cope; there had been no coordinated public order training; protective equipment, like shields and helmets, were outdated and in short supply. The RUC, and the people of Northern Ireland were to pay a heavy price for the lack of investment in training, manpower and equipment and the failure to divorce the police role from day-to-day political control. In dealing with the disorder, the RUC and the Ulster government were forced to operate in the unprecedented glare of the international media spotlight, with the bones of fifty years of unchallenged Unionist hegemony being picked over ever more critically by amazed outsiders.

There was particular criticism from onlookers that, on the frequent occasions when the RUC were caught in a confrontation between opposing crowds, they invariably turned their backs on the Protestants and faced the Catholics.

Although the Specials, whose controversial past had ensured their presence on the list of reforms, were not mobilised in the early stages of the crisis, they figured prominently in the propaganda war. Catholic politicians called for their disbandment when five off-duty Specials, in plain clothes, were found to have been involved with Protestant counter-marchers at Armagh in November.

In January 1969 a civil rights march, mainly consisting of radical students from Queens University, Belfast, set out for Londonderry. There was trouble at virtually every town on the route but on the last stage of the journey it was viciously set upon at Burntollet Bridge by a Unionist mob armed with clubs, pickaxe handles and nail-studded cudgels. Paddy Devlin, a prominent trade union figure who was a Labour MP at Stormont, subsequently tabled 442 parliamentary questions seeking to establish if named people, some carrying cudgels and other weapons, identified from photographs of the ambush,

THE B SPECIALS 25

were members of the Specials. It was established that forty-seven of those named were former members and another twenty-five were serving, but no evidence was ever adduced, in court or elsewhere, that they had participated in the incident, one of the ugliest events of the period.

By July 1969 the seams holding the beleagured RUC together were coming apart. The force was exhausted and outnumbered by the growing trouble. In the spring, some B men had been called out to guard strategic installations, after extremists, who turned out to be Unionists, not, as was thought, the IRA, blew up water and electricity installations serving Belfast.

With the start of the marching season the increase in tension and demands for police deployment forced the authorities to put the B Specials on standby. Fifty of them were called out at short notice when a major disturbance erupted in Dungiven, County Londonderry. Two tenders of police guarding the Orange Hall were attacked by a mob and the police were forced to take refuge in the hall for a time before being able to get out and fight their way to the local police station which was then besieged by the crowd.

The force of B Specials were drawn up at the home of one of their commanders and then deployed into the village to break up the crowd. At first they were armed only with batons, but when shots were fired at them revolvers were sent for. The detachment succeeded in dispersing the angry crowd after firing shots over their heads. However, controversy about the incident flared with the death of a man who was said to have been fatally assaulted during the baton charges.

In the early days of August, as the level of trouble increased throughout Northern Ireland, unarmed B Specials were deployed to keep the peace in the Protestant Shankill Road area of Belfast, following Catholic-Protestant clashes at the unfortunately named Unity Flats after some unusually impartial action by the police had soured their relationship with some of those on the Protestant side.

All attention was, however, focused on a Protestant march in Londonderry on 12 August which the government decided not to ban. It was no surprise, therefore, that late in the afternoon, trouble broke out when stones were hurled at the procession by Catholic youths.

Several days of intensive rioting, now known as the 'Battle of the Bogside' ensued. Barricades were thrown up around the area as petrol bombs and other missiles picked off the exhausted and ill-protected police like tenpins in a bowling alley. Over the next twenty-four hours, despite CS gas being used against the rioters for the first time in the United Kingdom, the trouble worsened and spread throughout the Catholic areas of Northern Ireland, forcing the government to mobilise all 8,000 members of the B Specials.

There was initial confusion about their profile. At first it was said they would perform duties armed only with batons and not be used for riot control, but because of the general lawlessness this order was later rescinded and they were authorised to carry their firearms.

Tension further increased on 14 August with a statement by the Irish prime minister that his government would 'not stand idly by' and an announcement from Dublin that military field hospitals were being established on the border, a move interpreted by many Unionists as the precursor to an invasion of parts of Northern Ireland by Irish forces.

Late that afternoon, with the entire six counties in a state of what a senior RUC man later described as 'incipient civil war', British soldiers were deployed in Londonderry.

Elsewhere, especially in Belfast, the police and Specials continued to deal alone with ongoing violence. Late that night a party of twenty-five RUC and twenty Specials was trying to deal with a riot involving several hundred Catholics and Protestants in the city of Armagh. Seventeen more armed Specials from the Tynan area near the border arrived in four private cars and were delegated by a senior RUC officer to deal with a crowd at Cathedral Road. As they arrived they found a blazing car, an angry crowd and the road strewn with items, including a garden seat, to form a barricade. The officers, completely untrained in riot control, unsupervisd by the RUC and faced with a threatening crowd, panicked and opened fire. Eyewitnesses said that there were thirty or forty shots. When the crowd had cleared the body of Mr John Gallagher was found to be lying in the street and two others were wounded.

It was not the most serious incident during a bad night throughout Northern Ireland. Before morning in built-up parts of Belfast, the police, firing Browning machine guns attached to armoured cars, had lost their nerve and control of the city. Four people lay dead at their hands and an armed rioter had shot a Protestant dead. By the end of the day the troops had also been deployed in Belfast and James Callaghan, the British Home Secretary, had flown in to take control of the situation. As army reinforcements were rushed in from bases in Britain and Germany, few gave any thought to other than the immediate peacekeeping objective. In the first heat of the crisis nobody believed for a moment they would still be there more than two decades later. One of those who feared that they might was the perceptive Callaghan, later to be prime minister. 'It's easy to put the troops in,' he told Gerry Fitt. 'But it'll be the devil of a job to get them out again.'

The General Officer Commanding, Lieutenant-General Sir Ian Freeland, had immediately assumed command of all peace-keeping duties and the RUC and Specials were subject to his orders as Director of Operations.

Feelings were running at fever pitch on both sides and many Catholic politicians and community leaders alleged that armed Specials, in plain clothes, had played a central role in the sectarian trouble in Belfast and elsewhere. The Protestant community, which believed that a full-scale IRA uprising had only narrowly been averted, was in an equally frightened state. They believed that calls for the Specials to be disbanded, if heeded, would leave them defenceless.

These fears were exacerbated by moves to call in and store the Specials' weapons in central armouries, first in Belfast, then in Londonderry and elsewhere, for what the British described as security reasons. The move, bringing the Specials into line with the army and territorial army, would enable the weapons to be issued when required for specific duties, at the discretion of military commanders.

Freeland was forced to issue a public statement denying there was any threat to the future of the Specials or that they were being disarmed. He asked the men to give him their support and carry out their duties with their customary loyalty.

Once in Belfast, Callaghan moved with urgency, inaugurating a vigorous drive to push through the long overdue reforms. To tackle the most pressing problem, creating a formula for acceptable policing, Callaghan called in Lord Hunt, leader of the 1953 expedition which was the first to conquer Mount Everest. His team consisted of Robert Mark, later to become a celebrated Commissioner of the Metropolitan Police, and Sir James Robertson, the Chief Constable of Glasgow.

Despite Freeland's soothing tones, the British government was deeply concerned at the shortcomings of the RUC and Specials, which had become all too apparent during the previous ten months. The fatal incident in Armagh, involving as it did the Specials, had inevitably become a source of particular controversy. It was later closely investigated by the judicial enquiry, headed by Lord Scarman, whose painstaking report on the 1969 disturbances was published in April 1972.

The tribunal found that it was impossible to discover who had fired the fatal shot and concluded: 'After making all allowances for the strange, difficult and frightening situation in which they found themselves, there was no justification for firing into the crowd – as the Ulster Special Constabulary themselves implicitly admitted by their strenuous denials that they had done any such thing.'

But Scarman also said that 'grave as was the misconduct of the USC ... the Tribunal considers that a measure of responsibility rests with the [RUC] County Inspector, who put an untrained but armed party of USC drawn from a country area into an alarming town riot without briefing or leadership.'

Other Specials deployments in that turbulent period were examined by the Tribunal which decided that opening fire without police supervision during another incident in Dungannon, in which a number of people were injured, was 'a reckless and irresponsible thing to do'.

The Tribunal noted that, while some Specials in Londonderry had participated in an exchange of petrol bombs and missiles with a Catholic crowd, there was nothing to justify any general criticism of the force in the few hours it performed riot duty on the streets of Londonderry. Tribute was paid to its role in protecting Catholic owned public houses in Protestant areas and the way in which the force had carried out patrol duties in the Shankill Road after the Unity Flats clashes.

Scarman summed up by noting that on several occasions USC patrols outside Belfast showed a lack of proper discipline, particularly in the use of firearms, and in Belfast 'their presence, while evoking the hostility of the Catholics was unable to restrain the aggression of the Protestants'.

The force, neither trained nor equipped for riot control duty and drawn exclusively from the Protestant community, the Tribunal pointed out, was: 'totally distrusted by the Catholics, who saw them as the strong arm of the Protestant ascendancy. They could not show themselves in a Catholic area without heightening tension.'

Another official report, published in September 1969, this time a non-judicial enquiry chaired by Lord Cameron, looked at the pre-July 1969 disturbances and recorded that for 'traditional and historical reasons' recruitment to the Specials was confined to Protestants.

> Though there is no legal bar to Catholic membership, it is unlikely that Catholic applications would be favourably received, even if they were made. Until very recent years, for drill and training purposes, the USC made large use of Orange Lodges and this, though it may have been necessary for reasons of economy and because of the lack of other suitable premises, tended to accentuate in the eyes of the Catholic minority the assumed partisan and sectarian character of the force.

The Hunt team did not, of course, have the advantage of reading these reports as they carried out their work but the sources of evidence they tapped clearly provided them with an identical analysis.

It was not surprising, therefore, that their report, published in October 1969, an impressive six weeks after being appointed, recommended, among forty-seven far-reaching reforms, the abolition of the B Specials.

The government should relinquish operational control of the police in favour of a broadly based, independent police authority. The RUC, they said, should be relieved of all its paramilitary duties, disarmed and, as a civil police force, be fully integrated into the British police service. Support for them should come from two newly created forces: one, a police volunteer reserve, would help the RUC with police work; the other, to be under the command of the army, would take over responsibility for guarding the border and other military duties.

The report, published on Friday 10 October, met with instant hostility among the Protestant community, especially the proposal to disband the Specials. The Saturday night after its publication, the army were called to help the RUC when a large crowd of rioting Protestants on the Shankill Road in Belfast, their passions fuelled by alcohol, could not be contained. After a policeman, Constable Victor Arbuckle, was shot dead, the first RUC victim of the troubles, a full-scale gun battle developed and throughout the night hundreds of shots were exchanged and the troops used CS gas.

When the trouble subsided three people lay dead and sixty-six were injured, including fourteen soldiers and three police-men with gunshot wounds. The government let it be known that despite the violence there would be no going back on the recommendations.

The next evening 137 Specials at Newtownards, County Down presented themselves at the local police station with their uniforms tied up in bundles and their guns. They said they were resigning in protest at the smear campaign against the force on television and in the press. Two Northern Ireland government ministers attended the station to talk to them and as they left their police car was pounded by an angry, jeering crowd.

It was not the first sign of discontent among the Specials. At the end of August a statement issued on behalf of the Specials said: 'The morale of the force has suffered a lot recently, mainly due to the appalling lies which have been reported in the press and it is most regrettable that only a very few MPs have spoken up in our favour.'

Some members of the force had even engaged, unofficially, a

firm of public relations advisers to improve the Specials' image. Among their efforts to enhance it was the publication of a letter from a senior Protestant clergyman assuring the Specials of prayers for them and their families, especially those injured in the execution of their duty.

After the Newtownards resignations, the USC Commandant, Lieutenant-Colonel Stephen Miskimmin, moved to quell what the authorities feared could be a serious revolt in the ranks. In a three-page letter to the force, he assured Specials that those 'who apply and are active enough' would be able to join the new forces, the police auxiliary or the local defence force, 'without any delay'. In the meantime, he emphasised, the USC would 'remain in being and quite unaffected right up to the moment when the new defence force comes into existence'. 'We must move with the times and needs of the day and out of these changes are bound to come many benefits to compensate for any cherished associations we may feel at the moment we are likely to lose,' he said.

Nevertheless, there continued to be reports of impending resignations as groups of Specials held meetings to discuss the situation. In Belfast a mass meeting rejected the Hunt report but said it would await publication of detailed proposals about the new forces before deciding what action to take. A similar view prevailed at a meeting of County Antrim Specials held in Ballymena where 150 men, about half the county strength, indicated their preparedness to resign.

Rumours abounded that the rejected B men were already planning to reform the Ulster Volunteer Force or form a new armed grouping to 'defend' Northern Ireland. There were well-founded fears that the nucleus of such an organisation had already sprung up throughout the community in the vigilante groups which had emerged since the beginning of the disturbances.

The detailed blueprint for the new forces emerged in November 1969 when the government published two White Papers announcing their intention to create a 1,500-strong RUC reserve, to perform part-time duty in support of the regular police and a second force, to be known as the Ulster Defence Regiment, would be a 6,000-strong regiment of the British army, under the command of the GOC, charged with providing military back-up exclusively in Northern Ireland. The proposal clearly divorced the police and military roles in Northern Ireland in line with the Hunt report.

There was at once another series of meetings at which the Specials considered their future. In South Londonderry, an entire platoon of twelve men resigned and at Cullybackey, County Antrim, fifteen members of the local unit quit. The broad reaction was, however, favourable 'with many reservations' according to a statement issued by an unofficial central committee.

During a rancorous discussion about the Hunt report in the Northern Ireland parliament at Stormont, hardline Unionists criticised their government for ceding control of the new UDR to the army, which was answerable to the British government. Harry West, a diehard Unionist MP, asked what would happen if the British government wanted to prune its defence forces and decided to axe the UDR. 'I hope the minister will tell us whether we have the right to establish our own force. I hope we would have the guts to establish our own force,' he said.

West also commented on the intention that, like all army recruits, members of the UDR should take the oath of allegiance to the Queen. He did not see how Nationalists joining it could reconcile their aspirations of a united Ireland with the defence role of the new force. 'If they are true to their ideals, they will be playing a double role,' he said. 'An ounce of loyalty is worth many tons of armaments.'

The Hunt report had meanwhile been warmly welcomed by Nationalist politicians, who generally urged Catholics to join both forces and play their part in the community. Their welcome was tempered in November when they discovered that 'application forms' had been sent to every member of the USC asking them their preference of the two new forces. Paddy O'Hanlon, an independent Nationalist, angrily waved one of the forms in the chamber at Stormont and accused the Unionists of trying to 'pack' the new forces and asked if there would be a block application from the USC when recruiting opened.

The question of the application forms and B Special membership also came up in the Westminster parliament when the legislation creating the new Regiment was being debated. Roy

Hattersley, the junior Minister for Defence, told the House that 'of necessity, the new force will draw substantially on the USC for its initial recruitment but there will be a campaign to enrol recruits from all sections of the Northern Ireland community'.

Mr Hattersley was forced to disown the occurrence as a slip-up and assure the House that there could be no question of any wholesale transfer from the Specials to the UDR because all applicants would be individually vetted for suitability. 'The recruiting instrument for the new Regiment is the normal army recruiting form,' he said. But the USC component was vital, the minister stressed, to ensure early viability of the new Regiment and, he continued, the USC was composed of a majority of men who had given good and honourable service to Northern Ireland. To placate snowballing fears that the UDR would merely be the Specials under another name, he listed seven points of distinction: the UDR would be controlled from Whitehall; British army officers would be in charge; there would be a firm training obligation; it would not be used for riot control; there would be free entry for all citizens; military discipline would prevail; and recruits would be security vetted. But the posting of application forms to serving Specials and the publication of recruiting advertisements in newspapers and on television before parliament had even passed enabling legislation angered several MPs and Nationalist politicians in Northern Ireland. They regarded the move as Unionist skulduggery to influence the army procedures to recruit the new soldiers. The whole episode had an uneasy similarity to the way the Unionists packed the Specials on formation.

Labour MPs also questioned the name of the new force. Eric Heffer asked: 'Defence against whom? Southern Ireland, or is it an internal defence force?'

Kevin McNamara said that as Ulster properly consisted of nine Irish counties, not six, surely the name of the new force was a misnomer. He wanted 'Northern Ireland Defence Force'.

The Mid-Ulster member, Bernadette Devlin, suggested 'Local Territorial Force', a name which would have 'no partisan bias and offend no one'.

Lord Hunt himself, initiator of the force, opposed the

proposed name when the legislation was debated in the House of Lords. 'I regret that this force has been given a name which is anathema to many Catholics who might be disposed to do their civic duty and join the force.'

The government was unmoved by the protests. Mr Hattersley asked that the force be judged by its characteristics and constitution, not its name, and replied that it was the practice, when raising new regiments of the British army, to incorporate names which have been used in the past. 'The word "Ulster" has played a distinctive part in British army history,' he said.

After an all-night sitting on 1/2 December, the bill was approved by the Commons and a week later by the Lords. It came into force on 1 January 1970 enabling recruiting to start. As preparations for the operational deployment of the new UDR on 1 April 1970 went ahead the formal disbandment date for the USC was set for April 30.

On 19 February, a USC patrol guarding a water pumping installation at Ballynahinch, County Down exchanged shots with unidentified raiders in what turned out to be the Constabulary's last engagement.

The government decided that every man would get a £10 discharge bounty in recognition of what the prime minister, Major James Chichester-Clark, described as the 'immense debt Ulster owes you'. He was speaking, on 22 March, at a religious service held at the King's Hall, Belfast to mark the disbandment. In keeping with the Specials' Protestant and Orange tradition, the service was conducted only by clergymen from the Church of Ireland, Methodist and Presbyterian religions.

Through the post, every member serving at the end later received a testimonial, signed by the prime minister, thanking them for their 'loyal and distinguished service . . . to the government and people of Northern Ireland'.

The Specials went out on a note of controversy with questions at Stormont about the whereabouts of their guns. The Northern Ireland government defended them to the end. All the guns had been accounted for, they insisted, pointing out that in the fifty years of the force's existence only twenty of the 50,000 weapons issued to it had ever been stolen.

2 The UDR: 1970–1975

On 1 January 1970 application forms to join the new UDR were made available at police stations and army careers offices throughout Northern Ireland. In a bid to widen the recruiting base in the community, the forms were also available from all post offices and public libraries.

The particular importance of attracting Catholic recruits was underlined from the start when the Ministry of Defence disclosed that, conveniently, the first two completed forms had come from Catholics.

There was more public symbolism and conditioning a few weeks later, on 18 February, when the first two recruits were publicly sworn in at the War Memorial Building in Waring Street, Belfast. 'Protestant and Roman Catholic take united stand,' reported the *Belfast Telegraph* as Catholic James McAree, aged 19 and Protestant Albert Richmond, aged 47, pronounced the oath of allegiance to the Queen. 'It seemed a good idea to join,' said McAree, a bookmaker's clerk. 'It will bring people of opposite religions together and I am sure it will be a moderate force both in persuasion and outlook.'

The swearing-in ceremony was watched by the GOC, Lieutenant-General Sir Ian Freeland and the man appointed as the first Commanding Officer of the UDR, Brigadier Logan Scott-Bowden. At 49 years of age, the cigar-smoking Brigadier had an impressive military record and wide experience of war and the world's theatres of conflict.

A native of Moresby, Cumberland, he was educated at Malvern College and the Royal Military Academy, Woolwich, and commissioned into the Royal Engineers on the outbreak of war in 1939.

In 1943, as a major with the special forces, he played a role in the reconnaissance before the Normandy landings, winning the MC and DSO for carrying out observations from midget submarines and swimming under the nose of the German occupation forces to inspect beach and sea fortifications. On D-Day, 6 June 1944, he helped pilot ashore the first wave of amphibious tanks from the 1st US Division at Omaha beach, where some of the fiercest fighting took place.

After the war he served in Palestine, Egypt, Libya and Greece. Following a spell at the War Office in London he went to Aden and later to Germany.

In 1969, while pondering the defence problems of India at the country's National Defence College, he was recalled to London and told he was to raise and command the proposed UDR. Backed up by nine majors from the British army, he arrived in Northern Ireland to begin his task.

About the same time Denis Healey, the Secretary of State for Defence, had outlined the military concept of the UDR in a White Paper published in November 1969 and later, in the House of Commons, during the debates on the legislation. 'This must be a military force, under military discipline and control,' he said.

Accepting the principle, enunciated by Hunt, that the police and military roles should be separated in Northern Ireland and brought into line with the rest of the UK, the UDR was therefore conceived as a locally recruited, part-time military defence force, under the control of the GOC, tasked to support the regular army on purely military duties carried out in support of the civil police. Members of the new UDR were to be subject to military law when on duty.

These duties were defined as protecting the border and the state against armed guerrilla-type attack and sabotage by undertaking guard duties at key points and installations, carrying out patrols and establishing checkpoints and road blocks when required. Any public order role for the regiment, either in crowd or riot control, was firmly ruled out from the start.

The UDR was to be organised into seven battalions, one for each of the six counties and one for Belfast, with an establishment of 6,000 officers and men. The Regiment would be an integral part of the British army, although it would not be called upon to serve outside Northern Ireland.

Each battalion would be commanded by a local member of the force supported by regular soldiers, 200 officers and NCOs in all, interspersed at various levels. A major, effectively second-in-command, would be responsible for training and administration. By military standards the force was to be lightly armed, mainly with standard army rifles. The basic vehicle was to be the Land Rover, for troop carrying, equipped with radio communication. Standard dress was to be army combat uniform, although a parade dress for formal wear was promised in due course.

The UDR would be called out for duty in defence of life and property against armed attack or sabotage and the legislation also provided for it to be placed on a whole time basis to defend the UK against 'actual or apprehended attack' or 'in circumstances of imminent national danger or great emergency'.

All male citizens of good character, aged between 18 and 55, normally resident in Northern Ireland, whatever their denomination, were deemed eligible for enrolment on a three-year engagement. The suitability of each candidate would be strictly vetted at the army headquarters. In parliament, Denis Healey stressed there would be no automatic right of transfer for ex-members of the USC and he said that in doubtful cases, the GOC 'will consult anyone whose opinion he values, on either the sincerity of the application or upon the veracity of the details'.

Such assurances were crucial if the UDR were to attract a strong Catholic element from the outset. The invitations to the old Specials had left a sour taste with many Nationalist politicians who had reservations about encouraging their constituents to enlist. When ex-commandants of the USC, most of them ex-soldiers anyway, were given commands of all seven of the new UDR battalions, these reservations increased. Gerry

Fitt complained at Westminster about the lack of Catholic officers.

Denis Healey had no qualms, however. Addressing the House of Commons on 19 November 1969 he waxed lyrical about the new dawn represented by the UDR.

> Ever since I first became Secretary of State for Defence I have been struck by the role of the services in Britain as an instrument of social integration – as a means by which men of all walks of life and from all parts of Britain and the Commonwealth can be welded into a living unit. This is true, above all, of the Northern Irish regiments of the British army. For many years, our Irish regiments have included both Protestants and Catholics. Indeed, they now have almost as many Catholics as Protestants. But while the Catholics and Protestants in these regiments remain equally proud of their faith and their special traditions, this is never a source of conflict in their daily work, and still less in battle. The religious affiliation of the individual officer or soldier has been completely irrelevant: at most, it is a matter for banter and leg pulling on mess nights.

Roy Hattersley concluded the debate by saying: 'I genuinely believe that the force can be commended to the House as an instrument for future peace and prosperity in Northern Ireland.'

Early in 1970 Brigadier Scott-Bowden was equally optimistic. He referred to his experience in Canada in 1942 training a joint force of men from the British and French traditions. 'In my experience in Canada and elsewhere I have been amazed how little religion or race matters once men get into uniform together,' he said. 'If you play with a straight bat and are constantly cautious you will not run into any great difficulties.'

The early signs were indeed most encouraging. During the first two weeks of recruiting, between eighty and a hundred applications a day flooded into army headquarters. In the first month of recruiting 2,123 men applied to join the UDR, 1,029 of them ex-Specials. According to their declared religion, 77 per cent of them were Protestants, 22 per cent Catholics.

It had been decided that the UDR would go operational on 1 April, working a one-month transition period with the USC, which would be disbanded at the end of April. By the end of

March the UDR strength was 2,440, including 1,423 ex-Specials. Catholics numbered 946.

The breakdown by each battalion area, according to information given to parliament, was:

	Applications	Accepted	USC	Accepted
Antrim (1UDR)	575	221	220	93
Armagh (2UDR)	615	370	402	277
Down (3UDR)	460	229	195	116
Fermanagh (4UDR)	471	223	386	193
Londonderry (5UDR)	671	382	338	219
Tyrone (6UDR)	1187	637	813	489
Belfast (7UDR)	797	378	70	36

Each recruit had been carefully vetted, according to Roy Hattersley. Two referees, nominated by every applicant, had been interviewed to assess their suitability and ensure they were of good character and 'not active supporters of any organisations on one or other extreme of the political spectrum'.

The vetting left some ruffled feathers. Robin Chichester-Clark, the Unionist MP for Londonderry asked in parliament why one of his constituents, a local government official and churchwarden, a man 'jealous of his reputation and good name', had been rejected. On both sides there were claims and names that either active civil righters or notorious ex-B Specials had been enlisted.

Hattersley said that he had instructed the army that if there was any doubt about applicants they should err on the side of caution but he also said that exclusion of an individual should not be taken as an indictment of his character. He disclosed that two clergymen, one a former officer in the Specials, had been turned down because the UDR had to be 'isolated from political and sectarian influence'.

In a similar critical vein a Unionist MP wanted to know why the Union flag had been omitted from the UDR's recruiting advertisements. Mr Hattersley said the flag was only used in national advertisements for the regular army.

While the new recruits were being vetted, Brigadier Scott-Bowden and his team were planning the operational role for the new Regiment in makeshift headquarters, a house inside the Thiepval Barracks complex at Lisburn, and drawing up training schedules for the men who had enlisted.

Those with previous military experience were put on a fast track refresher course, drilling on barrack squares, firing on the ranges, to sharpen up their already acquired skills. When the Regiment went operational for the first time on 1 April 1970, they provided the front-line soldiers.

One of the first duties the UDR assumed was providing the guard at Palace Barracks, Holywood, five miles from Belfast, one of the main army garrisons in Northern Ireland. Within the month, however, as the USC was finally phased out, the UDR was providing soldiers to help the army carry out road checks and guard key installations throughout the entire six counties.

On 30 April, 400 UDR soldiers combined for the first time with 1,600 regular soldiers in Operation Mulberry, an all-night search operation for arms, by setting up checkpoints on border roads across the counties of Armagh, Fermanagh and Tyrone, the first of many such major security operations involving the Regiment.

Those early days were a chapter of austerity and improvisation for the founding members of the force. Uniform clothing was generally old-style olive green battledress, with Second World War webbing. The choice of sizes was limited too, so the sight of those original units squaring up for duty in ill-fitting uniforms, with imperfect drill, was far from an impressive one, especially when combined with the long hair and thick sideburns which were the height of fashion at the time. Small wonder that the UDR was promptly dubbed 'Dad's Army', after the popular television programme which hilariously chronicled the activities of a Home Guard platoon in England in the early days of the Second World War.

That first winter one UDR unit was issued with white Arctic-wear duffle coats, totally impractical, as they made easy night-time targets of any soldier foolish enough to wear them. Another unit fared little better. It was given heavy jackets designed for motor-cycle despatch riders, which were not waterproofed and when it rained, became steadily sodden so that it was a feat of endurance just to stand up in them.

Weaponry was equally antiquated. The guns handed in by the B Specials had been sent back to England for refurbishment, according to the authorities, so old bolt action .303 Lee Enfields, the terror of former national servicemen, and war vintage Bren guns, became the standard issue. Other equipment was also hard to come by and one unit received an eagerly awaited crate only to find that it contained bulky instruction manuals for loading a Belfast airfreighter, a large transport plane then in service with the RAF.

Accommodation was also vintage and spartan. Battalion headquarters and company bases were established in a variety of makeshift locations. At Ballykinler, County Down, 3UDR was put together from huts dating back to the First World War. Elsewhere former Specials drill halls, Nissen huts, caravans, even rooms in police stations were pressed into service. Local companies established themselves in whatever accommodation they could find in their areas, and old vicarages, derelict country houses and spare factory outbuildings were commandeered. At least one officer operated from a former ladies' lavatory into which he manoeuvred a desk and chair, and old army stores lorries were fitted with bunks and parked at bases or guard points to provide unheated accommodation for units on stand-by duty.

Out on the ground things were hardly better. Transport was scarce, so soldiers going on and off duty frequently had to wait around until they could be picked up or dropped off. They had little radio equipment and what they had usually baffled the embryonic radio operators so it became standard practice to issue patrols with coins and tell them to find and use a public telephone to keep in touch and report incidents.

Other arrangements were equally rudimentary. Patrols detailed for guard duty at key installations were issued with a hurricane lamp, a box of sticking plasters and a lance-corporal's stripe and safety pin for the senior member of the patrol to attach to his uniform.

The manpower was frequently short of the required levels and there were, with hindsight, some massive security risks. At Dungannon, ten rifles and 200 rounds of ammunition were kept in a caravan in the town square, which functioned for a time as a UDR post. Many patrols had to travel unarmed to barracks to collect weapons and then return them for safekeeping because most UDR locations were locked up and unguarded during the day while the part-time soldiers were at their civilian work.

At Larne six soldiers, five of them ex-Specials, resigned in protest at the lack of administration and the risk of travelling to and from army bases in uniform to collect their weapons. Insult was added to their injury, they said, when nobody could even tell them how to resign. The Reverend Ian Paisley MP wanted to know why men guarding a telephone exchange at Newcastle, County Down were unarmed. One battalion commander reacted brusquely to the criticism. 'At the moment we are trying to form an instant army,' he said. 'People should give us a chance to get off the ground first before they start criticising.'

Despite the best efforts of the army and the fledgling UDR throughout 1970 and into 1971, the interlocked security and political situation in Northern Ireland deteriorated to un-imagined barbarism. In the spring of 1970, a militant breakaway faction from the IRA, which called itself the Provisional IRA, came into existence. At first it contented itself with manipulating riots and other public disorder, but soon, with financial and other help from sympathisers in the United States, it acquired weapons and explosives and began a campaign of urban terrorism. A no-warning bomb explosion at a bank in High Street, Belfast on 16 July was a harbinger of much worse to come. By 15 September 1970 there had been one hundred explosions and in February 1971, Gunner Robert Curtis, the first regular soldier to be killed, was shot by a sniper in the New Lodge Road area of Belfast.

At that time there were 7,300 regular soldiers in Northern Ireland as well as about 4,000 members of the UDR. The army was in control of the worsening security situation as the police struggled to regroup after its 1969 collapse, a task heavily aggravated by the escalating volume of violence, including murder, and the increasing turmoil in the community.

The army assessment, according to the GOC, Sir Harry Tuzo, was that they could achieve a gradual ascendancy over the IRA which would allow the politicians to work out a settlement, but that there was no permanent military solution to the problem.

In July 1971, Brigadier Scott-Bowden left Northern Ireland on promotion to major-general and a further appointment in India, this time as head of the British Defence Liaison Staff. He was replaced by Brigadier Denis Ormerod, a Catholic, aged 49. Educated at Downside School, Somerset, Ormerod joined the army in 1940 and served in India and then with the Gurkhas in Malaya, India, Italy and Greece, attaining the rank of major. After the war he was awarded the MBE and mentioned in despatches while attached to the Gurkhas in Malaya. On his return in 1950, he served with the Royal Irish Fusiliers for a time, the first of several postings including two with Irish formations of the British army. He was not long at his new post with the UDR before a major crisis developed.

With the intensified level of violence throughout the early part of 1971, the security forces regularly came under fire and the economic destruction, caused by bombs, mounted. By the end of July there had been a further 187 explosions. Final provocation came with the bombing of the *Daily Mirror* newspaper printing plant in Belfast and the abduction of a wounded terrorist, under guard in the city's Royal Victoria Hospital, by armed men in white coats disguised as doctors.

The British government, then headed by Edward Heath, who had come to power in the 1970 general election, reluctantly authorised Brian Faulkner's Stormont administration, who had been pressing for it, to introduce internment without trial. On 9 August 1971, in an operation code named 'Demetrius', about

400 terrorist suspects were rounded up in early morning swoops and detained. It proved to be a decisive turning point for both Northern Ireland and the UDR.

Any hopes that internment would contain the situation were immediately dashed. There was a dramatic upsurge of violence in the hours after the dawn raids which raised questions about the accuracy of the information used by the authorities in drawing up the arrest lists. The swoops sparked off severe rioting and pitched gun battles throughout Belfast and in several country areas. The IRA's leaders, the targets of the arrests, held a provocative news conference in a Belfast school, under the noses of the army, to prove that they had not been captured. Among the twenty-two victims of the intense violence over the next seventy-two hours was the first UDR soldier to be killed.

After the internment swoops, the entire UDR was mobilised for full-time duty, the first such call-out. Apart from 600 away on holidays and 300 in training, about 3,100 men were deployed throughout Northern Ireland on full-time duty for nearly two weeks. One of them was Private Winston Donnell, aged 22, a member of a patrol from 6UDR on road checkpoint duty near Clady on the Tyrone/Donegal border when two shots were aimed at them. About ten minutes later a burst of thirty to forty shots were fired from a car by a gunman with an automatic weapon. Private Donnell, one of four brothers serving in the UDR, fell dead.

More significantly in the long term, the introduction of internment ended the growing involvement of the Catholic community in a bid to find a peaceful way out of Northern Ireland's social and political problems. Over the preceding year a new grouping, the Social Democratic and Labour Party, comprised of moderate Catholic and Nationalist politicians, had been formed with the major policy goal of shelving any immediate moves to a united Ireland in favour of an accommodation with the Unionists to enable Catholics to play a full and fair part in governing Northern Ireland.

They had engaged in dialogue with Brian Faulkner, who had

by then replaced Major James Chichester-Clark as prime minister. After a round of talks in July, Faulkner said 'nothing of this sort involving private and completely frank exchanges has been attempted before' and 'we all think it worthwhile to continue with this experiment'.

With the recent history of Protestant involvement in violence, including the sabotage of water and electricity installations and the killing of a police officer, Catholics were shocked that the internment swoops were directed exclusively against people suspected of IRA links or those identified with the civil rights movement. Such blatant one-sidedness cut the feet from under the SDLP who had no answer to Catholic accusations that nothing had changed or would change. Their anger was amplified by the knowledge that as he talked peace with them, Faulkner was clearly immersed in planning the biased security swoops. Internment confirmed growing resentment that the extensive arms searches of the previous year had been exclusively targeted in Catholic areas. A forty-eight-hour search and curfew operation by the army in the Lower Falls at the beginning of July 1970, when families were forcibly confined in their homes for most of a weekend, especially infuriated Catholic opinion.

Although the Regiment did not take part in the arrests, these factors had implications for the substantial Catholic element in the UDR, then about one-fifth of its entire strength. Their membership was a reflection of the desire among most Catholics at that time for a peaceful existence through full-blooded participation in the Northern Ireland state. The one-sided application of internment, therefore, smacking, as it did, of a return to the bad old days of Unionist repression, left the Catholics in the UDR in a disillusioned and vulnerable position. This time Catholic reaction was made worse by the British government's clear connivance, despite its assumed impartiality and the mood of fair play and reform it had so clearly stimulated since 1969.

Internment was not the only problem for Catholics in the UDR, who were already becoming disenchanted at the way the Protestants, especially the former Specials, were being given the key jobs and promotion. One Catholic member recalls how uncomfortable he was made to feel every time he reported for duty at what was a former B Special drill hall, previously forbidden ground to anyone of his faith. Others spoke of more subtle intimidation, being cold-shouldered or ignored. 'It was made clear we weren't wanted,' said one, who later resigned.

Others objected to the military policy, complaining about the routine roughness and frequent brutality meted out by the regular soldiers, and the emphasis on patrolling and oppressing Catholic areas on the basis that they were the monopoly suppliers of disorder.

Their 'loyalty' was also being called into constant question by Unionists despite the fact that all Catholic soldiers had taken the required Oath of Allegiance to the Queen. There was also a certain hysteria, understandable but ill-founded, that there would be an armed invasion across the border, and Unionists remained in constant anxiety about the reaction of the minority in the UDR.

This sense of betrayal and uneasiness among those who had joined the UDR was vented at a private meeting of some thirty-one Catholic soldiers held at St Mary's Hall in Belfast on 18 August. They were addressed by Austin Currie, a civil rights activist and one of the SDLP MPs at Stormont, whose own brother was in the UDR. He told them:

> I object to the role which the army has played in interning people without trial and the role which the UDR has played in helping (regular) soldiers to be available for this sort of activity. As a result of army action and the policy of the British government, I am no longer obliged to say to Catholics that they should go into the UDR.

The position of the Catholics was already precarious because for some time they had been coming under pressure from the IRA. Barely a month after the UDR's first appearance on the streets, a pattern of intimidation began to emerge. At Clady, a border village in County Tyrone, one soldier of only three weeks' standing had his front door daubed with the slogan: 'Get out of the UDR or be shot – IRA.' Two weeks later, as the man, his wife and five young children slept in their house, shotgun blasts were fired at it, shattering several windows, but not causing any injuries.

Two other members of the Regiment were approached in the Falls Road area of Belfast by two men who handed them .38 bullets and said that they would be shot if they did not resign from the UDR.

In the bitter aftermath of internment, this sort of IRA intimidation was stepped up, especially as reports began to circulate that the army had ill-treated and even tortured some of the persons taken into custody. Against this background seventeen soldiers at the Belfast meeting decided to resign, another five had already done so and many others, not at the meeting, decided to reconsider their position. Within a month eighty resigned and there followed a steady exodus of Catholics from the UDR.

On 3 September another UDR member was murdered on duty. Private Frank Veitch, aged 23, a farmer, was shot dead by gunmen firing from a car outside the RUC station at Kinawley, County Fermanagh. He was hit in the head and neck by at least five shots as he walked from the station gate to a sandbagged look-out post nearby. His killers sped off in a car towards the nearby border.

Three more serving soldiers and a former member paid for their UDR connection with their lives in a four-day period in December, cold-blooded killings that were all the more poignant with the proximity of Christmas. On the evening of 7 December, Private Dennis Wilson, aged 31, went to bed early suffering from a cold. At about 10.30 pm three armed men forced their way into his farmhouse at Curlough, near Caledon, just three hundred yards from the Irish border, and while one of them held members of the family at gunpoint, the others went upstairs and killed him.

At 8 am on 10 December, two men in a civilian Land Rover

were ambushed as they made their usual stop at Lisdoo, near Clady, County Tyrone to give a third man a lift to work. Sergeant Kenneth Smyth, a former Special serving with 6UDR, and Daniel McCormick, a Catholic and former UDR private, who had recently resigned after threats, were shot dead.

But it was the second of the three horrific incidents, at New Barnsley, Belfast on 8 December, that was arguably the most significant, because it involved a serving Catholic UDR soldier. In the early evening, after returning from work as a steel fixer, Sean Russell was sitting on the sofa, watching television surrounded by his five children, girls aged 2, 7 and 10 and boys of 5 and 8. His wife, Jean, was in the adjoining kitchen preparing the evening meal, when a masked gunman rang the doorbell and burst into the house past one of the boys who had answered it.

As the gunman asked, 'Are you Sean?' Russell rose to grapple with him but as he did so three shots were fired, hitting him twice in the head and wounding his 10-year-old daughter in the thigh. As the dying man fell to the floor, the gunman pushed through the screaming children and, according to eyewitnesses outside, escaped on foot with smoke coming from his gun barrel.

That week alone at least forty Catholics fled from the UDR. Joe Russell, the dead man's brother, said: 'When Sean joined the UDR he never thought he might have to face the gunmen. He just saw the Regiment as playing a part in the running of the community and with Catholics taking a hand in it for the first time.' Although he had not quit, the dead soldier had been affected by the disillusionment among Catholic UDR members before his death. Relatives spoke of his worries about ex-B men getting the important jobs and he had confided he was scared, probably because he had been threatened himself or knew fellow-Catholics who had been. Only a week earlier two UDR Catholics had been fired on, over their heads, and then told by the gunmen to quit or next time the shots would be for real. Others had been receiving threats by telephone, or through the letterbox by post. Letters, bullets and even excrement were delivered. In addition wives were insulted and boycotted in shops and the children of Catholic soldiers were taunted and bullied at school.

By November, according to official statistics given to parliament, the Catholic proportion in the Regiment had halved to just 8 per cent. By the end of the year the potent combination of disillusionment and threat to their personal safety among the Catholic soldiers had dealt a body blow to the Regiment's desire to be a mixed force, from which it never recovered.

Internment itself turned out to be a profound misjudgment. In the seven months beforehand, thirty people had died in the civil disturbances but by the end of 1971 the toll had reached 173, including the first five casualties suffered by the UDR. The level of shootings and bombings also soared. There had, for instance, been only 78 explosions in July, but after the introduction of internment the numbers increased steeply – 131 in August, 196 in September and 117 in October.

At the end of September, with the army publicly saying that it had infiltrated and was getting on top of the IRA, a major expansion of the UDR was announced by Major-General Robert Ford, the Commander of Land Forces in Northern Ireland. The UDR manpower 'ceiling' of 6,000 was increased to 8,000 then 10,000 and the formation of three additional battalions was put in hand. 8UDR was formed by dividing 6UDR, then the largest battalion, and became operational in December; 9 and 10UDR battalions, drawn from 1 and 7UDR, the Antrim and Belfast battalions, went in to operation in January 1972, while a fourth extra formation, 11UDR, went into action in September 1972, bringing UDR strength up to an all-time peak of more than 9,000 and making it not only the youngest but also the largest infantry regiment in the British army.

The growing terrorist threat during this same period led to the UDR being given more modern rifles, the 7.62 mm SLR, at that time the standard NATO rifle used by the British army. In addition the UDR was given fifteen Shorland armoured patrol vehicles, equipped with machine guns.

Early in 1972, some elements of the Regiment went

waterborne, when high speed Dory patrol boats, capable of travelling at 20 knots were supplied to them. These fibre-glass, twin-engined boats were introduced to enable the soldiers to patrol the 240 square miles of inland waterway, including Upper and Lower Lough Erne and Lough Neagh, as well as the Ulster coastline, to inhibit gun running and the movement of explosives. They operated in pairs with one boat equipped with a machine gun providing cover while a boarding party from the other checked out vessels and their crews.

The time to get a volunteer into uniform and on active service was cut to two weeks for vetting and initial enlistment and another six days for basic training. Greater use was also made of the expanded and better equipped UDR, with more men deployed guarding key points in their own local areas and a higher frequency of armed reconnaissance patrols put into the border areas, many of them by Wessex, or the new Puma, troopcarrying helicopters drafted in to provide greater mobility for the soldiers.

During this period many UDR members, principally in the isolated rural areas along the border, were permitted to keep their rifles at home partly for their own protection and partly for greater efficiency, if they were called out quickly in response to an incident. At the same time, where a threat was judged to exist, many soldiers were also issued with Walther pistols for personal protection when off duty.

There was still great political sensitivity about permitting UDR soldiers to be armed off duty and the army tried to restrict the issue of licences. The selective approach caused trouble within the 200-strong unit based at Carrickfergus, County Antrim where some soldiers refused to report for duty. After the intervention of the MP, James Molyneaux, the problems were smoothed out when more protective equipment, including flak-jackets, was supplied to the soldiers.

The rapid expansion of the UDR throughout 1972 and the intensification of security measures reflected the level of violence in the community that year, which reached a pitch unthinkable even when measured against the violence of Irish history.

In January, members of the Parachute Regiment killed thirteen unarmed civilians while trying to break-up a civil rights march in Londonderry. The intensity of the reaction against the army was aggravated by their brazen insistence that they had been fired on, a doubtful claim which has never been convincingly substantiated.

The shock-waves from 'Bloody Sunday' – as it became known – broke through Whitehall and before they had even subsided it was discovered that the presumed legal basis for army operations in Northern Ireland was entirely unfounded. On 23 February, a Northern Ireland Act, setting out a legal framework for the use of the army and, in a highly unusual provision, retrospectively legalising all the army's actions since its first deployment in 1969, had to be rushed through the entire parliamentary process in one day.

After that the doctrine was established that responsibility and accountability for British troops on the Ulster streets had to lie with Downing Street and Westminster. The blurred overlaps and ambiguities between Belfast and London in determining security policy and how to react to the worsening situation had to be removed. In March, Faulkner visited London to be told that control of security was therefore to be taken back from his Stormont administration. After nine hours of talks he returned to Belfast, where the proposition was unacceptable to his Cabinet, and they all resigned. The British government then announced the indefinite prorogation of the Stormont parliament and that direct rule from London was being introduced. It appointed a senior Cabinet minister, William Whitelaw, to head a new Northern Ireland Office.

Faulkner's hand had been forced by hardliners in the Unionist ranks, not prepared for any sort of compromise with the minority. They had fought his pragmatic strategy and campaigned for draconian security measures, including the creation of a 'Third Force', arguing that the UDR did not match the B Specials. They insisted that tough security policies, not reforms –appeasing the IRA – as they saw it, were the only answer.

Their figurehead was William Craig, the former Home Affairs Minister at Stormont, who was forced out of office by Captain Terence O'Neill for voicing thoughts about the Stormont government breaking away from Britain if the Unionists did not get their own way. In the months leading up to Direct Rule, Craig formed the Vanguard movement, which held a series of well attended rallies at which he inspected lines of men drawn up in military formation. 'God help those who get in our way, for we mean business,' he told a rally at Lisburn. Later he talked of building up dossiers in case of a need to 'liquidate the enemy'.

Craig and his supporters clearly represented an extreme reaction, but there was quite justified anger and fear among the less vociferous Protestant community. For months there had been an IRA campaign of indiscriminate car bombing, killing and maiming people without warning in Belfast and other places, devastating shops, offices and factories and throwing many out of work. An outspoken government minister, John Taylor, had narrowly survived an assassination attempt.

Further provocation was given to Protestant opinion by the existence of so called 'no-go areas' in Belfast and, above all, Londonderry. These were the Catholic areas that had been the battleground in the 1969 disturbances and where the security forces only patrolled with caution. In Londonderry the entire Bogside and Creggan areas were sealed off with barricades and behind them the IRA paraded openly with masks and arms.

Protestants generally feared that closing down the Stormont parliament left them vulnerable to what they thought was an IRA insurrection and that the authorities were both unwilling and unable to deal with it. The sense of vulnerability was increased by what was regarded as a loss of control over their own security. For the first time, Unionists had no security force, private or official, to defend their interests.

The discontent among the community was reflected within the UDR and there were many unofficial caucus meetings. Unit commanders were instructed to give pep-talks to their men, but nevertheless there were threats of resignations and at least one case of a unit refusing to go out on duty.

The general fears prompted the emergence of a Protestant group calling itself the Ulster Defence Association. Its origins lay in vigilante groups formed to patrol Protestant working-class areas in Belfast after 1969, who had now banded together under an 'Inner Council' led by a 'Supreme Commander'. Before long it boasted up to 10,000 members throughout Northern Ireland, a claim not easily discounted, for it twice put thousands of masked men, clad in second-hand military clothing, on to the streets in the turbulent summer of 1972.

In June 1972, a deputation was received at Stormont Castle by Whitelaw, who gave them the assurances which they sought that a plebiscite on the future of the border would be held and that firm action would be taken to open up the IRA 'no-go' areas in Belfast and Londonderry.

Whitelaw was not long in fulfilling his pledge about the 'no-go' areas. The end of a short-lived IRA ceasefire was marked by a blitz of twenty-two bombs, which exploded without warning throughout Belfast over a forty-five minute period, killing nine people and injuring 130, on Bloody Friday, 21 July. A week later, in the biggest land operation since the Korean War two decades earlier, the army moved in force into the Nationalist areas of Belfast and Londonderry. Altogether some 22,000 soldiers, twenty-seven infantry and two armoured battalions, were involved in 'Operation Motorman'.

It was a major watershed in security policy which gradually turned the tide against the IRA and diminished street militancy on the Protestant side. The Catholic areas were dominated by intensive patrolling and intelligence-gathering activities co-ordinated by computer. The army carried out a virtual door-to-door census and compiled detailed data on every household, right down to the number of bottles of milk they received each morning. Such details were useful when people on the street were stopped for screening. Anyone unable to give the right answers for the address he claimed to belong to was taken into custody for a more thorough check. The movements of those suspected of active terrorism were put under close scrutiny and houses were searched to find the hiding places for arms and explosives.

To deter the bombers, the commercial centre of Belfast was sealed off with a ring of forty-one barbed wire entanglements and eight-feet high steel fences across the streets, with every shopper and worker searched as they entered. 'Control zones' were set up elsewhere with car parking banned unless someone was left sitting inside the car, a ploy to prevent vehicles packed with explosive being positioned.

The UDR, who provided 5,300 soldiers to back up Motor-man, played a key role in the new security arrangements. In October, members of 9UDR, from outlying towns, Antrim, Carrickfergus, Ballyclare and Lisburn, were mobilised for a short period of full-time duty and drafted into Belfast to help guard the city centre segment. They were billeted in the army headquarters in the city, the former Grand Central Hotel, where spartan military accommodation had replaced the former opulence.

The risks of being a UDR soldier increased progressively throughout the year, with members of the Regiment being murdered, both on and off duty. Sergeant Maynard Crawford, who worked as the foreman on a building site, was sitting at the wheel of his van on 14 January, waiting to take his workmen home when the gunmen struck, killing him instantly. His 9-year-old son may have inadvertently helped target his father. Some months earlier an anonymous caller to the family home had asked: 'Is your daddy a policeman?' The boy had replied proudly: 'No, he's in the UDR.'

On 16 February, Thomas Callaghan, aged 45, a bus driver and a Catholic, was dragged from his vehicle by armed men while working in the Creggan area of Londonderry. Two hours later his body, hooded and with gunshot wounds to the head, was found dumped nearby. Train driver and part-time Sergeant Harry Dickson, aged 55, another ex-Special, was shot dead when two gunmen called at his home in Lurgan on 29 February. His 11-year-old daughter was hit in the leg and wounded during the attack.

Less than ten hours later, four gunmen arrived at the small border farm of forestry worker, Tommy Fletcher, near Garrison, County Fermanagh. He was held up as he drove down the lane and taken back to the house where the raiders started to search for guns. After taking a pistol and shotgun, they told his wife that they were taking her husband, a part-time UDR soldier, hostage. About 150 yards from the house they frog-marched him into a field and fired twenty-two shots, killing him instantly. As his wife ran to him, the four killers strode off across the nearby border.

Within days five families of UDR members abandoned their homes and farms near the border in the Garrison area. Troops and police stood by as their furniture and other possessions were loaded on to farm trailers and taken to new homes. Their livestock was taken to the market at Enniskillen and auctioned. All said that they had left after threats to their lives and families.

Captain Marcus McCausland, a Catholic, who had submitted his resignation to the UDR because he feared for the safety of his family, was abducted on 4 March while returning across the border after visiting friends. At 8 am his hooded body, shot through the head, was found on a snow-covered laneway leading from the border into the Creggan area of Londonderry. At the subsequent inquest the coroner, Hubert O'Neill, asked: 'How could any Irishman take out another Irishman and shoot him like a dog?'

Over the next few months, Lance-Corporal Joseph Jardine, Private Samuel Trainor and Corporal James Elliott were all murdered. Between May and September, Lance-Corporal William Gillespie, Private Edward Megahey, Corporal Roy Stanton, Private Harry Russell, Private Robert McComb, Lance-Corporal Harry Creighton, Lance-Corporal Alfred Johnston and Lance-Corporal Victor Smyth also lost their lives.

On 21 September, Private Thomas Bullock and his wife were watching television in their farmhouse at Killynick,

Fermanagh, only a mile from the border, when three gunmen drove up. Mrs Bullock was instantly shot in the chest at the front porch and the gunmen then stepped over her dead body and went inside, where they shot her husband several times in the head and neck, also killing him. Later in the evening, a hostile crowd from a dance hall blocked the path of two hearses which were on their way to collect the bodies.

In October and November, Staff Sergeant John Ruddy, Private John Bell, Lieutenant Irwin Long and Private Samuel Porter were all killed off duty and out of uniform.

On 5 December, at about 7 pm, Private William Bogle took his wife and three small sons on a shopping trip to Killeter, a Tyrone village a few miles from the Donegal border. He parked while his wife went into a shop. Almost at once, a gunman fired on the car, despite the presence of the children. Private Bogle tried to reach the shop across the road, but collapsed in the doorway. His wife, cradling her husband in her arms, said: 'Willie, don't die.' He replied: 'No, I will never leave you.' By the time a doctor arrived, he had stopped breathing and was pronounced dead. Five years later, at Tyrone County Court, his son, David, aged 2 when he saw his father shot dead, received £500 compensation for nervous shock.

The murders before Christmas of Private Frederick Greeves and Private George Hamilton brought the year's death toll to twenty-nine, making it the worst year for casualties in the UDR's history.

Altogether in 1972, 467 people lost their lives as a result of the Troubles. One of the most sinister developments was the outbreak of tit-for-tat sectarian assassinations, with seventy Catholic and thirty-six Protestant victims losing their lives. Some suffered horrible tortures and beatings before being shot or stabbed to death for no other reason than their religion. The RUC said that the murder rate had increased ninefold on the previous year and that investigations were being hampered by lack of information from the public. The offer of a reward and the introduction of confidential telephones, to encourage people to provide leads to the police met with a sparse response from people who were generally too frightened to help.

Many of the Catholic victims were found to have fallen foul of the UDA, and others allied to them, who played a prominent part in the year's disorder. After Stormont was closed down, the organisation had adopted an increasingly anti-British posture and its leaders openly favoured going it alone from the rest of the United Kingdom, saying that they would rather be 'first- class Ulstermen than second-class Britons'.

There was much fanciful talk of raising armies to defend Ulster, independence financed with Russian aid by allowing Ulster to become a European Cuba, and even of a *coup d'état*, to overthrow direct rule and establish a Loyalist administration at Stormont.

Echoes of these sentiments were heard clearly on 14 July when a masked man, clad in UDR uniform, was the centrepoint at a news conference chaired by the Reverend William McCrea, a Paisleyite preacher who was later to become an MP and gospel-singing star. Assuring those present that the man was a genuine UDR soldier, McCrea spoke with belligerent ambiguity, hinting that there were those in 'a fighting position' in the Regiment prepared to take the campaign against terrorism into their own hands.

Throughout that difficult spring and summer, the UDA persistently defied the law on several counts, holding illegal marches and assemblies, wearing paramilitary uniform, sealing off areas of Belfast with barricades manned by men carrying cudgels and other weapons. Firearms were also used with increasing frequency.

The Parachute Regiment, which prided itself on being tougher than any other in the British army, clashed with the UDA on several occasions, especially in the Shankill Road area of Belfast. During the disturbances in early September, in which two people were shot dead, the UDA described the Paras as 'gun-happy louts'.

The UDR was drawn into the controversy when a group of fifty of its members, purporting to represent 150 soldiers from

Belfast, held a meeting and decided to go on strike unless the Paras were withdrawn from the Shankill area.

The simmering tension between the UDA and the army exploded into life again less than a month later. After serious clashes with the army in East Belfast, during which two people died, on 16 October, a UDA leader said: 'To hell with the British army. To hell with the Whitelaw administration. The British government and British army are now our enemies.' The UDA claimed that one of the casualties had been 'brutally murdered' by the driver of an army Saracen armoured vehicle.

The GOC ordered the call-out of 1,000 UDR soldiers for duty in the troubled areas, to help soothe Protestant feelings, but in further disturbances in the Shankill Road, there was rioting and then gun battles, in which the army calculated that five hundred shots had been fired at them. After talks between the UDA and a government minister a truce was arranged and the 'two-day war' was declared to be at an end by the UDA.

Meanwhile large contingents of uniformed and masked UDA members marched in ranks at the funerals of both the men killed in the rioting and volleys of shots were fired over their coffins.

Two other people lost their lives in the Shankill disturbances. A woman was killed when a blast bomb exploded and a man died from gunshot wounds. He was later identified as John Todd, a private serving in 10UDR, who was off duty at the time of his death. The Regiment did not acknowledge him as a member and he does not figure in its Roll of Honour even now. When his funeral cortège passed the UDA headquarters at Wilton Street, armed men in civilian clothes fired several volleys of shots over the coffin in a pseudo-military salute.

Given these events, there was easily predictable Catholic outrage, a week later, when the UDR commander, Brigadier Ormerod, said on television that if one of his soldiers also belonged to the UDA he would take no action. Within a few days, addressing Belfast Rotarians, the Brigadier returned to the subject. Joint UDR-UDA membership was not welcomed, but this was not on grounds of sectarianism: 'Apart from anything else we do not want our men exposed to the problems of divided loyalties,' he said. 'The important thing is that if a man's conduct arising out of his membership of the UDA constitutes a military offence, disciplinary action will be taken against him, either under the Army Act or the UDR Act, whichever is applicable, and this could include dismissal.'

The Brigadier's remarks were all the more surprising because they were directly at odds with sentiments he had expressed a month earlier in the UDR's internal magazine *Defence*. Stressing that the UDR had to be seen as non-sectarian, the Brigadier wrote: 'Our enemies would only be too ready to do us down on sectarian issues. That must never happen. It is vital for the future of the Regiment that we maintain the highest standards of impartial behaviour at all times.'

The public remarks were also clearly far removed from the ideals enunciated by Roy Hattersley when the Regiment was being set up. Hattersley said that it had to be 'isolated from political and sectarian influence' and its members could not be 'active supporters of any organisations on one or other extreme of the political spectrum'.

The *Belfast Telegraph*, the voice of moderate opinion in Northern Ireland, discussed the problem on 9 November in an editorial saying that:

> doubts about the loyalties of . . . UDR members . . . must be nailed without delay.
>
> There is no attempt to deny that some of the UDR's part-time soldiers are at the same time members of the Protestant para-military UDA. In fact, the commanding officer of the UDR is trying to excuse it.
>
> Last week, he surprised many with his statement that member-ship of the UDA was not necessarily a bar to joining the UDR, and on Tuesday added that dual membership was, however, 'not welcomed'. This comes as some relief, but it is hardly enough to dispel fears.
>
> The UDA . . . is the nucleus of the 'private army' which militant leaders like Mr William Craig say is ready, if necessary, to fight the British.
>
> In these circumstances, membership of a British regiment should be totally incompatible with membership of a sectarian organisation

which has publicly defied at least one law, on the wearing of
paramilitary uniforms.

Brigadier Ormerod is prepared to judge his men on their conduct
and, if necessary, discipline them, but this may be regarded as too
little, too late. Criticism of dual membership should not be taken as
criticism of the whole UDR force . . . and its best defence is to
ensure that the vast majority of truly loyal members should not be
tarred by association with the UDA.

To the UDR's great cost, these wise words were not heeded.
Indeed, Ormerod's ambivalence was given further credibility
and political approval by one of the Northern Ireland ministers
in November, when he voiced the same form of words: that
UDA members would be dismissed only if they committed a
military offence. In December it was disclosed that forty-four
UDR members had been discharged for military offences or
unsatisfactory conduct, but no details were given. The Reverend Ian Paisley waded into the fray, querying the cases of three
men involved, one of whom, he said, had resigned from the
UDA and opted to stay in the UDR, when confronted with dual
membership.

By January 1973 the army was again firmly ruling out dual
membership of the UDR and any sectarian associations. It was
most anxious for people to assume that there had been a purge
but, as future events would show, if there was, it was far from
effective.

The episode was to have lasting significance for the UDR in
that it blurred what should have been from the start a clearly
defined line between its own legitimacy and the lawlessness of
the paramilitary groups.

If an IRA activist, or even sympathiser, had been found in the
ranks, there would have justifiably been a Protestant outcry.
Catholics saw the UDA in the same light as Protestants saw the
IRA – they feared them.

At a time of accelerating Catholic exodus from the force,
with a fall in representation during 1972 from 6.6 per cent of
6,648 soldiers to 3.9 per cent of 9,102 at the year end, and
growing Catholic doubts about its impartiality, the Regiment
and the government lost a golden opportunity. If they had

unambiguously asserted the incompatability of dual membership, disowned and isolated the malignant influences that were
to corrode the integrity of the force and mar the gallantry and
sacrifice of the overwhelming majority of its members for years
to come, the UDR story could well have been one of triumph.

By failing to abide by the Regiment's self-proclaimed
standards, the government and army extinguished all hope of
meeting the impartial ideals which had been set for it. From that
point on the UDR, which was increasingly embraced by
Unionist politicians as 'their' force and last line of defence,
became irrevocably alienated from the Catholic minority.
Everything that happened afterwards was merely a confirmation of Catholic suspicions and fears concerning the UDR, all
now freshly aroused.

The British government, which was well aware of these
sensitivities and implications, chose to stand back and ignore
them for merely short-term reasons. There was in the army, and
government, an unwillingness to confront openly the Protestant
majority and face a war on two fronts. The army had long
realised that it could not beat the IRA militarily and that the
odds would be even more heavily stacked against it if it were to
take on the hardline Protestants at the same time.

There are good grounds for believing that the army was, in
fact, adhering to an unwritten understanding that all but the
blackest sheep within the Loyalist community were acceptable
as UDR members. The authorities, according to senior soldiers
who served at the time, believed that the UDR provided a
safety valve for people who might otherwise have joined a
paramilitary group and taken the law into their own hands.

Indeed many senior soldiers, and ministers, cynically
regarded the existence of the UDR as nothing more than a
controlled outlet for the militant sections of the Protestant
community, officered by the regular army to monitor and curb
the worst excesses. 'Better to have them out on the street in
uniform where we can keep an eye on them than in the UDA or
UVF where we can't,' one very senior soldier remarked at the
time.

The other compelling reason for turning a blind eye to hardline Loyalist links with the UDR arose from what the army called 'overstretch', the growing strain on army resources, making it increasingly difficult to maintain the commitment to Northern Ireland which had become unexpectedly long term.

Back in 1969, shortly before the army went on the streets, at one of the 'study days' so beloved of army staff commanders, a young officer had vigorously shaken his head in disagreement when the GOC said that he could not see even a baton and shield role for the soldiers in Ulster. 'What advice would you give then?' the young officer was asked. With perceptive flippancy he replied: 'Join the golf clubs.'

The army force level, in those pre-Troubles days, stood at 3,000 and the post of GOC Northern Ireland was seen as a preretirement sinecure for elderly generals with a taste for shooting and fishing. From the summer of 1969, however, the force soared steadily to 13,000 a year later, reaching a peak 22,000 in the summer of 1972 at the time of Operation Motorman.

The brunt of the Ulster commitment was borne by the British army of the Rhine, before the fall of the Berlin Wall and the Iron Curtain, the 55,000 troops committed to NATO charged with defending the inner German border against the Warsaw Pact armies of Russia and the Eastern bloc. Training for the feared war in Europe was heavily disrupted by the need to prepare for the very different threat in Ulster and there was some anxiety among the NATO allies at the constant hole in the defences caused by the absence of 'teeth-arm' units actually on duty in Northern Ireland, training for Northern Ireland or catching up on leave after a tour in Northern Ireland.

Training for the special circumstances of Northern Ireland was an exacting, time consuming task. In conventional war the soldiers were part of a battlefield team controlled by the generals back in their command posts. In Ulster the 'brick' on the street, four- or six-men patrols, have to act on their own initiative, exercise judgment in both legal and public relations terms, often in a split second. There is usually no officer to turn to, only the policy outline drummed into the patrol leaders during training. No wonder senior army officers often say that Northern Ireland is the 'Corporals' War'.

Some battalions were posted for twenty-month tours, accompanied by their wives and families, occupying permanent barracks such as those at Omagh, Holywood and Ballykinler. Lack of accommodation elsewhere and the operational need to have troops at the flashpoint areas meant that most units were serving four-month unaccompanied tours billeted in a variety of converted church halls, community centres, schools, police stations or even patched up derelict buildings.

The accommodation was rough and ready with soldiers sleeping in three-tiered bunks and eating meals off their knees. They were worked hard, often doing twenty-hour days, with only a five-day 'rest and recreation' break, back in Britain or Germany, during each tour. The overstretch was so acute that main front-line infantry units were actually doing one tour in Ulster every eighteen months.

With what one GOC described as the 'endlessness' of the Northern Ireland campaign clearly evident, there was an unpublicised desire to ease the strain by having the UDR play a greater role. This sentiment, although it was not spelled out in such stark terms, clearly lay behind remarks by Brigadier Ormerod in October 1972. Speaking to the Royal British Legion at Ballymoney, County Antrim, he complained that only 2.7 per cent of the eligible men in Northern Ireland had the 'determination and guts' to serve in the UDR.

In April 1973, just before relinquishing command and going to a new post in Germany, Ormerod returned to the subject. 'Far too many people in Northern Ireland are leaving the dirty work to far too few people,' he said. 'The UDR men need help. Some of them have been working flat out for nearly three years. It is time other people took a turn.'

The Brigadier, noting a fall-off in recruiting and admitting that people not turning up for duty had been pruned out, ended his command on a note of frustration. 'If the IRA were out in the open we would defeat them and that would be the end of it, but they are not, and we need all the help we can get.'

Shortly afterwards, the UDR moved to get more help – by opening its ranks to women. There had been a small cadre of women members of the RUC since 1944 and the Reserve was already recruiting and training women members. In January 1973 the first three of these had entered service in Belfast. However, before the UDR could enlist female soldiers, parliament at Westminster had to pass enabling legislation, as the 1969 UDR Act only permitted the recruitment of men. The matter came before the House of Commons in July when Peter Blaker, the Under-Secretary of State for the army said that the recruitment of women members for the UDR

> will be welcomed . . . for three excellent reasons.
>
> First, it will add significantly to the effectiveness of the role which the Regiment is already playing. Secondly, the UDR symbolises the determination of reasonable, peace-loving citizens to work out their future without violence. Thirdly, the bill allows us to acknowledge, albeit in only the most limited way, the unbounded debt of Northern Ireland and, indeed, of Great Britain to the women of the province who have borne such a terrible burden and strain in the present emergency. We know that some of them want to be allowed to play an active role alongside the men in the work of the UDR.

Apart from the benefits to the UDR force level through recruiting women for clerical duties, operating radios and telephones there was also a more pressing operational requirement for women members of the security forces to counter the increasing involvement of women in terrorist activity.

In March 1973, several women lured four British soldiers to a flat in the Antrim Road, Belfast, on the pretext that there was going to be a party. During the evening gunmen were admitted to the flat, shot three of the soldiers dead and wounded the fourth.

Women were also used extensively by the IRA as lookouts, couriers and weapons carriers, frequently helping male terrorists by concealing weapons in prams or on their persons. Others played an even more active role. Three women, disguised as nuns, produced weapons from under their habits and robbed a bank in the centre of Belfast. Two women bombers had left a device on the doorstep of the Unionist Party headquarters in the city. 'Pregnant' women frequently planted bombs. Others, wearing fashionable platform-soled footwear, hollowed out for the purpose, smuggled cassette-incendiary devices into the city centre shops past security guards and caused huge fires in the commercial heart of the city.

The dozen-strong IRA team which carried out the first bombings in Britain, at the Old Bailey and Scotland Yard, in March 1973, contained three women, one of whom, Dolours Price, was the leader. The authorities tried and failed to extradite a Belfast woman from the Irish Republic, where she had taken refuge and received treatment for gunshot wounds, after being involved in a gunbattle during which a soldier was also wounded, at Andersonstown in Belfast.

In the year since Operation Motorman in July 1972, sixty-six women were charged with specific terrorist offences and three others were detained without trial. Mr Blaker said that there were not enough women in the RUC or the Women's Royal Army Corps to search women suspects at checkpoints and during patrols, a situation he described as a gap in security arrangements.

Several MPs were concerned about the safety of the women soldiers and urged that they should be armed. Addressing the House of Lords, Lord Carrington, who was the Minister of Defence, had said: 'I cannot bring myself to believe that even those who are murdering British soldiers and members of the UDR and RUC in Northern Ireland will bring themselves to murder women of the UDR.'

Captain Laurence Orr, the Unionist MP for South Down, summed up the reaction of several Northern Ireland representatives when he replied:

> I cannot share his view. Anyone who has watched the indiscriminate destruction of the lives of innocent women and children in Ulster as a result of bombs callously thrown without regard for human life could not possibly believe that the people who are brutally murdering UDR men will scruple to murder UDR women if they feel that it is in their interest to do so.

The government was unmoved by the argument and stood firmly, if naïvely, by the principle that the women would be protected by the armed, male members of the force, when on duty. Accordingly, they would be trained only in drill, how to report incidents, map reading, driving, field craft, first-aid, anti-ambush procedures, the formation of vehicle and personnel checkpoints and procedures for searching. Parliament approved the measure and in August 1973 the first women joined the UDR.

There was no shortage of volunteers. Before formal recruiting for the 700 vacancies had even begun, sixty written applications from potential female soldiers had been received at UDR headquarters in Lisburn. When the first women went on duty soon afterwards they were given the call-sign 'Greenfinch'. The name stuck and before long the 'Greenfinches' had established themselves as an integral element of the Regiment.

Within a year 500 had joined the ranks and were playing a full part in the work of the Regiment and proving their value. A woman, searched at the entrance to the Belfast shopping segment by a Greenfinch, was found to be carrying a round of ammunition in her handbag.

Writing in *Defence*, the UDR newspaper, in autumn 1974, Private Surgenor, a woman member of 1UDR, provided a graphic account of how the 'venturesome one-year-olds' had taken their first military steps:

> The pressing of our uniforms for a smart turn-out seems routine now, but in the beginning most of us found our outside and inside pleats very confusing and irritating.
>
> In the Ops Room a year ago we quaked at the thought of having to say: 'Zero, OK, Over.' Now we enjoy keeping in touch with our mobiles, for voice procedure has become second nature to us and grid references hold no terrors. We no longer panic at a contact report but calmly wait for details and help to set the wheels of further action going.
>
> We are no longer embarrassed at accepting a hand up into the back of a Land Rover or at piling out into nettles at the side of the road on an ambush drill. What is a muddied skirt or torn tights compared with the relief of knowing it wasn't the real thing?

We have grown to love helicopters, even those of us who get dizzy cleaning the upstairs windows. Helicopter lifts are regarded now as one of the perks of the job.

And how nervous we used to be. We remember the dry throat before asking to see a woman's handbag, asking her to lift her hands for a quick frisk. Now we are veterans, working efficiently and patiently, always ready with a smile or sociable word to ease an awkward situation but able to stand abuse without embarrassment when we have to.

So much of our time is spent on search and on mobile patrols that we have learned to endure cold and wet, knowing that to moan about what we cannot change is pointless and that the job must be done.

Doing it was, however, not without its embarrassments. One Greenfinch, on patrol in Omagh, who described herself as an 'independent women's libber' became entangled in a barbed wire fence and ended up, in her own words, 'dangling by the knickers'. Efforts to free her from her predicament were delayed by the fact that the other members of the patrol were doubled up with laughter.

By now it was abundantly clear that the IRA regarded the UDR as prime terrorist targets, both on and off duty. Twenty-one members of the Regiment were wounded or injured during attacks and the killings continued throughout 1973. Catholics, in particular, were being targeted, accounting for eight of the first twenty-one victims. This further deterred the dwindling band of Catholic soldiers and ensured that the Regiment was made up almost exclusively of Protestants.

At about 11 pm on 4 January Captain James Hood and his son returned to their home at Straidarran, County Londonderry. The UDR officer, second-in-command of Company 5UDR, got out of the vehicle, while his son drove to the adjacent garage. As the captain approached the door of his home, his killers crept up behind him and shot him in the head. He was survived by a wife and twin sons, one a member of the RUC, the other a UDR soldier.

Eleven days later Corporal David Bingham, aged 22, was

apprehensive about keeping an appointment at the Royal Victoria Hospital in Belfast because it meant travelling into the Lower Falls, an area where the IRA was rampant. His fears were well founded, for as he drove into the area his car was stopped by armed men and hijacked. Although he had a pistol in a shoulder holster, he was unable to prevent himself from being abducted.

Clearly, he was stopped at random by terrorists looking for a car. Later in the day it was destroyed in an explosion at a shop in Great Victoria Street. The terrorists undoubtedly discovered his UDR connection once he was in their custody and killed him.

The alarm was raised by his wife on the evening of his disappearance, when he failed to return home. Next morning police and bomb disposal officers found his body, with three gunshot wounds in the head, in the boot of a stolen car parked on the fringe of Belfast city centre.

On 3 March, three days after he had been abducted, the hooded and gagged body of Sergeant David Deacon was found on the Derry-Donegal border. He had been shot. (Eight years later, his wife, Mrs Sylvia Deacon, joined with four other women whose husbands, RUC and UDR members, had been murdered to form 'Widows' Mite' to tell the world their side of the story and counter IRA propaganda. Mr Deacon's gold wedding ring, recast into the shape of the ancient mite and engraved with the symbol of a lighted candle, was dedicated at St Anne's Cathedral, Belfast. The Mayor of Londonderry, Mrs Marlene Jefferson, said the symbol 'shows the sacrifice of those . . . who have either died as the innocent victims of terrorism or who have been murdered in the fight against it.')

Less than a fortnight later, on 16 March, Private William Kenny was abducted while on his way to Girdwood Barracks, Belfast to report for duty. Nobody missed him. The UDR presumed that he had not turned in. His wife thought he was working. That evening, at 8.40 pm, just as his wife had begun to worry and think about reporting his failure to return home, his body was found dumped in an alleyway behind houses in the New Lodge Road area of Belfast.

The dangers for a UDR soldier going about his daily business were again vividly highlighted on 10 May. That morning at 9 am, Corporal Frank Caddoo drove his tractor down the lane to leave a churn of fresh milk at the side of the road for collection by the creamery lorry. As he neared the collection point, gunmen pulled him from the tractor and, after a scuffle, shot him twice in the head at close range. Six weeks later, near Omagh, three terrorists died when a 50 lb bomb which they were transporting exploded prematurely. One of them, Patrick Carty, had been named on a wanted poster circulated within the security forces by detectives hunting the killers of Corporal Caddoo.

By the end of the year, the killings of Private Kenneth Hill and Private Matthew Lilly brought the total number of UDR murders in 1973 to twenty-four.

In May 1973, Brigadier Harry Baxter had assumed command of the UDR from Ormerod. Born in Kilkenny, he was the fourth generation of his family to serve in the British army. Handicapped by the loss of his right eye in a shotgun accident when he was a boy, Baxter showed incredible determination in learning to shoot off his left shoulder after joining the army in 1941.

For six years, most of the period being during the Second World War, he served with the Indian army in Burma. In 1947 he transferred to the Royal Irish Fusiliers, seeing service in Palestine, Egypt, Greece, Germany and Malaya, where he earned a mention in despatches for distinguished service. He later spent some time as a staff officer to Lord Mountbatten. In 1959 he was awarded the George Cross, the highest peacetime award for bravery, for his actions after an unexploded IRA bomb was discovered at Gough Barracks, Armagh in May the previous year.

A sentry, on duty at the armoury which contained a large amount of gelignite, heard a ticking sound from a zip bag placed against the wall. Baxter, then a major in charge of the barracks, the depot of the Royal Irish Fusiliers, was told of the alert. Within minutes he had carried the bag outside, placed it on the back of a lorry and with Captain Henry Chavasse at the wheel, drove off at speed, heading for waste ground on the outskirts of the city. On the way through the streets a detonator exploded but failed to set off the bomb which was later made safe by a bomb disposal expert.

From 1963 to 1966, Baxter was in command of the North Irish Brigade Depots at Eglinton and then Ballymena, before serving as a staff officer at the British army headquarters in Berlin. Awarded the OBE in the 1968 Queen's Birthday Honours list, he was promoted to the rank of brigadier on assuming command of the UDR.

Baxter largely presided over a period of consolidation during which the UDR pruned out the passengers in its ranks and increased its operational efficiency.

By now the building programme to replace the sandbagged Nissen huts and makeshift accommodation which the UDR had lived in since formation was bearing fruit. In April a new headquarters building for the Regiment, inside the Thiepval complex at Lisburn, was opened. The first purpose-built operational centre for the Regiment had already opened at Ballykinler, County Down in February, providing a drill hall, training and lecture rooms, an ops room, offices and mess accommodation. It was named the Anderson Centre in honour of General Sir John Anderson, who is widely known as the 'Father of the UDR'. The General, who died in April 1988, aged 79, was both a distinguished soldier and a brilliant academic, born in London from Irish stock. For many years the family home was at Ballyhossett, County Down, not far from Ballykinler.

Educated at Winchester and Oxford, Anderson joined the army in 1929 with a commission into the Royal Inniskilling Dragoon Guards. At the outbreak of war, ten years later, he went to France with the ill-fated British Expeditionary Force, earning the DSO for conspicuous gallantry. At the end of the war in 1945, he was appointed CBE.

During his service, the General was known as 'the nicest man in the army'. 'He could, and did, dispense honey but was, by no means, unequipped with a sting,' wrote a correspondent in the *Journal of the Royal Inniskillings* in 1963.

In 1969 he was invited to join the Senate of Queen's University, Belfast as Pro-Chancellor and for eleven years he devoted much energy, despite periods of ill-health, to promoting the university cause, work recognised by the conferring of an honorary Doctorate of Law in 1980. During this same period, as the founding Colonel Commandant of the UDR, a post he held until 1979, he played a pivotal role in the raising of the Regiment, chairing the UDR Advisory Committee, a board of three Catholics and three Protestants, whose job it was to advise the GOC on the running of the UDR.

At his memorial service in August 1988, at Down Cathedral, Downpatrick, the Right Reverend Arthur Butler, the former Church of Ireland Bishop of Connor said that the biggest disappointment in Anderson's life was the decline in Catholic involvement with the UDR. 'In his plan there was no place for bigotry. When the Regiment was first formed, 18 per cent were Catholic and his hope was to double this. While he understood the reasons for the decline, he was bitterly disappointed and remained so to the end of his days.'

By the end of 1974 eleven similar new brick buildings to the Anderson Centre had been completed to accommodate battalion and company headquarters, at a cost of some £250,000 each. Fifteen old large houses had been converted for the same purpose at about £150,000 each. One of them, the Deanery at Clogher, County Tyrone, had once been the home of Dean Swift, the author of *Gulliver's Travels*. At some of the other forty-two locations inhabited by the UDR, permanent building projects were either under way or hutted accommodation, designed to last fifteen years, had been provided.

The constructions were no ordinary ones. Incorporated into each building were measures designed to keep the occupants safe from terrorist attack, which have since been constantly reviewed and updated to take account of the scale of threat.

The Regiment was now just over 7,000 strong and fielding an

average 549 soldiers on duty at any time of the day and 1,180 by night, putting it increasingly in the firing line. Incidents involving them, logged during a random thirteen-day period in November 1974, provide a typical snapshot of the problems and incidents which they encountered.

On 7 November at the Lisnahull housing estate in Dungannon, gunmen stopped a van, loaded it with a 500 lb bomb and ordered the driver to take it to the local UDR barracks, where J Company of 8UDR were based. When the van arrived it was driven straight into what the army called a 'critpit', a deep pit, large enough to hold a lorry, dug out of the ground and lined with sandbags, designed to cushion the effect of any bomb delivered to the base in a vehicle.

When the device exploded, less than an hour later, the force of the blast was largely absorbed and the only damage was a few broken windows in the base and at an adjoining school and church. It was the first time such a pit had been used and the army were pleased with its effectiveness.

On the evening of the same day, a UDR soldier was uninjured when shots were fired as he answered a knock at the front door of his home at Newtownards, County Down.

Next day there was renewed concern about the personal security of UDR soldiers when the IRA claimed that they had obtained army documents after holding-up a Royal Mail van. The terrorists said that the documents contained UDR names and addresses as well as details of people intending to join.

At Belfast City Commission, three local women were jailed for a total of seven years for illegally possessing a revolver and six rounds of ammunition, found when they were stopped at a vehicle checkpoint, operated by the UDR some six months earlier.

On 10 November, four UDR soldiers from 10UDR, the Belfast battalion, represented the Regiment at the annual Festival of Remembrance in the Royal Albert Hall, London. Next day, Remembrance Sunday, all UDR battalions took part in wreath laying ceremonies in towns and villages throughout Northern Ireland. During the day, ten high velocity shots were fired, from across the border, at soldiers from 5UDR operating a vehicle checkpoint near Middletown, County Armagh. The patrol returned fire at three men seen in a firing position but no casualties were reported.

Two days later, a UDR patrol found 200 live .303 rifle rounds, wrapped in a fertiliser bag, concealed in a hedge near Coalisland. Ten rounds of the ammunition had been filed to give a dum-dum effect if it had been fired at anyone.

The UDR refuted claims that two Londonderry men, murdered and dumped at the border with County Donegal, were members of the Regiment. The Regiment said that both were civilians and had never been associated with it.

Two Greenfinches from 4UDR escaped serious injury on 13 November when a 120 lb bomb in a milkchurn exploded at the rear of the second vehicle in a mobile patrol operating near Kinawley in County Fermanagh. The command wire for detonating the bomb ran south over the border and at the firing point the Irish security forces discovered a heavy coat and ten rounds of ammunition. The women soldiers were taken to hospital after the incident.

On 14 November, at Tyrone County court, a 30-year-old UDR lance-corporal, caught in a landmine blast two years earlier, was awarded £53,000 compensation for his injuries.

On the same evening, about forty minutes later, at Clough, a member of 3UDR became suspicious of three men who approached his home. He fired two shots out of the window to alert his father. Six shots were then fired by the intruders who made off after a further exchange of fire. There were no casualties during the incident.

The next evening a 1UDR patrol, who had been operating a vehicle checkpoint near Larne, discovered a Sterling sub-machine gun, a shotgun and a bag of ammunition lying in the roadway. They concluded that the weapons had been dumped from a vehicle waiting in the line of traffic at the checkpoint.

In two other individual incidents, logged that evening, an 8UDR patrol, operating at Pomeroy, came under fire but none of the twelve shots caused injury, while a 1UDR Land Rover patrol travelling through Ballymena was hit by a single revolver shot.

Next day, 16 November, a member of a mobile patrol operating in Newry was not so fortunate. Gunmen firing from a block of flats aimed two bursts of shots at the rear vehicle, hitting a soldier in the back as he ran for cover in a nearby alleyway. Private Thomas McCready, a farmer, who had served part-time in the UDR for three years, and was due to be married in less than a month, was rushed to hospital, but died two hours later. At Belfast City Commission in November 1975, four youths and a girl were imprisoned in connection with his murder. An 18-year-old girl was sentenced to eight years for possessing firearms and assisting the gunmen to escape. Another 18-year-old was given five years for assisting the escape. A 19-year-old youth and two men, aged 20 and 23, were convicted of murder. The youth was ordered to be detained at the pleasure of the Secretary of State, while the two men, said to have been chosen by the IRA because they were 'the best shots in town', were jailed for life. As he was led from the dock one of them defiantly shouted 'Up the Provos'.

That evening an off-duty lance-corporal, serving with 9UDR, was assaulted with a bottle while in the street. In the resulting scuffle his assailant suffered a gunshot wound to the leg with the soldier's legally held firearm. Both were taken to Dundonald Hospital for treatment.

Next day, in Newtownards, a soldier, whose home had been fired at three days earlier, was again fired on while out walking his dog. Although hit twice in the thigh, he managed to fire his legally held weapon at the car in which his attackers escaped.

Twenty-four hours later, an unmarked bus carrying off-duty members of 10UDR was halted at traffic lights in north Belfast when masked men were seen running into an adjacent bank. The police were alerted and, together with an army patrol, wounded two of the raiders, arrested five others and recovered the stolen cash.

At about the same time, four men hijacked a car at Jonesboro in County Armagh, loaded it with a bomb and forced the driver to take it to the RUC station at Bessbrook. There, soldiers from 2UDR, providing the station guard, helped clear the area, including carrying two children to safety, shortly before the 30 lb bomb went off, causing only damage to the building.

The period ended with the funeral of Private McCready, the last of seven UDR soldiers killed in 1974. The other victims that year had been: Private Robert Jameson, who died on 17 January when he was shot at Trillick, County Tyrone. The IRA issued a statement in Dublin acknowledging their responsibility for the murder and called on all members of the force to resign or be considered as targets; Captain Cormac McCabe; Corporal Robert Moffet, Company Sergeant Major David Sinnamon, and Corporal John Conley, who were all killed by explosions; and Private Eva Martin, the first Greenfinch to lose her life.

On 2 May a group of UDR personnel were chatting in the sergeants' mess at the Deanery base at Clogher. At about 11.10 pm a heavily armed terrorist gang, estimated at forty strong, launched a well-planned assault on the base from two positions, firing mortars, rockets and guns. Nine vehicles had been hijacked and placed to block roads in the area. The UDR detachment defending the base exchanged fire with the terrorists for fifteen minutes using their rifles and the heavy Browning machine-gun on an armoured car. During the attack, Richard Martin, a full-time clerk in the regiment, grabbed his gun and, running down the stairs from the mess after hearing what seemed like an explosion, stumbled over a body. 'It was dark at the time and it was through touch I knew it was my wife Eva. I picked up her head and shoulders in my arms and felt her blood on my hands. I felt her pulse and I think it stopped while I was feeling it,' he told a subsequent inquest which heard how she had been hit by a burst of machine-gun fire while trying to take cover.

Private Eva Martin, aged 28, was one of the first women to enlist in the UDR and the first female member of the security forces.

Such horrific acts were all too commonplace during Baxter's

eventful years at the head of the Regiment as the civil disturbances continued in Northern Ireland. After many months of intensive political negotiations, William Whitelaw had managed to persuade the Unionist and Nationalist politicians to share power, a deal concluded in December 1973 under what became known as the Sunningdale Agreement. The power-sharing executive, led by the Unionist Brian Faulkner and his deputy, Gerry Fitt, the leader of the SDLP, took office in January 1974. It was the first time that Catholic politicians had ever sat at the Cabinet table in Northern Ireland, or run ministries, and there were high hopes that after such a fundamental breakthrough the settlement would last and bring a measure of political stability.

However, before the fledgling executive could get into its stride, a confrontation developed in Britain between the powerful miners' union and the government. Ostensibly, the issue was about pay in the coalfields but in reality it was a trial of strength between the powerful trade union movement and the Edward Heath government, which became a 'who rules the country' issue. Heath narrowly lost the general election held in February 1974 and a Labour government took power in Britain with Harold Wilson becoming prime minister.

In Northern Ireland, where Merlyn Rees became Secretary of State, the issues were, of course, entirely different and hardline Unionists turned the election into a referendum on the power-sharing settlement, sweeping all but one of the twelve seats at Westminster, West Belfast being retained by Gerry Fitt. This landslide against the Sunningdale settlement undermined the confidence of the potentially radical executive before it had been able to fulfill its promise and fuelled the determination of its opponents to bring about its downfall.

After the election a new, shadowy group called the Ulster Workers' Council, made up of delegates from the entire spectrum of Unionist/Loyalist/Protestant groupings, began to plot the overthrow of the executive by calling a general strike. In May 1974, through intimidation and road blockades by members of the Protestant paramilitary organisations, the UWC spearheaded a general strike.

Within a few days, they had imposed a throttle-hold on the life of the entire community by their carefully prepared subversion of key workers in the electricity generating industry. With the power stations under their control and electricity rationed, even those who wanted to defy the strike were unable to do so. If the strikers progressively shut down the generators to the point where the power failed, the pumps would stop and raw sewage would be discharged into the streets of Belfast. They forced the resignation of the executive on the fourteenth day of their campaign.

The strike called into question, as no event had done before, the integrity of the RUC and UDR, for both forces were caught between the community and the British government in a difficult conflict of loyalty. Nationalists criticised both forces for standing back and permitting paramilitary groups to set up road blocks and intimidate those who wanted to go about their usual daily business. On the other hand, the hardline Unionists or Loyalists, as they were now more frequently being described, chided the RUC and UDR for not mutinying and throwing their weight behind the rebellion.

Whatever the beliefs of individuals in uniform, the underlying reality was that the local forces, the RUC and UDR, were, like the British army, impotent. Early on, the army made a judgement that there was little it could do in the face of such widespread a revolt. Their longstanding axiom that they could not fight on two fronts still stood.

There were calls to put the army into the power stations to run them and indeed technicians from all three services, the army, navy and RAF were involved in consultations. The UWC had exposed for the first time the raw nerve of modern society – its dependence on power and the complex skills, possessed by a small number of people, which provide that power. But the GOC pointed out that even if the army had managed to keep the generators going there were not enough soldiers to protect the distribution grid from sabotage, for every sub-station and indeed pylon, would have had to be guarded. Both the RUC and UDR, taking their cue from the army, kept their heads down in the face of their impotence. It is to the UDR's general credit that it did not mutiny in this fundamental test of its loyalty, despite the ripples of revolution that ran through the community and the Regiment at that time.

The aftermath of the strike ushered in a crucial review of British security and political policy in Northern Ireland. During the stoppage, Prime Minister Wilson had angered the Ulster Protestants in what became known as his 'spongers' speech.

During a nationally broadcast television address, on 25 May, Wilson said:

> The people on this side of the water – British parents – have seen their sons villified and spat upon and murdered. British taxpayers have seen the taxes they have poured out, almost without regard to cost –over £300 million a year this year with the cost of the army operations on top of that – going into Northern Ireland. They see property destroyed by evil violence and are asked to pick up the bill for rebuilding it. Yet people who benefit from all this now viciously defy Westminster, purporting to act as though they were an elected government, people who spend their lives sponging on Westminster and British democracy and then systematically assault democratic methods. Who do these people think they are?

When the strike was over there was further evidence of British exasperation, not only with the strike leaders and its supporters but with the Ulster Unionists generally. At a news conference in Stormont Castle, Merlyn Rees talked of the emergence of 'Ulster nationalism as a major force which the government will have to consider when rebuilding its long-term Irish policy.'

Rees and his most senior advisers, headed by Sir Frank Cooper, Permanent Under Secretary at the Northern Ireland Office, subsequently embarked on a complete rethink of the political and security imperatives. Rees devoured books on Irish history and regaled his visitors by reading extracts from a heavy tome called *Gladstone and the Irish Nation*, which particularly influenced him.

Many of their ideas were formulated at what Rees called 'chewing the fat' sessions with his team, drinking gin or

Bushmills whiskey, clustered around the blazing fire in his office at Stormont Castle, often far into the night. Frequently their deliberations were interrupted by aides coming in with notes outlining the details of yet more violence.

Throughout 1975, as their work progressed, the remorseless targeting and killing of UDR personnel continued with another seven soldiers giving their lives, four of them from the same battalion, 2UDR, all of them murdered when off duty. Some became victims of the vicious tit-for-tat killings concentrated in the County Armagh area during the year.

On 2 June, three men returning from exhibiting their prize labradors at a dog show in Fermoy, County Cork, were intercepted at an illegal IRA road block just after crossing the border into Northern Ireland at Killeen, County Armagh. Three gunmen each emptied the twenty rounds in their Armalites into the car, killing the three occupants. One of the victims was Sergeant Alfred Doyle, a part-timer serving with 11UDR.

The targeting of the three men on the main road between Dublin and Belfast created intense Unionist fury about the inadequacy of security tactics in the border area generally and South Armagh in particular. Their anger was aggravated by the fact that, nominally, since December 1974 there had been an IRA ceasefire and that government officials, authorised by Rees, were conducting secret talks with the IRA.

This raised Protestant fears and emotions to fever pitch and the Secretary of State's commitment to ending detention without trial by the end of the year, and the steady trickle of releases of Catholic terrorists from the Maze prison despite the continued killings by the IRA created a high degree of tension. 'I've never seen the province in such turmoil,' Sir Jamie Flanagan, the chief constable of the RUC remarked at the time.

The inevitable killing continued. Corporal James Fraser, Lance-Corporal Joseph Reid, Lance-Corporal John Bell, Colour-Sergeant Joseph Nesbitt and Private Robert Stott were all added to the UDR's roll of honour.

Against the background of community turmoil that summer

of 1975, the killing of the three men, intercepted at the border while returning from the dog show, is now regarded as the trigger for two controversial incidents that were to have long-term consequences for the reputation of the UDR and irrevocably undermine the already low level of Catholic confidence in the Regiment.

At 1.45 am on 31 July 1975, a minibus pulled away from the Castle Ballroom in Banbridge, County Down. On board were five members of the Miami Showband, who had just finished playing at a dance and were on their way back to Dublin, where they were based. A short time later as they travelled along a stretch of dual carriageway, north of Newry on the main Belfast-Dublin road, the driver stopped when signalled by a man with a red light, clad in military uniform and carrying a sub-machine gun. He thought he had been halted by a routine army checkpoint.

Other military-clad figures appeared when the vehicle stopped and one of them, speaking through the driver's window, ordered all five musicians off the minibus and told them to stand in a line facing the hedge. As they were being searched and asked for their names and dates of birth there was suddenly a huge explosion, followed by bursts of gunfire. The force of the explosion had blown one of the musicians, Des McAlea, over the hedge into a field and after a time he got up, uninjured. The minibus was blazing and there were bodies in the field beside him. He stopped a passing car and was driven to Newry police station, where he raised the alarm.

Police who rushed to the scene of the incident found three members of the band, Fran O'Toole, Brian McCoy and Anthony Geraghty, shot dead and a fourth, Stephen Travers, seriously injured. Two other mutilated bodies, found in the wreckage of the minibus, were later identified as those of Harris Boyle and Lesley Sommerville. It was quickly established that a bomb which they had placed on board the minibus had exploded prematurely as they were priming it. Both dead men were acknowledged as members of the Ulster Volunteer Force and given pseudo-military funerals. Shots were fired over

Sommerville's coffin, which was escorted by some fifty men in combat uniforms, wearing dark glasses.

Glasses, in fact, were to prove a vital clue in tracing the killers, for in the confusion after the premature explosion one of them had dropped his glasses. The RUC were able to trace these unique spectacles to their owner, James McDowell. The manufacturing optician later said in court that of the 10,000 prescriptions he had fulfilled, no other matched. Indeed, he said, the precise optical needs of the patient would only recur once in half-a-million people.

But the police also had a different and equally potent lead on the killers. Three green berets that had been found at the scene were UDR issue.

Within a few weeks, therefore, they had traced and arrested not only McDowell but another man, Raymond Crozier, the former a sergeant, the latter a lance-corporal in the Regiment. In October 1976 Lord Justice Jones found them guilty of murder and sentenced them to life imprisonment with the proviso that they serve a minimum of thirty-five years, at the time, the toughest sentences ever imposed on terrorists.

During the trial Crozier was asked how he felt about serving in the UDR and UVF at the same time. 'They were both legal organisations,' he replied.

Later, in September 1980, a third man, whose brother died in the Miami explosion, was charged. Fourteen months later he was found guilty of four murders, that of the three musicians and another man killed in a separate pub shooting in November 1974. He too was sentenced to life with a minimum term of thirty-five years in custody.

Meanwhile, just before midnight on Sunday 24 August, less than a month after the Miami interception, two Catholics, John Farmer and Colm McCartney, were both shot in the head and back, not far from the border, at Cortamlat, near Newtownhamilton, County Armagh, while returning north from a football match in Dublin. Although it has never been conclusively established, the authorities believe they were also stopped by terrorists masquerading as a security force patrol and then murdered.

An angry six-man delegation from the SDLP, led by Gerry Fitt, had a meeting with Rees at Stormont a few days later to vent their fears about rogue elements in the UDR. Fitt produced a UDR cap badge, which had been bought from an army surplus store in Belfast for a mere 85p, as evidence of the slack security involving the Regiment. He wanted legislation to outlaw not only the unauthorised wearing of military uniform and insignia, but also the resale of it.

In relation to the dilemma of people facing road blocks, Fitt maintained that the situation was crazy. 'If you don't stop when you are flagged down by somebody who looks like a soldier, and he is a genuine member of the security forces, you could be shot. If you do stop and the man turns out to be a terrorist, you could also be shot. What do you do?' he asked.

Rees wasn't able to say very much more than that measures were being taken to improve identification of security force checkpoints and that the police were investigating. The UDR were not only playing a vital role in the security effort but were crucial to Rees's plans to heavily reduce the regular army garrison in Northern Ireland. Any strike at their fragile morale would have compromised that objective.

On 23 December, after another bad weekend in South Armagh, with three more victims of terrorism during a gun and bomb attack on a public house, and at the end of a turbulent year in Northern Ireland, 300 UDR soldiers were mobilised and airlifted into the area to improve security cover.

The local SDLP politician, Seamus Mallon, called the deployment 'the most ill-advised military decision taken by the Northern Ireland Office' and said it was only a sop to hardline Unionists calling for tougher action in South Armagh. They were meanwhile haranguing Rees, during a meeting at Stormont, for even more draconian measures, including once again the rounding up of released internees.

In a Christmas message, Rees, who had been under constant fire from both the Catholic and Protestant sides for what they perceived as the ineffectiveness of the security strategy, appealed for greater responsibility from both sides and called on them to support the security forces as wholeheartedly as they deserved. He said that people in the rest of the United Kingdom found it difficult to understand how both sides in the conflict took up similar positions when it came to criticising the security forces. Dismissing the detractors as ill-informed and mischievous, Rees said that they were only 'armchair warriors'.

3 1976–1980

In the spring of 1976, a top secret report entitled 'The Way Ahead' was distributed to all those responsible for implementing security policy in Northern Ireland. It was prepared by a highpowered working party of officials, with police and military representatives, appointed by Rees. The group was chaired by a top civil servant from London, John Bourn, who later became Comptroller and Auditor General. It also included John Hermon, the future Chief Constable of the RUC. Their report was the most searching rethink of the situation since the 1969 RUC collapse.

The central conclusion of the far-reaching report was that there should be 'Ulsterisation' – setting a policy objective to disengage the British army gradually by putting the locally recruited forces in the forefront of the campaign against terrorism. The process, one senior official said at the time, was not a question of turning off one tap and turning on another. 'The handover from army to police will be a conscious, synchronised one,' he said.

The RUC, still shell-shocked by the whirlwind of civil rights disorder in which it had been engulfed and the ferocity of the subsequent IRA violence, was to be put back in primary charge of the security campaign.

For the RUC to give a convincing lead in the fight to defeat terrorism, it was to adopt, in the chilling words of the report, a 'high-risk profile', in areas virtually abandoned to the army in 1969. From this bridgehead it would be progressively able to restore a police presence in the hard and most dangerous districts of North and West Belfast and the Bogside and Creggan areas of Londonderry.

It was considered especially vital to re-establish the police as the backbone of security policy, for by failing to do so, the report argued, security policy would drift and the army would be left to shoulder the Ulster burden indefinitely, through a system that amounted to undeclared martial law.

There were also political imperatives for the Labour government in taking steps to disengage the army. A fledgling 'troops out' campaign had begun among the hard left of the Labour movement and there were clearly fears that if it gained any momentum, it could threaten the precarious coalition of socialist causes which passed for Labour unity.

To enable the RUC to adopt the 'high-risk profile', it was to be expanded substantially, undergo a rigorous re-training programme and receive new equipment. A particularly controversial aspect of this was the decision to reaffirm the responsibility of the police for dealing with public disorder: the force would be trained in riot control techniques developed and perfected by the army and be equipped with Federal riot guns and plastic baton rounds for this purpose.

The most visible evidence of these new policies quickly became the grey-painted, armoured Land Rovers, known as Hotspurs, which took to the streets as the basic police patrol vehicle. The RUC was also equipped with the then NATO standard SLR high-velocity rifles and M1 Carbines, as well as more powerful hand guns, to provide it with greater protection against terrorist firepower.

It was, as the designation implied, not only a high-risk, but a very costly, profile. During the month of May, seven RUC officers died at the hands of terrorists as the new policy came into force, as many in one month as in the whole of the previous year.

The UDR was also given an expanded role under the new strategy and, like the police, was to be remoulded into a more effective force, with better training and greater responsibility. The permanent cadre was to be increased in size and the UDR was to become more widely involved in the security campaign, taking on tasks which it had not carried out before and relieving regular soldiers of some duties, such as manning vehicle checkpoints. Instead of having the UDR as support for the regular army, the Regiment was to be trained up to carry some of the army's workload – but not riot control.

One of the most significant, or, as some saw it, sinister developments, was that for the first time the UDR was to play a role in intelligence gathering. In the security report there had been much emphasis on the crucial importance of intelligence to the anti-terrorist campaign, and much greater effort was to go into gathering general intelligence about terrorist personalities and activities. The information would, in turn, be used to target the hard-core terrorist activists with a view to securing convictions against them in the courts.

As detention without trial was firmly ruled out as an option in all but the most violent of circumstances, attrition through the courts was to be of fundamental importance in neutralising the terrorists. This aspect was to be the responsibility of the police, whose criminal investigation activities were to be reorganised and enlarged. The UDR, it was envisaged, could play a vital role in the primary phase by helping to identify those in the community who played an active terrorist role or provided support networks. The tradesmen: postmen, milkmen, meter readers, who populated its ranks part-time were ideally placed to provide such information, gleaned on their daily rounds. In the small communities in the rural areas the local UDR men knew the colour and character of every family around them.

Unionists believed that this local knowledge had been the real strength of the old B Specials in getting to grips with the IRA and had long urged that the UDR be allowed to play its part by exploiting information from its soldiers. 'Only local troops can recognise the sound of the elephants going through the bamboo,' said one UDR officer who had previous military experience in the Far East.

Each UDR unit formed an intelligence cell, both to receive and disseminate incoming intelligence and to process material for issue to patrols on the ground, more necessary now that they were to play a more detailed role in hunting the IRA.

The UDR's new role in intelligence gathering was such a sensitive issue that it was never disclosed in public statements by the government for there was, of course, continued concern among Nationalists about the integrity and impartiality of the UDR. This was given real focus by the murder incidents during 1976 where 'bogus' UDR soldiers were reported to have mounted roadchecks and assisted with abductions, such as the Miami Showband incident.

Doubts about the reliability of many members of the UDR were now widely held within the RUC. There were, of course, professional rivalries and even personality clashes, throughout the system but underlying these was a suspicion that the UDR might misuse information which they received. Those on the inside knew that the vetting system, designed to keep undesirables out of the UDR, was largely a veneer. Regularly, applicants adversely reported on by the police were accepted. The RUC knew, too, of the close links, especially in Belfast, between certain members of the Regiment and Loyalist terrorist groups. Furthermore, there was concern about the vulnerability to intimidation of those living in Loyalist areas of the city.

UDR officers pleaded, almost fought, according to one, to be allowed access to intelligence material, but without success. That officer recalled once haranguing the Commander Land Forces about why intelligence was denied to the Regiment.

The reasons were all too apparent. Most of the information came from carefully cultivated sources in both communities. The consequence for these sources, if their identities became known, was death. Both Republican and Loyalist groups had no qualms about murdering informers.

The police went to elaborate lengths to protect their intelligence sources. Each was designated only by a number and his or her true identity was known only to the one or two police 'handlers' who maintained contact. In this context, the politically pragmatic decision to involve the UDR in the sensitivities of intelligence work, both by giving them a role in obtaining it and providing them with access to existing material, was to have important consequences for its longer term reputation and, as later events showed, many of the misgivings expressed turned out to be very well-founded indeed.

More immediately, the enhanced role for the UDR was welcomed by those interested in the Regiment. The Northern Ireland peer, Lord Dunleath, who had recently served a two-year stint as a captain, had outlined a shopping list to the House of Lords shortly after standing down:

> The real enemy is boredom. If members feel that they are getting somewhere, they will put up with personal danger, inconvenience and detriment to family life.
>
> Two things must be rectified. First a meaningful role must be devised, whereby officers and men can feel that they are doing something positive rather than mainly being nightwatchmen at key points. Second, no member of the Regiment should have to suffer financial loss because he voluntarily gave up his time and endangered his life to try and bring peace to Northern Ireland.

'The Way Ahead' unmistakeably gave the UDR a greater sense of purpose than before. Building up the Regiment to cope with its new responsibilities fell to a new commander, Brigadier Mervyn McCord, who arrived at Lisburn to take over the Regiment in March 1976. The son of an officer in the Royal Ulster Rifles, he was born in Armagh, Northern Ireland on Christmas Day 1929. Educated at Coleraine Academical Institution, Queen's University, Belfast and the Royal Military Academy at Sandhurst, he was commissioned into his father's regiment in 1949.

After a two-year tour of duty in the Korean War, where he earned the MC, he served in several posts, including periods in Canada, Malaya, Hong Kong, the West Indies, Cyprus and Germany, before becoming commander of the 1st Battalion The Royal Irish Rangers in 1971 in the rank of lieutenant-colonel. He was appointed brigadier in 1975 shortly before assuming command of the UDR.

Building up the capability of the UDR called for a greater level of military skill and professionalism than before. For the first time, units of the Regiment were taken out of Northern

Ireland for more rigorous training on military ranges in Britain. Well away from the omnipresent terrorist threat on the UDR's home ground, units travelled to Warcop in Cumbria where, for a week, they spent time on the ranges improving signalling techniques, practising anti-ambush tactics and honing their marksmanship with live fire. Specially trained search teams were formed within the Regiment and they were shown how to comb the countryside and derelict buildings for dumps of illegal arms and explosives. The danger of booby-traps and the need for constant alertness was stressed during the exercises.

Although the UDR fleet of vehicles numbered some 400, including more than fifty Shorland armoured patrol vehicles, used in the border area, the Regiment was increasingly taking to the air, being dropped in and taken out by helicopter, so the range training included flights to carry out simulated snap patrols and road checks in areas where terrorist activity was likely.

Some of the UDR units travelled by road to the training area, crossing from Larne to Stranraer on the ferries. Others were moved by the Royal Fleet Auxiliary landing ship, *Sir Percivale*, sailing from Belfast.

While the training programme was an intensive one, a good deal of recreation and relaxation was built in. Trips were organised to the bright lights of Blackpool and a series of events, including a disco, tug-o-war and football matches were laid on to entertain the troops. One party of 400 soldiers, which included only twenty-two Greenfinches, did complain that there were not enough women at the disco.

The time and training at Warcop was, however, only a brief respite from the continuing Troubles. Throughout the year, in the aftermath of several major incidents, the UDR had played an ever-increasing role.

A typical follow-up took place in January, after fifteen people died in two days of sectarian attacks. These included ten Protestant mill workers, ambushed by the IRA, lined up beside a minibus and scythed with automatic gunfire at Kingsmills, near Newry, County Down. The Catholic driver of the bus was singled out and told to run away by the killers.

3UDR was immediately tasked to mount as many patrols as possible to reassure the local population and deter further reprisal attacks. The battalion had planned to field four patrols from its part-time element that evening, but within an hour of the Kingsmills attack it had mustered enough soldiers to put out ten patrols.

Later that evening the Brigade Commander called the battalion out for four days' full-time duty. Over that period, nine out of ten members turned out for duty and three-quarters of them, both men and women, carried out as many as five long patrols of up to twenty-four hours' duration.

There was another major UDR call-out in August, after the normal seasonal tensions were exacerbated by rioting in Belfast and Londonderry and a series of firebomb attacks on provincial towns. Altogether five battalions, some 4,000 men and women, were involved.

Putting the UDR soldiers on the streets enabled regular army units to be deployed to deal with the widespread street disorder. Despite its enhanced role, the UDR was still specifically precluded from having any responsibility for maintaining public order. Nevertheless, it was involved throughout Northern Ireland in search and check operations for terrorist arsenals and suspects.

The upsurge of terrorism in 1976 claimed 297 lives, making it the most violent year since 1972, when 467 people died. Again, the UDR were singled out by the IRA, its members, both on and off duty, being regular targets for the gunmen and bombers. Fifteen, including the second Greenfinch to die, lost their lives during 1976, all but two of them being off duty at the time.

At the beginning of the year, Private John Arrell and Private Joseph McCullough were both targeted and killed. In April, within the space of forty-eight hours, Private John McCutcheon and another member of the same unit, Staff-Sergeant Robert Lennox, were murdered.

On 5 April, Corporal William McConnell, aged 32, was walking the short distance along a lane from his cousin's farmhouse to his own at Tullyvallen, County Armagh, when he was confronted and killed by three gunmen who had come across the fields from the nearby border. He was the sixth UDR soldier to die in the area in ten months. About eighteen months later at Belfast Crown Court, John McCooey received seven life sentences. The court heard that he had driven the IRA killers to Tullyvallen Orange Hall in September 1976, when five Protestant men were murdered. Later he had driven the gunmen who killed Private McCullough and Corporal McConnell. Sentencing him, Mr Justice McDermott remarked that 'the great debt the public owes to UDR volunteers who fearlessly face the dangers of death and mutilation can never be repaid.'

The second Greenfinch to become a terrorist victim was killed on 6 April when IRA gunmen, concealed on a wooded bank overlooking the Armagh-Middletown road, opened fire at night on a UDR patrol travelling in two Land Rovers. The first vehicle escaped the gunfire while the second crashed and overturned after the driver, who had been hit in the ankle, lost control. The gunmen continued firing and unarmed Female Corporal Jean Leggett, aged 33, travelling in the rear of the vehicle, received a fatal gunshot wound to the head. The mother of two boys, aged 7 and 9, and a former member of the Women's Royal Army Corps, English-born Mrs Leggett had enlisted in the UDR eighteen months earlier after her regular army husband, Hugh, was transferred to a staff-sergeant's post with 2UDR in Armagh.

In July, Private Robert Scott was killed by a booby-trap device.

Lieutenant Joseph Wilson, a father of nine, met his death on 26 October at the bacon counter in the Armagh supermarket where he was working when a man suddenly produced a gun and fired three shots. Just over a year earlier, the part-time soldier had narrowly survived an attempt on his life when a teenage gunman had opened fire at point-blank range, shattering the windscreen of his car, as he drove away from the supermarket. Cardinal William Conway, the leader of the

Catholic Church in Ireland, who lived in Armagh, said that the death of Mr Wilson was 'a cowardly murder which has once again stained the city of St Patrick with blood'.

Postman Stanley Adams, a part-time lance-corporal, was lured to his death at a remote house near Pomeroy, County Tyrone. That morning gunmen held the woman occupant hostage and watched while the postman arrived. As he walked back to his van they opened fire, killing him. The police said that the killers had posted the letter, which they took away with them, to lure their victim into the trap they had laid for him.

Later on the same day another part-time UDR man was attacked. As William Bond, who served as a part-time captain, walked the short distance from the Housing Executive office, in the centre of Londonderry, to his home, two gunmen struck. For ten days, doctors fought to save his life, but he died on 7 November.

Within forty-eight hours another member of the Regiment fell. On 10 November, three men drove into the forecourt of a garage at Desertmartin, County Londonderry and approached the proprietor, Mr James Speer. They asked him to look at a leaking radiator and shot him in the head. Mr Speer was a part-time lance-corporal who had served in the UDR for more than four years. Among the eighty-six wreaths received by the family was one of chrysanthemums, sent on behalf of the Secretary of State, Mr Roy Mason. A few days after the funeral, his wife Mrs Ruby Speers took the wreath to Stormont Castle in Belfast, where it was handed back to an official. She said that a couple of weeks before he died, her husband had said the wreaths sent by Mr Mason to the funerals of terrorist victims were nothing more than a mockery and should be sent back. 'This is something I don't like doing but I feel I have to because my husband would have wanted it. A lot of UDR men's wives feel the same way as I do and they are all asking: "Who'll be the next to go?" '

In September 1978, Ian Milne, aged 24, who had figured with two other terrorists on the very first 'wanted' posters ever published by the RUC, was cleared of murdering Mr Speer, but he was sentenced to life imprisonment for the earlier murder of Private Robert Scott.

In November, Lance-Corporal Winston McCaughey, Private George Lutton and Corporal Derek Kidd were all murdered. Mr Harold McCusker, the local Unionist MP, said of Private Lutton that he had died doing his duty to the community. 'He was protecting those who were lying with their feet up in front of the fire watching television – people who are always eager to criticise but not always prepared to do their share.'

After the spate of attacks on the Regiment in November, the IRA admitted responsibility and accused the UDR of being 'part and parcel of the Loyalist murder gangs which have accounted for numerous sectarian killings'.

While the Catholic/Nationalist community at large did not approve of the IRA campaign against the UDR, which was roundly condemned by church and political leaders, there was continued deep-seated apprehension about the Regiment's partiality, which was regularly recharged by repeated evidence of wrong-doing by UDR soldiers and fears that the overwhelmingly Protestant Regiment was aligned with hardline Loyalists.

After the Ulster Workers' Council strike and the fall of the power-sharing administration in May 1974, Merlyn Rees had set up an elected constitutional convention to come up with proposals for political progress. After prolonged debate the Unionists said that they would settle for no less than the restoration of majority rule, an option firmly unacceptable to the British government, who rejected the report of the convention.

Faced with this continued political intransigence and deadlock, Roy Mason, a pugnacious former Yorkshire mineworker, who had replaced Merlyn Rees as Secretary of State, decided that he would suspend the search for a political solution and concentrate instead on alleviating both the security and economic situations. The years of violence had shattered economic confidence in Northern Ireland. Many existing jobs had been lost and there was a marked lack of investment in new ones because of the very real fear of being bombed.

The Protestant/Unionist mood at this time was highly un-settled. The provocative excesses of the IRA campaign and what was widely seen as a pussyfooting attitude by the British government in dealing with it was typically reflected by the UDR widow who returned the wreath to the Northern Ireland Office. There were also strong suspicions, widely held, that the British government, which had flirted with the IRA at arm's length during a ceasefire between December 1974 and the early part of 1975, was preparing to withdraw from Northern Ireland. Unionist fears that they would then be left at the mercy of, at best, an unsympathetic Dublin administration or, at worst, the IRA itself, bred insecurity and led to an increase in support for Loyalist paramilitary groups, regarded as the last line of defence for Ulster.

There was again much talk of Ulster going it alone, after a unilateral declaration of independence. One Loyalist grouping formed itself into a research team to investigate the possibility but after labouring for some nine months had only agreed on the design for the flag of the new country and that the UDR should be the army.

The Reverend Ian Paisley was at the forefront of the discontent about security policy and in May 1977, backed by some of those who had planned and carried out the 1974 stoppage, he called a general strike. The ostensible reason for what he called a 'constitutional stoppage' was to demand tougher security measures against the IRA.

Paisley and his supporters wanted the security forces to 'go on the offensive' against the IRA and believed that the RUC and UDR were being asked to operate 'with one arm tied behind their back'. However, many of those behind the strike call were embittered that they had not gained enough in 1974, when having reached the point where the electricity system was on the verge of breakdown and the well-being of the entire community was threatened, they had not used this advantage to demand a restoration of the Stormont government. Most believed a unique opportunity had been thrown away.

This time they intended that the electricity workers would

again run the system down to breaking point so that they could force the British government into accepting the convention report and restoring Unionist majority rule.

From the outset the British government, which had learned its own lessons from the events three years earlier, was determined to put down the strike. By calling some of the key power workers to Stormont, where Mason laid on a slap-up buffet and fast-talked them, the government fought and won a battle for their hearts and minds and prevented power cuts. This in turn enabled other workers to stay at their desks or benches, sometimes protected, by the police and army, from often determined intimidation by hardliners.

This tough strategy directed by Mason himself, broke the strike in a few days and humiliated Paisley. More important were the long-term consequences, for the credibility and grip of the Loyalist paramilitary groups was loosened. From then on their membership declined and their activities became more and more centred on Mafia-style racketeering and extortion.

A common thread running through this era of Loyalist discontent and rebellion was that in the eyes of hardline Unionists, the UDR could be relied upon to defend Ulster from being 'sold-out' by the British. The RUC were no longer seen as 'reliable' by the hardliners, who genuinely believed that the British were actively conspiring to pull out of Northern Ireland. Thus they increasingly looked to the UDR for their security. They laid claim to it and sought to control and strengthen it in order to protect their own interests.

Protestant politicians quite rightly shared a strong empathy with the UDR, but some adopted what could best be described as a proprietorial attitude to it. They were constantly fed with internal information which they paraded in public to illustrate their intimacy. They complained incessantly about operational restrictions on the Regiment, how it was prevented from going after the terrorists and how the IRA had death lists of soldiers for assassination. There was no mistaking that in many Protestant hearts it was regarded as 'our' Regiment.

The case of David Burnside, dismissed from the Regiment in

1975, provided firm evidence of the close affinity between the UDR and extreme Unionist organisations. Burnside, aged 23, who later became a senior publicity executive with British Airways, joined B Company 10UDR in Belfast in the summer of 1974. The following March he became the press and research officer for Ulster Vanguard. This was a militant Unionist political group, led by the former hardline Stormont Home Affairs Minister, Bill Craig. He was the man who had ordered the RUC to confront the civil rights marchers in Londonderry in October 1968, a decision now seen as triggering off the two decades of the Troubles. Vanguard was a quasi-military organisation, its members often appeared at rallies, wearing uniforms, drawn up in ranks. Craig had carried out 'inspections' of them before delivering what were usually bloodcurdling and threatening speeches to those opposed to the Unionist viewpoint.

In May, Burnside had issued a press release outlining his view that if the union between Britain and Northern Ireland was to be defended, it could only be defended by a resurgent Unionist majority prepared to oppose Republicanism in a way British governments had failed to do since the Troubles began.

This was unmistakeably a subtly coded call for people to consider taking the law into their own hands. After the statement was published, the commanding officer of the UDR battalion called him in on 26 May and said that his political beliefs were in conflict with his duties as a member of the UDR and that it was time he and the Regiment parted company. Burnside protested at his dismissal but an appeal was later rejected by the GOC. In October 1975, answering a question from a Unionist MP about the case, the Defence-Under-Secretary for the army, Bob Brown, said: 'A member of the UDR may be a member of a political party, including the Vanguard Unionist Party, but he may not take any active part in the affairs of any political organisation or party.'

The way in which the UDR had become a political football, tossed backwards and forwards over the sectarian and political divide, is well illustrated by exchanges during Northern Ireland

Question Time in the House of Commons at Westminster in December 1976. A Unionist MP attacked the 'political maggots' of the SDLP, who had been responsible for the recent deaths of UDR men because of 'a vicious and wicked propaganda campaign' against the Regiment. A Conservative MP joined in, deploring the 'vile slanders' made against the Regiment.

The SDLP leader, Gerry Fitt, protested against the allegations and said that every member of his party had condemned the murder of UDR soldiers. His party law and order spokesman, Michael Canavan, who was not an MP, later said that the MPs had 'used the vicious IRA attacks on UDR men to arouse emotions and avoid facing the real issue about the UDR – the danger of Loyalist paramilitary infiltration. The prospect of a law and order agency with paramilitary associations is unthinkable.'

The strength of these associations was one of the central issues concerning the UDR examined in November 1977, when a documentary about the Regiment was televised by Radio-Telefís Eireann, the state broadcasting organisation in the Irish Republic.

The programme confirmed the worst impressions of the UDR held by the Catholic/Nationalist community. In it, a major in the Regiment, serving in the South Londonderry area, said that he was suspicious of half the Catholic community in his neighbourhood. A Belfastman said that he had been serving simultaneously in the UDR and the paramilitary Ulster Defence Association for three years. He disclosed that only two days after serving a four-month prison sentence for riotous behaviour, he had resumed duty with the UDR.

Andy Tyrie, the so-called 'Supreme Commander' of the UDA, said that he encouraged his members to join the UDR to get military training and suggested that in a crisis situation they might refuse to go on duty against the Loyalist population. The UDR dismissed the programme as an attempt by RTE to discredit the Regiment.

There is no doubt that many individual UDR members

shared the fears of the Unionist community about the future of Northern Ireland in the face of the unremitting terrorist campaign and that many were actively associated with the paramilitary groupings. To its credit, however, the Regiment stood firm throughout what was a tense and testing time for its integrity. Whatever the strain of the divided loyalty of many soldiers, the overwhelming majority remained true to the UDR but there was a distinct lack of vigour in weeding out the 'bad apples'. In high places the view still prevailed that the Regiment provided a safety valve for strong feelings which might otherwise have to be expressed in violent ways. Certainly, between 1975 and 1976, 1,000 people were dismissed from the UDR and, in the same period, 10,000 applicants for the Regiment were rejected; but as subsequent developments showed, this clearout did not go far enough.

During the summer of 1977 the Regiment, by now not only the youngest, but also the largest in the British army, enjoyed a rare opportunity to show its ceremonial side. As part of her Silver Jubilee tour of the country, the Queen carried out a two-day programme of engagements in Northern Ireland. The UDR mounted a guard of honour at Hillsborough Castle on the first day of the visit, surrounded by an unprecedented security screen. Three officers and ninety-eight men, made up of detachments from each of the eleven battalions, were involved together with twenty-four pipers and drummers wearing the traditional ceremonial uniform of the Irish regiments: saffron kilt, green jacket and shawl, and the distinctive hats, known as 'corbeens'. That year, too, in what had become a grim routine, the UDR pipers were frequently called on to play the final lament as the IRA continued its murder campaign against members of the Regiment, on and off duty.

Major Peter Hill, who carried on the family fashion and furnishing store in Londonderry, founded by his grandfather, returned from work soon after 6 pm on 23 February 1977 and was shot in front of his house. Major Hill had been in the UDR for over two years. Shortly before his death he had submitted his resignation, on grounds of ill-health, and it was still being processed when the terrorists struck.

Private John Reid, Corporal David Graham and Private David McQuillan all lost their lives in March. McQuillan's 14-year-old son witnessed his father's murder: 'He tried to run away but he didn't have a chance. I ran across and turned him over, but I knew he was dead. He must have been dead before he hit the ground.'

Lance-Corporal Gerald Cloete and Captain Eric Shiells died in April. The gun used in the killing of Captain Shiells was a Kalashnikov AK-47 rifle and police ballistics experts established that this was the twentieth murder in which it had been used since it was first identified in 1974. They later discovered that it had been smuggled to the United States, where it was auctioned for $30,000 at a fund-raising function held by Irish-American IRA supporters.

Over the next few months, Corporal James Geddis, Lance-Corporal Gerald Tucker, Corporal James McFall, Corporal Hugh Rogers, a Catholic, Lieutenant Robin Smyrl and Private Robert Bloomer all lost their lives.

On the evening of Saturday 8 October, Margaret Hearst, aged 24, a civilian clerk at the UDR barracks in Armagh, who also served as a part-time private with 2UDR, and her 3-year-old daughter were asleep in their mobile home. It stood a few yards away from the main family farm house at Doogary, close to the Armagh-Monaghan border.

In a confession to the police, Ian Hegarty, who lived in the same district, just over a mile away and was just 16 at the time, described how he had obtained a rifle and ammunition three days earlier and hidden them. On the night of the incident, with two teenage companions, he picked up the Armalite rifle and two magazines from the hiding place close to the border and went to the Hearst house, where the family's grandmother, in her seventies, was looking after the two youngest sons of the family, aged 9 and 13.

Hegarty said:

> As we approached the house we saw a light on in one of the rooms and a milk churn was thrown through the window. I poked the gun through and told the woman and boy inside to stand against the

wall. I asked them where the UDR girl was and I was told that she was in a caravan at the back.

While I was running towards the caravan I saw a woman looking at me from the door and then going back inside. The door was closed and I smashed it open with the butt of the gun. When I got inside I saw the woman sitting on the bed. I didn't say anything to her. I just shot her. I don't know how many shots I fired – I think it was in two bursts.

A pathologist who examined the body said that the woman was hit in the head, shoulder, arm and chest by nine or ten shots fired at close range. One of the bullets pierced the internal dividing wall in the mobile home and ripped through a soft toy lying on the bed beside the 3-year-old. After the shooting Hegarty said: 'We then went back across the border and went to a dance at a hotel in Monaghan. On the way we hid the rifle and magazines in a hedge.'

After changing his plea to guilty, on the seventh day of his trial, Hegarty was sentenced to indefinite detention. He escaped a life sentence because of his age. His accomplices also changed their pleas. The first, aged 17, was given a ten-year term for manslaughter, the other, a 16-year-old, who admitted assisting the others and possessing the gun, was ordered to be detained for five years. Mr Justice Kelly, who heard the case, remarked that the murder of Private Hearst was 'a grim and savage murder even by the standards of terrorism in Northern Ireland today.'

But tragedy for the Hearst family did not stop there. Three years later, in September 1980, Private Hearst's father, Ross, was abducted and murdered after crossing the border and having a drink in a pub with a long-standing family friend. Armed men took him away in his own car. Next morning it was found burned out, forty yards from where his body had been dumped.

The fourteenth UDR victim of 1977 was William Kerr, an assistant bank manager, who served as a part-time Lieutenant with the UDR. On the morning of 27 October, as his son and daughter, aged 6 and 12, and a young friend waited for a lift to school, he went into the garage and started the car. There was a loud explosion and the wall of the garage collapsed. He was rushed to the local hospital in Magherafelt where surgeons were forced to amputate both his legs. As he fought for life against further serious abdominal injuries, fifty soldiers, including many of his UDR colleagues, donated blood to help. Five days later, on 2 November, he died.

Despite this steady haemorrhage of its membership and the constant threat it faced, the latter years of the 1970s were a period of consolidation and expansion for the UDR in the wake of 'The Way Ahead' report. This was overseen by Brigadier David Miller who was 46 when he took over command of the Regiment from McCord in March 1978. Born in Essex, Miller was educated at Loughton School and Sandhurst and commissioned into the Border Regiment in 1951.

In 1971, shortly after taking command of his regiment, Miller served a short tour in Northern Ireland. A year later he gained more detailed knowledge when they returned for an eighteen-month tour, after which he was awarded the OBE. Before promotion to brigadier and joining the UDR, Miller held staff appointments at the National Defence College and the Ministry of Defence.

By 1980, when the Regiment celebrated its tenth anniversary, the 'Dad's Army' image had been well and truly shaken off. There was a new military professionalism and a greater sense of purpose about the UDR. At Maghera, for instance, an eight-strong 'brick' from 5UDR had formed a ski patrol. Every winter, when there was snow on the ground, they dropped in by helicopter and carried out checks across a 27-square-mile patch of the Sperrin Mountains in County Londonderry.

Since 1976, the UDR's front line role had steadily widened with, four years on, eight of the eleven battalions providing first line military support for the RUC in new TAORs, Tactical Areas of Operation. In territorial terms this made the UDR responsible for supporting the RUC over some 85 per cent of the Northern Ireland landmass. Previous operational arrangements had always placed UDR companies under the command of regular battalions. Now the position was reversed and regular units often found themselves assigned to assist UDR companies. On average the UDR was fielding about 1,000 soldiers most nights of the week.

In line with the objectives outlined by Rees, the regular army commitment to Northern Ireland had been progressively cut. One of the three brigades was withdrawn and the overall force level had been reduced from its peak 21,200 in July 1972 to 12,000. Standing arrangements existed to fly in immediate reinforcements if necessary. At all times a 600-strong regular battalion was designated as 'Spearhead', ready to move at short notice. Vehicles and other equipment, such as riot shields, were pre-positioned in Northern Ireland for use in such an event.

Only in what became known as the 'hard areas' – West Belfast, the Bogside and Creggan estates in Londonderry and the border areas of East Fermanagh and South Armagh – did the regular army retain the first line back-up role for the police because of the scale of the terrorist threat. Because these were Catholic areas, heavily populated with IRA supporters, they were 'out of bounds' to the UDR.

The strength of the UDR had peaked at about 9,000 in 1972 and dipped in the mid-1970s, due to the weeding-out of a few who were considered unsuitable and many more, who could not be relied on to report regularly for duty. Others who felt that they had done their bit also pulled out. By the beginning of the 1980s, however, recruitment was on the way up again, younger men were coming forward and the Regiment had some 7,000 members on its books. With many of the older founder members and former B Specials retired and about one-third of the complement now full-timers, the average age of members actually dropped a good six years to between 25 and 28.

But there was smouldering resentment inside the UDR, which still exists, that far too many people in the community, especially those in the middle classes, were taking an 'I'm all right Jack' attitude. They reasoned that the fight against terrorism was none of their business. Particular hostility was reserved for the growing number of business people who objected to the UDR and deterred their staff from being associated with it, either on the grounds that having a soldier about the place invited terrorist attention or that it was bad for business in offending customers who might be opposed to the Regiment.

There were now three categories of UDR soldier in all. The part-timers remained the largest element by far. They still carried out duties two nights a week and two weekends a month, subject to call-out for full-time duty in an emergency.

The permanent cadre were full-time soldiers who enjoyed terms and conditions broadly similar to members of the regular army but, being members of the UDR, their service was confined to Northern Ireland and they were not trained or expected to take part in crowd or riot control operations. Unlike regular soldiers, they could resign on a month's notice. Like their part-time counterparts, the permanent cadre soldiers lived away from their barracks, in the community with their families, sharing the risk of terrorist attack on and off duty.

The third category of soldiers were those from the regular army posted for tours of duty, usually of two years' duration, with the UDR. The Commander UDR, a brigadier, was always a regular, as were some of the key staff at UDR headquarters in Lisburn and at each battalion headquarters.

The Regimental headquarters at Lisburn dealt essentially with administrative and policy matters, including recruitment, training, career management, discipline, security, public relations, resettlement and welfare.

The security vetting of recruits was carried out by another department based at Lisburn. Run by the Ministry of Defence and staffed by civil servants, usually ex-police or military officers, this department was charged with screening applicants for suitability to join the Regiment.

Operational command of the battalions was vested in the two territorial brigadiers, who were respectively responsible for areas, roughly east and west of the River Bann. They worked closely with the RUC Divisional Commanders, who determined the scope and nature of the military assistance that was required in each district. Soldiers, whether UDR or regulars, were never formally under police command. Technically they were providing military aid to the civil power but, under emergency legislation exclusively applying to Northern Ireland, they enjoyed certain powers to stop, check and search while carrying out their duties.

The commanding officer of each battalion was a regular lieutenant-colonel. Officers attaining that rank always aspired, in a highly competitive environment, to command a battalion of their own regiment. Increasingly, the command of a UDR battalion was seen as a good second prize for those on the way up the narrowing military pyramid. A UDR command, in the active service conditions of Northern Ireland, gave an ambitious officer a chance to show what he could do, and a good tour enhanced his promotion prospects.

Many of the British military officers who subsequently distinguished themselves in the wars in the Falklands and the Gulf cut their military teeth with the UDR. Regimental plaques and hand-cut blackthorn walking sticks are still prized possessions and mementos of days in Ulster. One former UDR battalion commander remembers his time in command of 3UDR as 'the happiest days of my army life'.

Apart from the commanding officer, the deputy commander, in the rank of major, was normally a part-time officer. The posts of quartermaster and training officer were assigned to regular majors, as was that of regimental sergeant-major, but the advent of more full-time, locally recruited UDR soldiers saw a number of posts, intelligence, operations and administration, increasingly allocated to those of captain rank.

The typical UDR battalion, in a structure which has now become standard, would therefore have a headquarters company commanded by regular and full-time officers. There may be up to five more operational companies, one or two permanent cadre commanded by full-time officers, the others part-time.

Greenfinches served in both a full- and part-time capacity.

Most of them were locally recruited but some were military personnel who had asked to stay on in Northern Ireland after serving there. From time to time their ranks were boosted by the wives of commanding officers, often ex-servicewomen themselves, who found a spell serving with the UDR to be a worthwhile commitment during their husbands' posting.

The capability and role of the women in the UDR had widened, too, and apart from first aid, radio and clerical duties, they were now to be seen increasingly out on the ground with male colleagues in mobile and foot patrols, even in and out of helicopters. They were particularly useful for searching women and children during security operations. The terrorists frequently used females and children as couriers or messengers to smuggle bombs or weapons, even concealed in a pram under a baby.

Although the Greenfinches were never armed on duty, they were given firearms familiarisation training. When on patrol, they were protected by their armed, male colleagues, but after the murder of Private Hearst, some of them were allowed to have personal protection firearms.

The UDR had now settled into an efficient operational pattern. The permanent cadre units essentially worked up to seventy hours a week during the day, with the part-timers assisting or relieving them at night. At weekends, in what became known as the Province Reserve, UDR units, both full- and part-time, would be sent away from their local areas. Thus some of those normally deployed in Belfast would find themselves down on the border, manning checkpoints, or taking part in a comb-out, across rural areas, looking for arms and explosive hides.

Conversely, rurally based units often found themselves directed to Belfast, where they would be used to patrol the city centre shopping area and carry out checks on pedestrians as part of the precautions to prevent property being bombed.

6UDR also pioneered the new concept of a 'fit and fast' operational platoon, designed to go anywhere in the Fermanagh, Tyrone and Londonderry areas. The men for this were handpicked for their fitness. They were asked to do step-ups for five minutes, with those whose pulses were under the yardstick being judged fit enough to undergo an intensive three-week training course designed to improve their ability to find and handle explosives, carry out air and land observations and use their weapons well enough to stay alive in the most difficult circumstances.

With the annual training trips to Cumbria now being supplemented by further training at the Barry Buddon base near Dundee in Scotland and at Otterburn in Northumbria, the UDR was steadily acquiring a greater level of military skill. Basic training had also been improved with the provision of a Regimental Training Centre at Ballykinler, County Down, where all new recruits learnt some basic infantry skills, with permanent cadre soldiers undergoing a nine-week induction.

For the officers, there was a testing one-week course at the Royal Military Academy, Sandhurst, as well as specialist courses at other establishments. Over the years the army had also opened its worldwide resources and encouraged members of the UDR to involve themselves in sporting and character-building activities designed to boost their operational effectiveness and widen their experience. Trips away from Northern Ireland also provided a break from the unremitting stress of continuous active service. So men and women from the Regiment went off to parachute with the 'Red Devils' team from the Parachute Regiment; help in a South Pacific underwater archaeological exploration; freefall with the RAF; ski in Scotland and trek in Norway. UDR teams also distinguished themselves in various sporting events, notably tug-o-war. At the annual army shooting contests at Bisley, where the cream of military crackshots compete, teams and individuals from the UDR have picked up medals and trophies every year. UDR teams have also competed with distinction in the annual Nijmegen march in Holland, an international test of fitness, endurance and discipline.

Speaking at a dinner in Belfast City Hall to mark the tenth anniversary, General Sir Edwin Bramall, the Chief of the

General Staff, said that the service and sacrifice of the UDR had been admired and recognised throughout the United Kingdom.

When, exactly ten years ago, the UDR became operational and joined the British army's order of battle, it took its place uniquely in the annals of military history, not so much because of its youth, but because of the circumstances under which it was raised. That place is no less unique today, because it has won so much distinction in such a short time, through a remarkable record of service.

Back in 1970, Ulster faced a far graver situation even than the disturbances and rioting of 1968 and 69. There were all the indications of a growing terrorist threat and a rising tide of violence, spreading like some contagious disease, beginning to affect directly or indirectly every household and every aspect of life in the province. Mindless, chaotic terrorism was the order of the day and the whole social and economic fabric of the community was threatened.

The very fact that the Regiment was born and baptised in such a violent situation is a stark reminder, if we ever need one, of the dangers the province faced and the desperate urgency of our need to counter terrorism and restore the rule of law.

Since then what a remarkable record the Regiment has had. It has been on active service continually. In 1970 it had no gentle period of peace in which to train for its role and it has had no period of respite since. For ten tough years it has held its position in the front line.

Margaret Thatcher, the prime minister, joined in the tributes. In a parliamentary reply to the East Belfast MP, Peter Robinson, she said that the government had the highest possible regard for the contribution made by the UDR in Northern Ireland, but she declined to recommend the Queen to confer the 'Royal' designation. Such an honour, she said, was only awarded 'most sparingly'.

On the day the Regiment marked its tenth anniversary, there were ninety-eight names of murdered soldiers on the roll of honour, each inscribed in gold paint on a board erected in the entrance hall at the headquarters. The first entry for 1978 commemorates Cecil Grills, aged 56, a corporal, who served part-time with 3UDR. During 1977 terrorists twice tried to kill him but on 12 January gunmen using a hijacked car took up position and ambushed him in the back streets of Newry as he took a short cut home from his job. The IRA said that he was murdered because he was part of the 'British war machine'.

Postman John 'Jock' Eaglesham, born in Scotland, settled in Northern Ireland after meeting and marrying a girl during the Second World War. He joined the UDR on its formation in 1970, attaining the rank of quartermaster-sergeant. On 7 February, after delivering mail to an isolated area called the Rock, near Cookstown, his van was fired on. Hit in the chest, he died instantly.

There was exceptional callousness in the way the terrorists targeted school welfare officer, William Gordon, who was also a corporal in the UDR. As a founding and experienced member of the Regiment he was well aware of the need for careful attention to his personal security. So, on the morning of 8 February, neighbours were not surprised to see him checking around his car in the cul de sac where he lived at Maghera, County Londonderry, before setting out to drop his children at school. As one recalled: 'Willie would never let the children into the car before checking it.'

However, that morning as he reversed and pulled away from his house, a length of fishing line wrapped around the valve cap on the front wheel at the driver's side tightened and detonated a three pound gelignite bomb concealed in the wheel arch. The 'unmerciful bang', in the words of a neighbour, blew the Ford Escort car apart, instantly killing the corporal and his 10-year-old daughter, Lesley, who was sitting beside him in the front seat. Her brother, Richard, aged 9, who was sitting in the back of the car, was hurled out of the wreckage by the force of the blast and survived, but sustained face and leg injuries. Only the skill of doctors saved the sight in his right eye. The atrocity was witnessed by Mrs Georgina Gordon and the family's other member, Lindsay, aged 4, who were outside on the doorstep as the car exploded.

In equally callous attacks, Corporal William McKee, Private Allen Ferguson, Captain Charles Henning, Sergeant Robert Bachelor and Private Robert McNally were singled out and murdered.

On the morning of 13 April, six days before he was to retire, Lance-Corporal Thomas Armstrong was out early feeding stock on the estate of Lord Caledon, near Tynan, County Armagh, where he worked as a gamekeeper. As he drove back home for breakfast, his van was ambushed, he was hit several times and died.

In the same month, Private John Graham and Private George Gibson were both shot dead and in June, Private Alexander Gore, Private John Hannigan and Private Joseph Porter were all murdered.

At about 8 am on 15 October, staff and teachers arriving at St Tierney's primary school in the Fermanagh border village of Rosslea, were held up by two armed men and hustled into the school dining hall. Outside in the playground, the children gathered and played games. Just before 9 am, the regular delivery of vegetables for the school kitchen arrived. As the driver reversed his lorry through the playground, the two armed and masked men, one with a rifle, the other a handgun, came out and shot him in the cab. Their victim was part-time UDR Corporal Herbert Kernaghan, whose wife was within a fortnight of giving birth to their fourth child. Condemning the murderer, Humphrey Atkins, the Secretary of State, said, 'Thugs and assassins who spill the blood of their victims in school playgrounds . . . are the enemies of peace whose shadow is cast over every desk and cradle in the country.'

The UDR suffered its biggest single bodyblow to date on the evening of 6 January 1980 when three soldiers were killed in a landmine blast on the road between Rathfriland and Castle-wellan, County Down. Some days earlier, terrorists had concealed a 1,000 lb bomb in a culvert under the road and run a command wire some three hundred yards to outbuildings nearby, which gave them a clear view of the stretch of road.

As the first of the two Land Rovers in the patrol reached the spot, the watching terrorists detonated the huge bomb, throwing the first vehicle fifteen feet into the air and blowing a forty-feet wide, twelve-feet deep crater in the road. As debris from the vehicle and pieces of wreckage were flung as far as three hundred yards from the seat of the explosion, the three soldiers in the vehicle were killed instantly. The force of the blast lifted the second vehicle more than a yard into the air and it toppled into the deep crater, which had rapidly filled with water from a broken main. Its four occupants suffered shock and minor injuries.

The three soldiers who died were: Private Robert Smyth, aged 18; Private Richard Wilson, aged 21; and Private James Cochrane, aged 21, who was a Catholic. All three were single and serving full-time with 3UDR. Their deaths marked a grim milestone in the cycle of violence since 1969 for they brought the total of UDR murders to 101 and the overall total of victims to 2001.

Richard Latimer, who was a part-time private in 4UDR, was another soft target for the terrorists. On the Saturday afternoon of 7 June, as he was serving behind the counter at the hardware shop he ran at Main Street, Lisnaskea, a man walked in and fired three shots. The murder was witnessed by two customers and Mr Latimer's 11-year-old son, who was helping in the shop at the time. Local people calculated that Mr Latimer was the fifty-fourth murder victim in the area in ten years, all but four of them Protestants. At his funeral a few days later, the local Church of Ireland rector, Canon Neville O'Neill, said: 'The situation here now is shocking and it seems to be getting worse. There is an awful feeling amongst people here that we are expendable.' Within a week, Mrs Thatcher received one thousand letters from the families of UDR soldiers and other murder victims, asking for tighter security measures in the area. Among them was one from Mrs Latimer.

Colin Quinn, 20, who was a part-time private in 3UDR, came out of the printing works in Belfast where he worked about 5 pm on 10 December. As he approached his car, gunmen crept up behind him and opened fire. He fell dead from bullet wounds to the head and back. Among those who saw the murder were two of his brothers, who also worked for the same printing firm. Some years later, in May 1984, it was revealed by a so-called 'supergrass' at Belfast Crown Court that the two killers later died violent deaths themselves. Roddy Carroll was shot dead by a special police anti-terrorist unit in Armagh in December 1982 while Gerard Barkely was one of sixteen fatal victims of an ideological feud between members of the outlawed INLA in 1983. The 'supergrass', Harry Kirkpatrick, aged 24, the third man involved in the murder of Private Quinn, received five life terms and other sentences totalling more than 1,000 years when he pleaded guilty to five murders and other charges.

It is a measure of the fatalism or stubbornness of the average UDR soldier that, despite the evident risks, most stuck to the routine of their jobs and lifestyles without compromise. Others who did, and who paid with their lives were: Private James Robinson, Corporal Alexander Abercrombie, Private John Clarke, Private James Hewitt and Private Norman Donaldson.

This succession of cold-blooded murders, especially in the vulnerable border areas of Fermanagh, understandably provoked strong and angry feelings. The fact that the killings were often planned and mounted from across the border or Republican areas, specifically out of bounds to the UDR, rankled with many in the Regiment and with Unionist politicians. Strident calls for the UDR to be allowed to 'search and destroy' terrorists in these areas were often made by hardline politicians. In November 1979, the Reverend Ian Paisley reflected this sentiment when he handed back two medals from 'disillusioned' members of the UDR to Mrs Thatcher during a meeting at Downing Street. According to Paisley, the UDR soldiers had said: 'Throw these medals at her. Tell her we want our country saved. We are sick to see the hands of the security forces tied when dealing with terrorists.'

These same frustrations surfaced again in January 1980 after the landmine attack at Castlewellan. The Reverend Robert Bradford, MP for South Belfast, who was himself to become an IRA murder victim within the year, said that the terrorist gunmen and bombers should be executed, like spies and saboteurs in a war situation. 'People would flock into the Regiment in their hundreds if the government were to say we are in a warlike situation, a military situation. In any war situation of that sort, the terrorists would be shot by the very men they are plotting against.'

Brigadier Miller, responding in a television interview, said: 'The UDR is part of the British army and there can be no doubt whatsoever that the UDR must continue to conduct its operations within the law set down. We believe this is the very best means of defeating the IRA.'

By the end of the Regiment's first decade, the level of violence in Northern Ireland had declined substantially and the UDR could claim much credit for the part which it had played in the reduction. Although the terrorist campaign continued, it was at a much reduced rate. In the ten years to 1980, shootings had fallen from a peak of 10,628 in 1972 to 645. Bombings were also down in the same period from 1,853 to 400. The annual death toll had fallen from 467 to 76.

The current situation was summed up articulately by Lieutenant-General Sir Richard Lawson, speaking to Northern Ireland Chamber of Commerce in Belfast on 14 February 1980, soon after assuming command of the army garrison in Northern Ireland:

> My feeling is that circumstances have been and are continuing to change, however slowly, for the better. Of course I do not believe in miracles and do not expect terrorism to end tomorrow. Sadly, we may still feel its effects in many parts of the province for some time to come. But, without doubt, the trend is downwards and I am of the firm opinion that if we can restrain each other to act and react with both patience and wisdom, no one can put out this bright flame of hope.
>
> There are a few who, out of sheer frustration and impatience, say to me: 'Go in hard, General, and flush out those terrorists, whatever the cost. What we want are bodies; what we want are skulls and we do not care how you get them.' Well, let my reply to those people ring out loud and clear: I am not in that business. I have not come here to destroy Ulster. Nor have I any intention of leading my soldiers to defeat. For such a wild and totally impracticable course of action is not only a guaranteed recipe for disaster, it is also a surefire way to give the terrorist his victory on a plate.
>
> Of course I sympathise with this deep, genuine and fairly

widespread feeling of frustration but we must remember that over the past years considerable progress has already been made. Let us not allow our present frustration to lead us into a course of action which will throw all that away.

Whatever its fearsome image in the eyes of the Catholic community and the apparent desire within the Protestant population for the UDR to 'go on the offensive', to its credit, the Regiment at large showed commendable restraint. Despite the extreme provocation to its members caused by the IRA campaign and the unavoidable stress it generated, only an unrepresentative minority have taken the law into their own hands. (This aspect of the UDR reputation is examined in chapter 5.)

But even when on duty, the UDR record for restraint is considerably better than its image would imply. According to figures quoted by John Hume, MP, the leader of the SDLP, in June 1990, 10 per cent of those killed during the Troubles of the previous ten years had been killed by the British army, 2 per cent by the RUC and only 0.29 per cent by the UDR. By the same calculations, the IRA and other Republicans – responsible for murdering about 70 per cent of the 2,850 victims of the violence –had notched up a rate of killing which was 250 times greater than that of the UDR.

Altogether five people have been killed by on-duty UDR soldiers. The first was a 16-year-old youth, Alec Moorehead, shot in October 1972. After an explosion near a cinema at Newtownstewart, County Tyrone, a mobile UDR patrol mounted a follow-up operation. When they reached the scene they saw a man climbing a fifteen-feet high security wall at the back of the cinema. When he failed to respond to three challenges, one of the patrol opened fire, killing him.

It turned out that the youth was almost totally deaf. His father said that he did not blame the UDR soldier who killed his son. In a cruel twist of fate, one of the members of the patrol, a sergeant, was an uncle of the dead youth, although he did not fire the fatal shots.

On 20 March 1981, a UDR patrol in a Land Rover spotted a

stolen car in Belfast city centre and gave chase. At Cullingtree Road, in the Lower Falls area, a corporal opened fire on the car, causing it to crash into a garden at the front of a house. The driver and front seat passenger ran away but the passenger was caught. Meanwhile other members of the patrol found a third person, with a gunshot wound to the stomach, in the back of the car. An ambulance was called but the joyrider, Patrick McNally, aged 20, was dead on arrival at hospital.

The next person to be shot by a UDR patrol was Tony Harker, who died in Armagh in January 1982. According to a police account of the incident, the patrol opened fire on a man acting suspiciously a short time after a break-in at a nearby supermarket and a short time later incendiary bombs exploded, starting a fire at a timber yard close by.

Sinn Fein said that the dead youth had been constantly harassed by the security forces and claimed that his death was 'political murder'. However, he had previously been sentenced to six months' imprisonment for assaulting police officers and, at the time of his death, was on bail after being charged with making and possessing petrol bombs and handling stolen property.

Only one of the UDR soldiers who has killed when on duty has subsequently gone on trial. The incident concerned took place in a Catholic area of Armagh in the early hours of 30 July 1983, when Corporal David Baird was a member of a fifteen-strong UDR patrol – thirteen men armed with the standard army 7.62 Self Loading Rifle and two unarmed women Greenfinches.

Baird and another member of the patrol stopped a group of three men and two women to check their identities. At first the women refused to cooperate with the request, which the soldiers were fully entitled to make under the emergency powers. What happened next is disputed by both sides. Clearly, scuffling developed between the soldiers and the group and when an estimated fifteen other civilians arrived on the scene a full scale fracas ensued.

At one point Baird's rifle was discharged at a range of some three to six feet, hitting an 18-year-old youth who died instantly from a wound to the chest. Whether Baird fired deliberately or whether he was jostled and the rifle was grabbed, causing it to go off, became a matter of fundamental dispute, sparking off major public criticism of the UDR.

The victim of the shooting was Martin Malone, a farm labourer, one of those who had joined in the row after the original five persons were confronted by the UDR patrol. At his funeral, a few days later, Cardinal Tomás O'Fiaich, head of the Catholic Church in Ireland, claimed it was deliberate killing and spoke of the 'suspicious circumstances'. He particularly criticised the UDR because one of the people concerned in the incident claimed he was assaulted with a rifle butt and prevented from leaving the scene to call an ambulance.

Priests in Armagh called for an 'urgent and vigorous' inquiry. This was in fact already under way and after the outcome was reported to the Director of Public Prosecutions in Belfast, he ordered that Baird should be charged with murder. After being arrested on 5 April 1984 and charged, he replied: 'I'm flabbergasted, that's all.'

When Baird went on trial in Belfast in November 1984 before Mr Justice Higgins, sitting without a jury, as in all cases brought under emergency legislation, a confused and contradictory version of events emerged.

Baird himself had given the police conflicting accounts of his behaviour. At first he had insisted, in a written statement, that during the fracas someone emerged from the crowd and grabbed his rifle. When it was pulled down it went off and shot the man. But in further interviews he admitted that he had cocked his rifle to frighten the crowd, stepping back, bringing it down to his level and pointing it at the crowd to frighten them. The next thing he experienced, was a flash and a bang. He did not know that the safety catch was released or how the rifle was discharged.

It was also revealed during his evidence that Baird had two previous criminal convictions: one for assault and disorderly behaviour at a Young Farmer's function in 1975; another for disorderly behaviour again in 1978, this one during his eight-year membership of the UDR. Asked by Crown Counsel if he found it difficult to control his temper he replied: 'No.'

A woman witness described how there was a lot of shouting and pushing between the soldiers and the civilians. She said she took hold of Malone's arm because she feared someone was going to be arrested, then she saw a flash and heard a bang. 'As a result Martin Malone fell. As he fell, I bent down to pick him up and that's when I felt my hands all blood. I shouted that he had been shot but nobody seemed to realise because it had happened so quickly.'

One of the men originally stopped by the patrol admitted in the witness box that he had changed his evidence to fit in with what other witnesses were saying, after discussing the case with them.

The judge eventually decided that the evidence of the civilian witnesses was totally unreliable and that he could not be satisfied beyond reasonable doubt that the soldier had the requisite intention for murder. But he ruled that because of Baird's conflicting statements to the police about the events leading up to the shooting, and the fact that they did not tally with independent forensic evidence, he did have a case to answer in relation to manslaughter.

Two weeks later, however, after further consideration, Baird was acquitted. The judge decided that having regard to all the evidence, he was not guilty because the prosecution had failed to prove that Baird did not fear for his safety.

During the course of the trial, in the late afternoon of 19 November 1984, another member of the UDR patrol involved in the Malone incident was driving his car along the Armagh–Caledon road. A bomb concealed behind a wall was detonated as he drove past, damaging the car and slightly injuring the soldier on the neck and hands. The RUC said that he had only escaped death or serious injury because the passenger side of the car had taken the force of the blast. After the attempted murder, the IRA said that the attack was directed at the man because of his involvement in the controversial incident.

The fifth person to die at the hands of the UDR was another young joyrider. Paul Kelly, aged 17, who died on 4 January 1985, was travelling in a stolen car which was fired on after crashing through a road check at Kennedy Way, Belfast. The very next day he had been due to appear at the city's Magistrates Court to face charges in connection with an earlier episode of car theft.

1980 also saw two significant changes at the top of the UDR. The first Colonel-Commandant, General Sir John Anderson, generally regarded as the father of the UDR, retired due to ill-health and was replaced by the former Commander, Brigadier Harry Baxter.

There was also a new Commander, the sixth. Brigadier Pat Hargrave, aged 46, a native of Worcestershire, joining the UDR in May from Cyprus, where he had been serving in the rank of colonel, as Deputy Chief of Staff and commander of the British contingent to the United Nations peacekeeping force. Like his predecessors, he had extensive military experience, seeing service in the West Indies and Aden, rising to command his battalion, the Worcester and Sherwood Foresters, and spending a period on the directing staff at the National Defence College.

Anderson had made a vast contribution to establishing the UDR and it was through no fault of his that the Regiment failed to fulfill the original cross-community ideal, outlined by Lord Hunt. Friends of his say that the amount of time this tough, but diplomatic, old soldier expended on UDR affairs cost him his health. For these reasons, his reputation is held high, even beyond the Regimental circle.

4 Commitment and Sacrifice

Whatever the controversy about the origins, background and make-up of the UDR, there can be no excusing or condoning the unjustified and merciless campaign of murder, maiming and intimidation against its members by the IRA. The litany of deaths of soldiers is but the visible crest of a largely submerged iceberg of tragedy and heartbreak suffered by the Regimental family at the hands of the IRA. Since it was formed, a member of the UDR has been murdered on average every thirty-nine days and another seriously injured every nineteen days.

At the end of 1990, mothers and fathers had lost 184 sons and 4 daughters, serving with the UDR, while 90 wives had been robbed of their husbands and 124 children had been deprived of a father. Several more children lost their father even before they were born. One girl actually died with her father in a boobytrapped car.

About 400 others have suffered unthinkable injuries as a result of bombing and shooting incidents including disfigurement, losing limbs, senses and their physical independence. Thousands more have been less seriously hurt. The overwhelming majority of the Regiment's fatal casualties have been due to cowardly attacks off duty and usually out of uniform.

The extraordinary commitment and sacrifice of the UDR in the face of this unremitting threat, can be seen at its most graphic in Fermanagh, where its members and their families have suffered or been the target of some of the worst excesses of the terrorist campaign, notably the Remembrance Sunday bombing at Enniskillen in November 1987.

Eleven civilian members of the community died, and many

more were injured, including a local schoolteacher who was still in a coma three years later, when, without warning, a large IRA made bomb detonated in a disused school building overlooking the local War Memorial, a short time before the religious ceremony commenced.

If the explosion, triggered prematurely by an incorrectly set timing device, had gone off some eight minutes later, during the ceremony as planned, most of the 114-strong contingent of 4UDR, officers, men and women, would by then have been formed up at the spot. Undoubtedly many of them would have perished or been injured.

The UDR contingent had been mustering in parade order at a car park, some 200 metres away, when the bomb went off. As panic-stricken spectators fled from the scene, many clutching their small, terrified children, the UDR personnel raced to the scene. That morning, instead of honouring the dead of two World Wars and the nineteen serving and four former members of the battalion who had been killed by terrorists, the men and women of the Fermanagh UDR were involved in a frantic rescue to claw, with their bare hands, the dead and dying from the smoking, choking rubble and dust.

One of the heroes of the morning was Captain Ian McDonald, a young regular army medical officer, nearing the end of a tour of duty with 4UDR, who was in civilian clothes, planning to photograph the occasion. Whether on duty or not, he habitually carried in his pockets a few lifesaving plastic airways. In the immediate aftermath of the blast he attended to twelve seriously injured casualties and his work and foresight is credited with saving the lives of three of those crushed under the masonry, unable to breathe without the assistance he provided.

Essential first-aid was also administered to many of the other casualties by members of 4UDR, whose battalion team had only recently beaten other UDR teams to win the Northern Ireland First Aid Championships. One of the Greenfinches involved was later awarded the BEM for her outstanding work. Her citation said in part: 'Although horrified at the extent of human destruction, her medical training and maturity stood her in good stead, enabling her to remain composed and play a full role in the subsequent rescue operation. After helping to treat and evacuate the critically injured casualties, she reported for duty at a vehicle checkpoint and remained for eight hours during the follow-up operation.'

The Remembrance Sunday bombing was not the first taste of tragedy for Enniskillen, a bustling country market town at the heart of the Fermanagh-South Tyrone parliamentary constituency, which embodies the contradictory extremes of the situation in Northern Ireland. On the one hand it contains some of the most breathtaking scenery in Ulster and, arguably, some of the best fishing in Ireland in the waters of Upper and Lower Lough Erne. Its people always warmly welcome the increasing flow of tourists, from Northern Ireland and beyond, who promise it a new prosperity. On the other hand, behind its deceptive tranquillity, ancient hatreds have all too often flared into the most brutal violence and caused its lush green landscape to be stained with blood.

Throughout the 1970s and 80s, over 200 terrorist murders, one-tenth of the total, have taken place in this killing field and only some thirty of them have been solved, with the killers being brought to justice. About three-quarters of the victims have been murdered by the IRA.

The active terrorists are well known to the RUC and UDR, whose level of intelligence about them now, after two decades of conflict, is probably more detailed and accurate than ever before. The problem for the security forces is to convert this intelligence into hard evidence that will stand up in court, for the terrorists go to painstaking trouble to frustrate them.

Intimidation of witnesses is routine and for every advance in forensic and scientific techniques there is skilful, evasive action: gunmen and bombers wear surgical gloves, boiler suits and even plastic bags over their footwear to avoid leaving fingerprints, footprints or other traces. To prevent hairs and fibres being used to incriminate them, all these items are burned rapidly after the crime, an aspect usually preplanned as thoroughly as the crime itself.

It is not uncommon, when prime suspects are visited in the immediate aftermath of an outrage, for them to be found in the bath or shower, washing away any lingering traces of firearms residue or explosives traces from their bodies especially from their hair, hands and under their fingernails.

Intensive interrogation of terrorists has long been one of the most effective techniques used by the police. Now they are finding that they cannot break suspects to the point where they will make a confession. The harder the terrorist, the harder he, and increasingly she, is to break. Those detained by the police are thoroughly debriefed on release by fellow terrorists, and information gleaned about police tactics is used to forewarn others and train them to resist interrogation. Experienced detectives describe how suspects will sit through interviews lasting several hours without saying a single word or reacting in even the slightest way. Terrorists are tutored to stare at a fixed point on the wall, an acoustic tile, a crack, a light fitting, to fend off questioning. The offer of cigarettes or tea is ignored. They will not even engage in small talk about sport or television. Some actively disrupt the interview process by lying on the floor, standing or even climbing on the furniture.

Those 'on the run' in the Irish Republic are usually on their best behaviour, to avoid coming to the notice of the Garda Siochana, and thus remain even further beyond the reach of the RUC. Many of these 'untouchables' number among their victims members of the UDR and it is in Fermanagh that the stubborn courage of the Regiment is most vivid, despite the exceptional dangers.

A part-time corporal lives on a farm with his brother and elderly parents just three hundred yards from the border. He has already survived two attempts to kill him there. As he tramps through the fields inspecting his cattle, he carries a pump action shotgun and a Browning pistol in his belt. He is well within Armalite range from across the border, marked by a stream which runs at the bottom of the sloping fields. His biggest fear is, however, that he will come home from duty in the early hours of a morning and find terrorists holding his family hostage. Yet, despite this fear and the constant risks to his safety, he will neither leave his farm or the UDR. 'If I left here that would be giving in to them. That's what they want. And even if I left the Regiment it would be no guarantee of safety. Sure forty ex-members have been killed, one nine years after he left.'

Another remains on a farm, three miles from the border, despite four threats on his life. His only concession to the situation was to write a note outlining the arrangements for his funeral. In a different border area a soldier described how, after he was officially warned of an imminent threat by the police and his unit commander, his family had lined up to stop him going on duty and force his resignation from the Regiment.

The vulnerability of men like this is clearly evident from a map on the wall of the operations room at the RUC divisional headquarters in Enniskillen. Every UDR home is marked by a coloured pin, a line of 'soft targets', in security argot, strung out on the isolated countryside along the border. Sometimes the closest neighbours are a mile away. The clusters of pins have been thinned out and moved back over the years by the removal of those representing murdered soldiers and others, intimidated or frightened to breaking point, who have abandoned their exposed front-line locations and moved back. These days the line of pins delineates an unofficial new frontier, ten to twelve miles back.

In the resulting no-man's-land, increasingly populated by Catholics alone, some once thriving farms are now left un-worked, the houses abandoned to decay, permanent shrines to the futile reign of sectarian terror imposed by the IRA on fellow-citizens whom they have scornfully derided as part of the 'British war machine'.

There is a well-practiced drill when one of these UDR members is threatened or a planned attack comes to light. Some of his comrades mount a guard on the property, the animals are rounded up for auction, a flit is organised, usually in a fleet of farm tractors and trailers. A short time later an auction notice appears in the *Impartial Reporter*, when a family has had enough and flees to England or Canada.

The stubborn ones refuse to sell. They are proud of links with their land, sometimes going back for generations and hundreds of years. They hold on in the hope of going back one day. Some let their fields or pay for cattle and crops to be tended, others have become so embittered that they leave the property unused and empty. It is a sore point that they cannot claim any compensation from public funds for their involuntary plight.

Farms and farmers are not the only targets. Builders, quarrymen, concrete suppliers, haulage firms, many of whom employ UDR men or carry out work at security force bases are also targeted. When they can no longer stand it, they put advertisements in the papers stating that they will no longer work for the security forces. More often than not an auction follows, for they are driven out of business. The auction notice contains no direct reference to the reasons for the clear-out but everyone knows and the lower prices obtained reflect the pressure to sell. 'I'm not happy living in a housing estate in Enniskillen,' said one. 'But at least I'm alive.'

UDR men have also been driven out of their jobs by threats or the risk of attack. Now many employers, even Protestants, do not want them, because they endanger the business and other employees by potentially attracting terrorist attention.

Ken Maginnis, the Unionist MP for the area since 1982, keeps a computerised count of all the killings in the constituency office inside his fortified house, on the outskirts of Dungannon. With the tap of a few keys he can analyse the pattern of the killings, which, in his view, are not merely sectarian, but genocidal. He believes that the IRA targets the eldest sons, the wage earners in the border families, the sons who run the farms and businesses, in a premeditated campaign to drive the Protestants inland from the border and claim their land and living.

As the entries on his computerised index flicker across the computer screen, it is clear from his remarks that these are not just names to him, or mere constituents, but former friends and comrades. For twelve years, Ken Maginnis was a school teacher by day and part-time UDR soldier by night, attaining the rank of major. Much of his time was spent ensuring the safety of his men, living and working in an exposed rural area. The solutions to their security problems as they went about their civilian jobs or lived in their homes were sometimes obvious, frequently make-do-or-mend.

One soldier was persuaded to make alternative arrangements to get his children to school in the mornings when he realised how he was enabling himself to be set up for murder. Bulletproof flak jackets were begged and borrowed for those whose jobs involved some unavoidable routine, like creamery drivers, milk roundsmen and busmen. Several sheets of armoured steel were obtained and installed in a Royal Mail van to protect a postman whose round required him to travel through areas where he was considered to be especially at risk.

There was widespread concern at the inadequacy and unreliability of the Walther pistol issued to these men for their protection off duty and in many cases Maginnis used his authority and influence to obtain approval for them to get a more powerful and proven weapon, the 9 mm Browning pistol, at their own expense. Finding the £200 to pay for the weapon, at a time when the UDR soldiers were earning £7 for a turn of duty, represented a considerable outlay and financial sacrifice for most of the men.

Since Maginnis left the UDR in 1982 to go into politics, he has consistently campaigned for better conditions, better protection and more public support for his former colleagues.

The vulnerability of the average UDR soldier is all too clear from a visit to what is in reality a UDR family, at Lisnaskea, County Fermanagh. Outside the village, the narrow side road to their farm meanders for nearly two miles up into the hills. The only way in or out, there is a potential ambush point every few hundred yards along it. It must be a heart-stopping experience to encounter a stranger or an unfamiliar vehicle along the way, especially in the early, eeriest hours of the morning, when returning alone from duty.

Four members of the family are at risk from their

membership of the security forces. One son is a full-time member of the RUC; another son is a full-time UDR soldier, a third is part-time. He is planning to get married, build a house on the family land and take over the farm from his father. Part-time service fits in well with these plans. His father has recently retired from the UDR, ending a forty-year connection with first the B Specials, which he joined at fourteen years of age, and then the Regiment. For months after quitting, he prowled around the house until the early hours of the morning. His body clock, his wife says, was so accustomed to the several nights a week duty from seven at night till two or more the following morning, that he could not relax. Now the telephone rings less often and he's getting used to watching a bit of television in the evening or taking his wife out.

The ingrained alertness for any threat to his personal security has not been dulled, however. The energetic dog is a constant alarm system, bounding round and round the farm, barking every time a car comes close. The road is a dead-end into the farmyard, so there is no passing traffic. A car approaching is watched carefully as it drives along the road towards the house. 'It's the fertiliser man,' he says, with clear signs of relief. If it was a stranger, there would clearly be tension. His wife would answer the door, he would hang back, watching from a window with a view over the back yard, listening, looking for something suspicious, ready to grab one of the guns which he is allowed to retain for his protection.

With their sons still involved in the security forces, they never totally relax. An unexpected car coming, a telephone call in the night, could herald bad news. They tell you not to set a pattern about your life, he says, and then describes how that security advice is impractical. Every morning and evening the cows have to be milked, the creamery van calls, cattle have to be fed, the unavoidable routines of farming. The range of threats which he must consider and the checks he must make are enormous. The car, the tractor, the byre door, could all be booby-trapped. The possibilities of walking into an ambush or a carefully concealed bomb out on the farm are endless. A sniper has ample opportunity to fire while gunmen could arrive at the farm anytime, if they were so minded, even walking across the fields, to ensure surprise.

His only defence is the revolver in his overalls and his fieldcraft, both as a farmer and an experienced soldier. He can tell if the cattle have been disturbed, if a gate has been opened. In moving around he uses what natural cover there is to protect him, skirting around potential firing points, going through a hedge rather than a gate in case of a bomb. It's really second nature, after his years of caution.

He talks in friendly terms about the neighbours. The closest are several fields away. They help each other out. Farming is that sort of calling. Fields flood. Cattle go sick. The crops have to be harvested when the weather is good. There is an unofficial cooperative where expensive machinery is concerned, to avoid duplication. No need for two costly balers when one would serve both. Better to invest in another piece of equipment. Some of the neighbours involved in this effort are Catholics. He says that they get on very well together. They visit each other and meet socially as well as through work. But, for him, there is always an unspoken reservation.

Seven of his comrades and friends have been killed over the last twenty years and, for every murder, the killers are still free. He talks of another former comrade who has already survived one attempt on his life and is now talking openly about being targeted and being killed sooner or later. He won't give the IRA the satisfaction of leaving the UDR.

Leafing through the bundle of black-bordered Orders of Service for their funerals, he says that in every case they were set up by neighbours, workmates or so-called friends, fingered for the IRA gunmen by people so close to them that they knew their every move. (Another farmer with UDR connections said he shared machinery and hay making with Catholic neighbours but, 'I would never stand with my back to some of them.')

He tells a story about the son of a neighbour, killed in a car crash, to illustrate how well concealed are the tentacles of the IRA. As is the custom, the neighbours, regardless of religion, turned up at the local hospital to escort the body home for the wake. He recalls that several members of the Regiment, in civilian clothes, were in attendance when, to their horror, the funeral approached, led by a piper and with a tricolour and black beret on the coffin. The dead youth had been a member of the IRA, unknown and unsuspected to them all. The UDR men quickly withdrew into the night, embarrassed and even more embattled.

'The feeling of distrust is always in the back of your mind. When middle-class Roman Catholics chat you up, you're never sure if they're sounding you out, sifting you. You always wonder is it genuine friendliness or are they setting me up? It annoys you, to say the least, that they know so much about you.'

About one hundred miles and three counties away, in the fishing village of Kilkeel, County Down, there are echoes of the same distrust within a small community. As Mrs Norma Johnston goes about her daily life, she encounters people involved in the murder of her son, Corporal Alan Johnston, aged 23, who was shot five times on 15 February 1988 as he arrived for work at the joinery in the village. Overnight the killers had held a schoolteacher in his home who was left bound and gagged while they used his car for the killing.

We are local. My father was a farmer here and we were people that never had any enemies. It's very hard to take. It's something that I'll never get over – the fact that local men, known to the family, were pointing him out. I feel they've taken part of me. I was born and reared here. This is the hard part to take. They know everything about you, more really than you know yourself.

We brought our family up to respect people. When it happens you sit down and wonder what they feel about your family and your values that they would do that sort of thing. The hardest part for a mother is to see the hurt on the faces of the rest of the family. Grief is a lone thing, no matter how many are in the family.

There is one fellow, the man who pointed the finger, who is doing time. I always pass the mother of that fellow, walking up the street. He was known to my son, through his being in the UDR. Probably he was being used by others. It's a very small town. It's also a very small courtroom you're sitting in, close to those people. I found that

very hard, very, very distressing but giving evidence was something
I had to do because I'd gone in with Alan one morning to his work,
when this fellow was watching.

At Belfast Crown Court, in December 1988, William Joseph
'Fatso' Harper, from Kilkeel, was sentenced to life imprisonment after being convicted for collecting and passing on
information about Alan Johnston's movements knowing that
the IRA was planning to murder him. UDR intelligence,
painstakingly collected and recorded, played a vital role in
identifying Harper and convicting him.

> I know another one who I'm perfectly sure should be doing time
> along with this fellow. I believe he's never been lifted or questioned.
> I'm almost 99 per cent sure listening to the court case that he had a
> part in it. That's the sad thing, he was known to Alan. I would say
> there are different ones we know but they cannot be prosecuted
> because of the lack of proof.
>
> It seems he was set up by the locals and the gunman was brought
> in. We have a name. A man from Lurgan, who is wanted for other
> things. When we hear his name or see his photo on television, it's
> part of the torture and grief. We hear he was the gunman for our
> son. Again, who has the proof? There were actually two of them,
> one a local, who's still on the run. I can't blame the police. What's
> the point? How do you get proof? I understand their difficulties.

She does. Her husband is a full-time member of the RUC
Reserve. Another son was in the Regiment for more than eight
years, but left after the murder of his brother. 'He was living in a
very vulnerable area. It was a great strain. When he came back
to live with us I was in constant dread. I was going up and closing
windows. I was so scared that they were coming back to get
him.'

Mrs Johnston believes that Alan knew he was being targeted.

> I saw he was under strain a couple of weeks before. I asked him but
> he denied it. There are things I still don't know about. He must have
> known they were waiting. The Sunday night before he died, he
> wouldn't go out to church. That was unusual. If he was apprehen-
> sive about anything, he kept it to himself. He didn't want to worry
> us.

About eight weeks before Alan died, Mrs Johnston witnessed an incident that she now thinks was significant.

> I walked down to the centre of Kilkeel to meet him every afternoon. It was a routine. I got a lift home. When I got there, there was a car pulled up beside him and one of the three men in that car was shouting abuse, using filthy language. On the way home I asked him what was going on. He just said, 'Mummy, forget about it.' It worried me that evening. For some reason after that I felt they were watching for him. But what can you do?
>
> He was an easy target, easy got at. They knew he was going to turn up at a certain time every morning. His brother wanted him to work around because he was such an easy target, leaving at the same time every day. We couldn't get him to leave. It was like a family in there, where he worked. I think they decided to shoot him because he was always very careful about checking his car. When he got out of it at the joinery works, he was carrying a toolbox and lunchbox. He had a personal weapon but no chance to use it.
>
> The morning he died was most peculiar. I had to wake him, so he was a minute or two late. I remember asking him if he had enough sandwiches. That's something I never did. He'd been away, working out for six weeks beforehand and was only back a few days. That leads me to believe he was set up by someone very close, for few knew he was back.
>
> If you're connected with the security forces you wonder if it will ever happen to you, the nightmare come true. I often wondered if it would happen. Over the years, we've known so many threatened people and listened to so much. What you'd do in the circumstances, you never know.
>
> Although I'd had this feeling about Alan, at the same time it's something you think is never going to happen. That morning it was totally unexpected. I heard the police siren at home here. I thought of a road accident. Then, a short time later, I looked down from the upstairs window and saw the police car. I knew something was wrong.

Alan Johnston was 23 when he was murdered and had been serving in 3UDR for well over four years. He had spent his entire life in Kilkeel, growing up with the Troubles as a constant backdrop, and, apart from a holiday trip to Scotland as a child, had only ever been away when he went with the UDR to summer training camps in Britain. He was educated at the local primary and then the High School.

His grandfather persuaded him to learn a trade – 'it's easy carried,' his grandmother told him – so he began serving his time at the local joinery works. His mother says he was a steady reliable lad, very close to his two older brothers and younger sister. He was a quiet, generous boy, whose greatest love was walking his dogs in the foothills of the Mourne Mountains nearby and visiting his grandparents, when they were alive. 'Nothing really meant that much to him except his love for the countryside where he lived and his friends,' his mother remembers. 'He was not a lad who would put his arm round you but there was a special bond.'

His other great interest was the Kilkeel Silver Band, which he joined as a small boy, graduating from the cymbals to drums. He loved drumming and the uniforms and three years before he died he also joined the Mourne Young Defenders, a flute and drum band of the 'blood and thunder' type. His mother was worried about the reputation of such bands for causing trouble and warned him: 'Any carry-on and out goes the drum, sticks and uniform.' However, such worries proved unfounded and both bands now remember Alan Johnston, the Silver with a mace, the Defenders with a bannerette, both presented by his parents.

He was not encouraged by any of his family to join the UDR. 'We didn't want him in the UDR,' says Mrs Johnston. 'He wasn't forced to go in. But these young fellows love their country. They see what's happening. They feel they must go out and play their part. He was a very dedicated young lad.'

At least two nights a week Alan would come home after his day's work, have a meal and be gone again for duty from 7.30 pm to 2.30 am, or later, the following morning. 'I remember once saying to him: Alan, why do you bother? I was afraid for his health working and going out at night. "Mum," he told me, "if it's only to stop some one person getting killed then it's worth it." That was the reason. They see the cancer of terrorism and they want to do something for the community. What people don't understand is that, when they live in a small area like this and something happens, there's a terrible pressure put on you.

You have to be careful what you say. There is the fear of a mother that they're coming back again and if you have any more family, that's the terrible thing.'

The killing brought her into contact with other bereaved mothers and widows. 'I was surprised, talking to them, that they all have this terrible, terrible fear that they're coming back for you. Before this I used to look at people and say, goodness, six years on and there's still tears in their eyes. Now I know what they're going through.'

So when anyone, especially a member of the security forces, becomes a victim of the terrorists Mrs Johnston gets in touch. 'Anytime there is a death I sit down and write a wee letter and put my phone number on it. You may get a reply. You may not. You say we know what you are going through. We share in your troubles. It's not easy to do. It bursts open your own wounds.'

She is now part of a network of those left behind to grieve. They exchange letters and visits, the most recent victims being counselled by the longer suffering but all drawing comfort from sharing their experiences and feelings.

> A natural death or an accident is a terrible tragedy but for us it's the thought that this dark evil is still out there roaming free. If someone was brought to court and imprisoned, it would help knowing that someone else was not going to suffer.
>
> There's no doubt that because these people are free, they're going to kill again, target someone else. If they were behind bars, at least you would feel they were in safekeeping for so long.

It was this shared desire to protect other families, UDR or not, from suffering a similar ordeal that compelled Mrs Johnston and four other UDR wives and mothers, whose husbands or sons were blown up or shot, to ask to see Mr Peter Brooke, the Northern Ireland Secretary.

'We wanted to put over to him the sorrow. Politicians talk and we've heard it. Probably they try to do their best but we felt if we could get in to him, we could bring something to him, from the families, that he probably didn't hear before.'

The meeting took place on 25 June 1990. Mr Brooke received the women, Ken Maginnis MP and Jeffrey Donaldson, a

Unionist candidate, in his office at Stormont Castle, Belfast. Over afternoon tea, they sat in a semi-circle around his desk and poured their hearts out.

Each of us had our chance, as much time as we needed. It was very, very emotional; from the heart. He did not say very much to us, just took notes and summed up at the end. I felt he was feeling for us. It surprised me actually. I do believe that if one man could do something for you, I genuinely believe he would try.

We told him we felt nothing was being done. Every time something terrible happens, it comes right back to you and you just feel a frustration. The government don't seem to understand what's going on. We feel, who's doing anything for us?

We put it to him, it was never going to help us again. Our loss was something he could never bring back. We wanted him to try and get something done to stop other families suffering what we suffered.

We suggested selective internment. Not going out and lifting your next door neighbour because you think he's in something but persons they believe have done a crime. The security people know. The intelligence is supposed to be very high compared to what it was at the start of the Troubles. Extradition from the South was another thing we brought up. It seems to me there's a lot more could be done there.

Basically we wanted more vigorous action within the law. Not an eye for an eye or a tooth for a tooth. It doesn't work outside the law. I was very, very frightened that somebody would do that. I know Alan wouldn't have wanted that and we didn't want that. No way. His friends have now become our friends and call to see us. I'm glad that Alan is not forgotten and prouder that I can go about and know none of those lads is locked up because of something they did for Alan Johnston.

It amazes me with what is going on, people being shot and bombed, that there isn't a bigger backlash. The first thing you want to do is go out and hurt for revenge. But if you hate, it burns you up. How do we come through then? How do we go on?

As a Christian person, I have my faith. I believe the Lord helped me through the court case. In my times of utter despair, sometimes you can't pray, but I know the Lord is with me, no matter what I'm going through. If I hadn't my faith I couldn't go on. Sometimes it's a struggle. You take two steps forward and one step back. I didn't take tablets. The most I've ever taken was an aspirin. I try to battle through. I don't let anyone see my tears. It's a struggle with just blow after blow.

Nine months after Alan Johnston was murdered, the IRA killed the local police Commander, Superintendent Alwyn Harris outside his home in Lisburn, County Antrim. 'That was a big loss. He came in here and sat and talked with me as a friend. The RUC were very good to us after Alan's death, as were the welfare people from the UDR.' A short time later, the family came within a hair's breadth of another tragedy when Alan's father, a member of the RUC, was on patrol in Castlewellan, County Down. An RPG7 rocket was fired at the car but missed, hitting a nearby building. 'The fear of another death in the family is always there with you. I'm not too sure how I would react if it happened again.'

In the churchyard at Kilkeel, Alan Johnston lies in a line of seven graves, all local victims of terrorism. Twelve people from this one locality, most members of the security forces, have been killed by terrorists. Alan Johnston was the fifth person on his father's side of the family to be murdered.

In addition, Kenneth Graham, a member of the family which operated the joinery works where Alan Johnston had been employed, was killed by terrorists.

> I admire the bravery of the people in Northern Ireland, especially the mothers. When you hear some of the terrible things that have happened, you wonder how they cope. The terrorists have you in a corner. But I think, because of bravery, because your son's been brave, that you can say: 'Do what you want to us but you'll never win in the end.'

After their encounter at Stormont, Mrs Johnston and the other women issued a statement which said:

> In meeting Mr Brooke we feel we are carrying on the fight, in the only way we know how, for justice and peace for which members of our families have died. We do not want their sacrifice to be in vain or forgotten. We want to indicate our support and deep concern for their comrades who still serve and for all the other families who like ours have already paid the cost.

Mr Brooke, replying later to Ken Maginnis, who had organised the meeting, said he found it 'extremely moving. I can only underline my admiration for the ladies' courage and sincerity. I shall never underestimate the contribution which the UDR has made and is making to the elimination of terrorism and I believe this is shared by all right-thinking people in the Province.'

Joining the UDR to help eliminate terrorism has been described as 'a form of public service unique to Northern Ireland', by Brigadier Pat Hargrave, a former commander. Another former commander, Brigadier Mervyn McCord, once said the UDR was a 'citizens' army.'

It was conventional military wisdom as expounded by many distinguished soldiers that local insurgency forces could only be defeated by locally-recruited counter-insurgency forces, the military doctrine which underpins the existence of the UDR.

Mrs Johnston puts it more succinctly. 'Local boys know what's going on around their own doors. They'll soon know if there's a strange car about.'

Over the years more than 40,000 Ulster men and women have been concerned enough about the future of the community to enlist and serve for a time with the Regiment. Some have lasted only a short time before giving up, others have soldiered on for up to twenty years. They have come from all walks and classes of life. In 1975, for instance, there were eighty-four married couples serving and fifty-three family groups of three or more. One entire family had enlisted in Fermanagh: mum, dad, three sons and daughter. There are still strong family groups in the Regiment today. Four Craigavon brothers are serving while the fifth member of the family is a Royal Irish Ranger.

When the Regiment was overwhelmingly part-time the range of occupations represented was diverse. Farmers were the most numerous but teachers, shopkeepers, nurses and housewives were pretty commonly scattered in the ranks.

At one time the Regiment boasted that it could have planned and built a fair-sized town with the architects, surveyors, stonemasons, bricklayers, carpenters, electricians, plumbers, estate agents, roofers and steel erectors it contained.

The clash of these diverse civilian backgrounds with the military culture embraced by the UDR often had startling and amusing consequences. One wealthy farmer, who ran a 300-acre farm, was selective in his respect for red-tabbed and be-pipped senior officers and only those whom he favoured earned the required salute. One evening, when he was on sentry duty at the main gate of his base, the eye-patch-wearing Brigadier Harry Baxter queried his lack of respect for a senior officer. 'Goodnight, sir,' said the soldier, who unabashedly grabbed the Brigadier by the hand and pumped it warmly. 'I hope your eye gets better soon.'

Another story, in the same vein, concerns a titled member of the gentry. Awaiting a drop of milk for his morning cornflakes, he was quite annoyed to find that his milkman had not delivered at the usual time and a ticking-off was administered when he duly arrived. That evening the titled gentleman, also a part-time UDR private, was late reporting for duty and was made to endure a lecture on the merits of punctuality from his part-time platoon commander, who was also his milkman.

There was, and is, no class barrier in the Regiment. The great, the good and the wealthy have served side by side for the benefit of the community. A UDR commander was once flying over his patch in a helicopter with a visiting senior officer from Britain. 'Look at that magnificent property down there,' the envious visitor said, pointing to a large house with manicured lawns. 'Who does that belong to?'

'One of my privates,' replied the UDR commander.

But why are so many people prepared to run the risks of UDR membership? What motivates them to join? There is no clear answer, but 'love of country' or 'Queen and country' are very commonly stated reasons. One UDR officer said that in his estimation, two-thirds of the members joined out of loyalty, one-third for the money.

This officer, a successful businessman and UDR major, was actively involved in moderate Unionist politics soon after the Troubles broke out at the end of the 1960s. He thought that there was a good chance of creating a new society, with fair and equal Catholic and Protestant participation. The outbreak and intensification of the IRA terrorist campaign changed his mind and he felt the most useful contribution he could make to creating a better society was by joining the UDR to combat violence.

Many joined through tradition. They may have been B Specials or had family connections, a very common factor among the Unionist community. Today many young men and women are following their parents into the Regiment, carrying on the tradition of service. Many of those serving now were not even born when the UDR was formed, a sobering comment on the enduring nature of the security problem and its political context.

The generations-old fear of the resurgent IRA and opposition to any whiff of a united Ireland was also a powerful motivator for many people. 'What would there be to stop the IRA if it was not for the UDR?' one soldier said. Another, interestingly a Catholic, said: 'I joined because I didn't like the idea of someone trying to force me into a united Ireland at the point of a gun.'

Basic public-spiritedness, too, has attracted many into the UDR. Northern Ireland, despite its religious differences, is a church-going, caring, extended family and those with the appropriate instinct have found a ready outlet in the Regiment at this troubled time in Northern Ireland's history.

'Everybody talks about what should be done,' one woman officer said. 'I joined up to do what I could.'

A married couple (civil servant and teacher), serving together in Belfast, share this motivation. 'It is easy to sit back and complain about the situation but better to get involved,' said the wife. 'The risk of death drifts into the subconscious,' said the husband.

More mundane reasons have undoubtedly motivated a substantial number of the UDR community. Although the Regiment is poorly paid and works long, unsocial hours, by comparison with the RUC, economic necessity and high unemployment have nevertheless made it an attractive career proposition for some. 'I'd be on the dole if I wasn't here,' said a young full-timer in Tyrone.

In the rural areas, many farmers and agricultural workers, struggling to eke out a living on marginal farms, have found that the steady pay from the Regiment has transformed their financial position. Young men, faced with high levels of long-term unemployment in their own districts, have also joined up, benefiting, not only financially, from the demanding life which they subsequently lead.

UDR members earn the same pay as their counterparts in the regular army. In addition they get a special Northern Ireland allowance, currently £3 a day (1990). The authorities refuse to call it 'danger money'. Part-timers who complete the required work-load of training and service obligations are also entitled to an annual bounty, which increases with service.

The work-rate of the UDR is impressive by any standards, with the Regiment now totting up in excess of twelve million man hours a year. Every soldier, on average, spends one night in three out of bed. Part-timers average ten duties a month, normally two nights a week and two weekends, frequently a forty-eight hour spell of front-line operational deployment. Full-timers, those in the permanent cadre, rarely work less than a seventy-hour week with many regularly clocking up eighty hours. When there is an emergency or a major incident the basic eight-hour duty period can be extended indefinitely for the same day's pay.

From the summer of 1990, a new family leave scheme was introduced for the full-timers. Those who have completed three years' service, are entitled to a travel warrant at public expense to bring their wives and children to any mainland British airport or to transport their car and passengers from Northern Ireland by ferry. This concession is clearly a recognition of the extraordinary risks faced by UDR soldiers and their families. The concession came at a time of growing disquiet among many of the men about the hours they are being required to work and the low rates of pay, without overtime, when compared to the police.

RUC pay, which includes overtime, and conditions are in line with those of the entire police service in Britain. In addition they get about £130 a month Northern Ireland allowance and a rent or housing allowance, which the Northern Ireland Office has now set about reducing substantially.

In these days of financial stringency, with the government demanding VFM – value for money – the cost effectiveness of the UDR is beyond question. However long it is called out, none of the soldiers are paid overtime, the factor which has swollen the RUC budget to some £1.5 million a day. By contrast the UDR costs only £1.2 million a week to run with an annual wages bill of £54.7 million. Although the disparity with RUC pay has been a long-running grievance it has affected neither the morale of the UDR nor its commitment to duty.

It is, of course, impossible to measure the full extent of the bravery and sacrifice of those who have served in the Regiment over the years and the stresses and strains it imposes on them.

For many of them, the very act of enlisting has been a brave one. Numerous others have shown outstanding courage during service, quietly resisting threats, intimidation and sometimes repeated direct attacks. For the protection of its soldiers, the UDR keeps its roll call of courage a secret, but a glimpse of the Regiment's bravery and selflessness can be obtained from the record of public honours which its members have been awarded.

By the end of 1990 about 300 UDR members had been decorated with the Order of the British Empire, Member of the British Empire, British Empire Medal, Military Medal, Queen's Gallantry Medal and Queen's Commendation for Brave Conduct. Another 600 had earned Mentions in Despatches or Commendations from the General Officer Commanding, Northern Ireland.

One of the eleven Queen's Gallantry Medals was awarded posthumously to Corporal David Brown, a 37-year-old dog handler. On 23 May 1986, the corporal and his dog, Oliver, a golden labrador trained to sniff explosives, were helping the police carry out a search at a garage in Kilkeel, County Down where they had good reason to believe that a bomb had been planted.

1a & **b** 1922: Newtownbutler Specials on patrol
with their Lancia cage car (*above*)
and members of a C Special patrol on
duty at Albertbridge Road, Belfast (*below*).
The Specials were the forerunners of
the UDR and were disbanded in 1970.

2a A modern UDR street patrol ready for action.

2b 'Greenfinches' searching women at a UDR checkpoint in the seventies.

3a A vehicle checkpoint in the countryside.

3b A UDR search party being briefed.

4a A sniffer dog helping a UDR patrol to search for arms and explosives.

4b A passing out parade at the Regimental Training Centre at Ballykinler, County Down, where all new UDR recruits learn some basic infantry skills, with permanent cadre soldiers undergoing a nine-week induction.

5a Brigadier David Miller,
   Commander UDR 1978–80

5b Brigadier Pat Hargrave,
   Commander UDR 1980–2

5c Brigadier Roger Preston,
   Commander UDR 1984–6

5d Brigadier Michael Bray,
   Commander UDR 1984–6

6a Corporal
David Brown
and his
explosives
sniffer dog,
Oliver, who
were both
killed during
a search
operation
at Kilkeel,
May 1986.

6b The twisted
remains of a
booby-trapped
car in which
Private Victor
Foster died,
January 1986.

6c Four UDR
soldiers died
when this Land
Rover was caught
in a landmine
explosion at
Downpatrick,
April 1990.

7a Part-time UDR soldier, Albert Cooper, died at his garage in Cookstown in November 1990, when a woman delivered a booby-trapped car for repair.

7b UDR colleagues carry Albert Cooper's coffin.

8a Brigadier Angus
Ramsay who was
appointed Commander
UDR in 1990.

8b John Stevens, Deputy
Chief Constable of the
Cambridgeshire police
force, appointed in
September 1989 to
head an investigation
into allegations of
collusion between the
security forces and
Loyalist terrorist
groups. The
subsequent Stevens
Report exposed
serious irregularities
within the UDR and
recommended more
stringent guidelines for
its control.

Knowing full well the grave risk to himself and the other members of the security forces supporting him, he made the decision to conduct a search of the exterior of the building as far as the abilities of his dog would allow. The dog quickly indicated something suspicious to the corporal, who ordered his covering party to ground. As he moved forward to investigate the suspicious area further, the dog triggered an anti-handling device incorporated in an oil drum packed with explosives. Both Corporal Brown and Oliver died instantly.

The corporal had been in the UDR since 1971 and had been a dog handler for eight years. At least three times he had turned down promotion to sergeant because it would have meant ending the work with dogs, which he loved. In 1983, this dangerous work, leading explosives search teams, had been recognised by a commendation from the GOC which read:

> He has been involved in innumerable search and clearance operations within County Down and further afield in South Armagh and elsewhere in the province.
>
> He has had to be ready to turn out in emergencies, at any time of day or night. His soldierly manner and his professionalism made an excellent impression on regular units who have come to rely on his advice with complete assurance.
>
> He has turned himself into a thorough professional. He has had long hours of hard work in all weathers and often in difficult and dangerous conditions and has made a valuable contribution to the reputation of the UDR and the cause of peace in Northern Ireland.

On 22 July 1987, Corporal Brown's widow and two of his four children were presented with his QGM by the Queen, during an investiture at Buckingham Palace in London. 'It brought it all back to me but I was proud to be there on behalf of my husband,' his widow said afterwards.

Another of the QGM's was awarded to a UDR private whose cool head and swift reaction undoubtedly prevented loss of life in a car bombing attack. The incident began when a neighbour received an anonymous telephone call saying that a bomb had been planted in a car on the housing estate where she lived. When she arrived at the soldier's house to tell him of the threat, she was panic-stricken. He managed to calm her down, extract all the relevant information and notify the police. Then he went outside, located a suspicious car, and single-handedly set about alerting and clearing neighbours from the vicinity. Having set this operation in motion, he obtained a torch to inspect the car further and confirm its colour. At this point he identified a triangular box on the back seat which began to bleep as he was inspecting it. Despite the danger of an imminent explosion, the soldier checked again that no one living in the street remained in range.

By now five minutes had elapsed and three RUC officers arrived at the scene. Seconds later there was a huge explosion which destroyed eight houses in the area and damaged sixty others. Thanks to the quick and efficient reaction of the soldier, all those within range were ushered to safety and escaped injury.

Private A, a founder member of the Regiment, who had refused to give in to threats on his life and a bomb attack, was commended after the way he dealt with a terrorist raid on his joint home and garage business on 30 August 1973.

During the course of the day two terrorists, one carrying a revolver, raided the premises just two hundred yards from the border. Those present, including the owner, were lined up at gunpoint and asked their names. When Private A replied, the terrorist aimed the weapon at him and pulled the trigger. Realising that the hammer was not cocked, the soldier jumped to the side and ran to his nearby bungalow where he assembled the firing parts of his UDR issue sub-machine gun. As the raiders made their getaway in two cars he fired first eight shots and then four shots at them, from two positions. A short time later a bomb which they had left behind exploded, destroying the garage building. The soldier's citation said that 'in circumstances which would have daunted many, he showed an aggressive spirit and willingness to engage the raiders which would have done credit to a much more experienced professional soldier. Throughout the incident he acted coolly with courage and determination and without regard for his own personal safety.'

A lance-corporal who showed great presence of mind and an aggressive spirit after being caught in an explosion was also honoured for his actions. He was in the turret of a Shorland armoured car in February 1974 at Garvagh, County Londonderry when a 200lb landmine went off between his vehicle and the one in front.

Despite the fact that both vehicles had crashed into the bomb crater, about twenty-five feet across and eight feet deep, and had come under fire from the terrorists, he managed to overcome the effects of shock and facial injuries and return fire from his General Purpose Machine Gun. As a result the raiders broke off the engagement and fled.

The lance-corporal then assisted other injured and shocked members of the patrol to escape from their crippled vehicles, which were by then rapidly filling with water and sinking into the crater.

Later examination by an army bomb disposal officer established the real value of his efforts, for the terrorists had abandoned two other devices at the side of the crater intended to be detonated from the same firing point as the members of the patrol attempted to get away from the effects of the main explosion.

A British Empire Medal was awarded to a part-time corporal in 1988 after an attack on him as he was leaving his civilian workplace. Two terrorists, firing at close quarters as he drove out through the gates, hit him in the shoulder. Three women workmates were in the car with him and became hysterical after the shooting, but he remained calm and, despite the effects of his injury, drove through the ambush until he reached the safety of a police station two miles away.

No account of the UDR's record of bravery would be complete without a mention of the Graham brothers from County Fermanagh, three of whom have been singled out and murdered by the IRA. 'They were the best fellas you could meet in a day's travel,' said a former colleague and family friend. 'They couldn't do enough to help you. They would have bent over backwards to help you.'

Albert Graham, their father, reared five sons and two daughters, in a railway cottage near Lisnaskea, working as a general labourer. He was a member of the B Specials for many years and when the UDR was formed in 1970, he joined, followed by three of his sons and a daughter, Hilary. She was knocked down by a car which crashed through a UDR checkpoint and sustained serious injuries, from which she never really recovered, despite months spent in and out of hospital. Friends say the accident undoubtedly caused her premature death.

The first of the brothers to be murdered was Ronnie, 38 years old and married with two children, a family whom he supported from the proceeds of a job in a local factory, a round delivering groceries and coal and his duties in the UDR as a lance-corporal.

One Thursday night in June 1981, he spent his last night on earth with other UDR colleagues, voluntarily lying out in the countryside to guard a soldier and his family who had been threatened and were moving out the next day. At breakfast time on the Friday morning, 5 June, he was asked to make a delivery to an isolated farmhouse, where his killers were holding a woman and her daughter hostage and lying in wait. As he drove up, the masked gunmen ran from the house and shot him dead.

Five months later, his brother Cecil was murdered. He had inherited the family farm and, having married a Catholic girl whom he met while working in a local factory, set up house in a mobile home while building a modern bungalow. Like Ronnie, Cecil was an industrious, hard-working man, holding down a job at Unipork, a local firm, running his farm and serving with the Regiment as a private.

In October, five weeks before his death, their first baby was born premature and required constant attention, so mother and baby moved in with her parents, at Donagh, a Catholic area, where Republican sympathies were undoubtedly strong. Although it was clearly a risky area for Cecil to visit, he called most evenings, arriving and leaving at different times. These cautious movements were obviously watched and betrayed, for late on Monday night, 9 November, as he was leaving at the end of a short visit, gunmen struck, hitting him sixteen times in the head, trunk and legs with shots from an Armalite high-velocity rifle. He was air-lifted by the army to hospital in Belfast, where he died from his wounds, two days later.

On 18 August 1983, the full horror of what took place was revealed at an inquest when his father-in-law, Mr Vincent Rice, described how the mortally wounded man lay helpless on the street and was left alone to drag himself from his car back into the shelter of the house where he tried to help him. He disclosed that he was a 'bit upset' that in the two years since the shooting none of the neighbours had extended sympathy or even mentioned the murder of his son-in-law.

One of the first police officers on the scene, after the shooting, said that he was not surprised that no one had come to the aid of the dying man. 'It is a hardline Republican area and decent people living there were probably afraid to come out,' he said.

The coroner, Mr James Elliott, described the incident as coldblooded murder and commented:

> It seems Mr Graham was either a brave or foolhardy man in that he visited his wife regularly at this estate which has been described as a hardline Republican area. It seems its inhabitants must have been to some extent terrorised – for none of the neighbours felt able to come on to the street to offer any assistance and none has offered any sympathy and that is to be regretted. It is a terribly tragic and sad state of affairs.

But the tragedy for the Graham family did not end there. On 1 February 1985, Jimmy Graham, married with two teenage daughters, agreed at short notice to take a party of school children to a swimming lesson. As he sat at the wheel of his bus, outside the primary school at Derrylin, County Fermanagh, a burst of shots were fired through the windscreen. He ran down the bus wounded, but one of the gunmen boarded the vehicle and fired again. He died from the effects of fifteen gunshot wounds in his head and body. Several eyewitnesses reported that as the killers drove off towards the border, eight miles away, they were cheering.

Jimmy Graham knew that he was living on a short timespan and had openly discussed the situation with colleagues after at least two IRA attempts on his life. In the New Year Honours list, only a few weeks before his death, he had been awarded the British Empire Medal for his courage during one of them in 1980 when he was attacked in his car outside his home. His personal protection Walther jammed but despite being wounded in the neck and shoulder, he succeeded in driving to his house, reaching his rifle and engaging the terrorists, who then escaped.

Jimmy Graham had asked for a military funeral, an honour granted by the UDR, with a piper playing a lament and the Last Post being sounded as his coffin was lowered into the Fermanagh earth. At the funeral service earlier, Dr Gordon McMullan, the Church of Ireland Bishop of Clogher, condemned his murderers. 'They are men and women whose work simply plunges us into grief and whose ultimate goal, if it ever was achieved, would be the destruction of Ireland, North and South.'

In October 1986, at Belfast Crown Court, an 18-year-old youth, Paul Smyth, was imprisoned for seven years for his part in the murder of Ronnie Graham. Mr Justice Carswell heard that, acting on written instructions, the youth, who was only thirteen at the time of the offence, moved two rifles from their hiding place in a barn in Lisnaskea to a hedge facing the house where Ronnie was to be shot as he made his delivery. The court heard it alleged that Smyth had been recruited and sworn into the IRA only a month earlier by a temporary woman teacher at his school.

There is another, usually hidden, side to the terrible toll the terrorists have exacted from the UDR. The Regiment has been on active service now for longer than the combined totals of both world wars and for longer continuously than any other British regiment since Napoleonic times.

The resulting stress and strain imposed on its members have caused at least forty-five of them to take their own lives. In October 1972, a 30 year-old left his house at Strabane on foot, apparently to report for duty. A short time later a 15-year-old girl found his body nearby with his UDR revolver lying by his side.

A 22-year-old second lieutenant, regarded as a competent officer, who was also studying for an honours degree at Queens University, Belfast, shocked friends and colleagues when he shot himself in April 1984. His father told a subsequent inquest that the only explanation was fatigue and tension. 'He had no worries.'

The shame of being arrested for suspected drunk driving after a traffic accident caused a 26-year-old UDR soldier to commit suicide in May 1985. After being arrested he was taken to the RUC headquarters at Strand Road in Londonderry, but instead of getting out of the police car he shot himself in the head with his personal protection weapon and died next day in hospital.

In 1988 two UDR soldiers, both in their twenties, took their own lives within thirteen days of each other at the same UDR base in Londonderry, again with officially issued firearms.

In July 1989, the wife of a part-time UDR soldier, who felt neglected because of his constant absence at work or on duty, filed for separation and after sleeping alone in another bedroom for a period, eventually moved out. The soldier, later described as a hard working and devoted father, wrote threatening to kill himself if the marriage ended. One evening, when he had brought the children back from a swimming outing and the wife admitted she was seeing another man, he pulled a gun out of a bag and shot himself in the head in front of her.

On 19 March 1990, Lance-Corporal Stanley Massey was showing his girlfriend how to load and unload his new .38 revolver. After ejecting several rounds on to the floor he said 'Let's play Russian roulette.' He put the gun to his head and fired. 'There was a bang, a flash and the smell of gunpowder,' she told a subsequent inquest. 'There was a startled expression on his face as if to say – I did not mean it.' The coroner described his behaviour as 'absolutely insane'.

The Troubles prompted a general rise in the number of suicides in the Northern Ireland community brought on by stress, financial worries, marital problems and other highly predictable factors. In 1972 there were 47 self-inflicted deaths but by 1983 the number had soared to a peak of 142 and since then has averaged about twice the 1972 figure.

The Samaritans in Northern Ireland reported concern at the high rate of suicides among under-25s and in particular those among the security forces, aggravated by the ready availability of a firearm. One of the most futile deaths took place in 1983 when a 23-year-old private killed himself in the guardroom at Girdwood Barracks, Belfast, playing 'Russian roulette'.

The suicide problem was a serious embarrassment to the security forces, both police and army, who regarded it as a poor reflection on their morale and manliness. As recently as December 1986 the Samaritans said that the security forces were 'somewhat resistant' to offers of help, but since then medical research and greater awareness of the stress problem as a legitimate reaction, not as a sign of weakness, has caused a more compassionate attitude to evolve.

Supervisory officers have now been trained to look for early signs of stress, post-trauma stress counselling has been recognised as a crucial need and the level of welfare care for those in the security forces has been substantially upgraded. Soldiers and police officers are now not dismissed as 'soft' or of suspect reliability because they show symptoms of strain or stress which, if treated sympathetically, can be overcome.

The daunting burden of UDR welfare is largely shouldered by the UDR Benevolent Fund. Set up in 1972, by General Sir John Anderson, it is now a private registered charity, independent of government or the Ministry of Defence, administered by twelve trustees who include the Catholic and Protestant members of the Advisory Council appointed by the GOC to advise him about the UDR.

Its purposes, as defined in the Deed of Trust which governs its operation, are to make immediate grants to the widows and dependents of UDR soldiers who die in service and to help the families of ex-soldiers killed in terrorist attacks if they are in need. The Fund can also help serving soldiers in need as a result of their service in the UDR.

Until the early 1980s, by which time it had reached £400,000 and was paying out between £50,000 and £95,000 a year, the Fund was mainly built up by the entire Regiment covenanting one day's pay a year. But inflation and the increasing demand on its resources, as the casualties and hardship caused by terrorism mounted, meant that the pay-out for a widow could only amount to a paltry £750. There was also concern about funding the longterm responsibility to UDR dependants. Most of the casualties were young men, who often left young wives and children deprived of a wage-earner. There was also an increasing number of pensioners to care for.

Accordingly, in 1983 a drive to raise a £1 million capital fund to enable more realistic payments to be made to widows and dependants, to supplement statutory pensions and compensation, and secure the long-term welfare of the UDR family, was put in motion by the then Commander, Brigadier Peter Graham.

The fund-raising was launched at a dinner in the Mansion House, in the City of London in March 1983, attended by Prince and Princess Michael of Kent. Addressing the guests, James Prior, then the Secretary of State for Northern Ireland, paid tribute to the men and women of the UDR, whom he told a distinguished audience, were at risk twenty-four hours of every day.

> They do not live in fortified barracks, but in their own homes spread throughout the community. They are often an easy target for the terrorists. It takes a brave or dedicated man or woman to join the Regiment under these circumstances. This is an heroic effort; there are no Goose Greens for the UDR; few opportunities for headline-catching acts of gallantry; but the risk of death is always present. And too often the terrorist uses a cowardly bullet in the back or a bomb under the car. The risk and the stress extend to the families of soldiers of the Regiment. They are always conscious of the threat and they, too, run the risk of the cowardly terrorist assassin.

By the end of the year the Fund had reached its £1 million target with the community, industry and commerce, the churches, trusts and individual donors, including one who gave £100,000, all contributing.

The payment to widows was immediately stepped up to £5,000, with an additional £200 for each dependant child, a practical cushion against the immediate effect of a murder and the inevitable funeral and incidental expenses. Since then the Fund, which works closely with designated welfare officers in each battalion, has become an important prop in UDR welfare and morale. Apart from its prompt aid to widows and dependants when tragedy strikes, it helps in a variety of ways. Soldiers with an injury sustained on duty which has stopped them doing their civilian job have been compensated. Families who have had to move home at short notice because of threats or intimidation have been assisted in covering the costs of the disruption. Interest free loans have been made available to soldiers whose cars have been damaged or destroyed to enable them to replace the vehicle before criminal damage compensation is awarded.

Less than a week before Christmas 1988, terrorists exploded a large car bomb in a residential area of Richhill, County Armagh. More than sixty houses were devastated in the blast with roofs blown off, doors and ceilings damaged, windows shattered and water damage from broken pipes. Several of the houses closest to the bomb sustained structural damage and four had to be pulled down. Among the families affected were those of seven UDR soldiers. The Benevolent Fund stepped in and, with speedy assistance, enabled the families to replace Christmas presents for the children and begin to repair the damage.

Bereaved families receive special and sustained assistance from the Fund. Every year the older widows receive a week's holiday at a good hotel with all expenses paid. Those with young families are booked into a caravan or holiday camp. With the help of other generous benefactors in the United States, more adventurous holidays are provided for teenagers. In recent summers, groups of 13–18-year-olds have lived with American families and been enabled to see sights as varied as Disney World, the Grand Ole Opry in Nashville and even Gracelands, the former home of Elvis Presley.

The Fund has now paid out in excess of £1.5 million to assist distressed members of the UDR family. The pressures on it remain unremitting. At present it disburses about £200,000 a year but the total could soar, depending on the number of casualties. In one month, early in 1990, when eight soldiers were killed, the Fund had to pay out £66,000, half the total expenditure in the previous year. But generosity to the Fund continues on a noteworthy scale from the Northern Ireland community. For instance, all the major churches, except the Catholic ones, now hold a UDR collection Sunday each year. In two years the Presbyterians alone have donated almost £100,000.

Since 1982, when the Queen approved the proposal, the general courage and sacrifice of members of the UDR has also been recognised by the award of one of two special medals. Full-timers, who have completed fifteen years' service and 'whose character and conduct have been irreproachable', earn a circular, silver medal for long service and good conduct. Part-timers with twelve years' efficient service, receive the UD medal, also made of silver.

The Regiment itself has instituted a medallion, engraved with its crest and ivy leaves, bearing the inscription 'In proud memory', which is presented to the closest relatives of murdered UDR soldiers.

5 The 'Bad Apples'

At the conclusion of a murder trial in Belfast in January 1985, involving a member of the UDR, Mr Justice Murray proclaimed the two overlapping yardsticks by which the honour of the UDR should be measured. 'The life of a soldier is a life of discipline,' he said, adding: 'It is of vital importance that the public should be able to have confidence in the integrity of the security forces.'

Over the years, full-blooded community confidence in the discipline and integrity of the UDR has been seriously compromised by the repeated involvement of its members in murder and other serious criminal and sectarian activity. These soldiers have become known as the 'bad apples' and critics of the Regiment insist that they have infected the whole barrel. To assess the damage to the UDR's reputation and the consequences of this misbehaviour, it is first necessary to look at the Regiment's record. This survey begins with an account of the murder cases in which UDR soldiers were involved and convicted. It then looks at other cases over the years involving members of the Regiment and examines a number of instances where UDR weapons went missing.

Within forty-eight hours of the murder of UDR Private Samuel Porter near Maghera, in November 1972, two Catholics from the same part of South Derry died, apparently in reprisal. Joseph McAuley was walking along a country lane near his home on 21 November, when a gunman fired a shot from a passing car, knocking him to the ground. The car then reversed and several more shots were fired into his body. He died from his wound, ten days later in hospital.

A day after the first shooting another man, Liam Chivers, was murdered. He had just taken his dog out for a late-night walk and was only a short distance from his home when members of his family heard several shots fired close together and then, after a pause, a single shot. His teenage son found him lying dead, face down in a pool of blood. A post-mortem later established that he had been killed by the single shot to the head, fired as he lay wounded from the earlier shots, discharged from an automatic rifle.

The three killings came at a time of high tension, with local Unionist politicians calling for Loyalists to unite and 'take action to eradicate the IRA once and for all'. Nationalist leaders had been to Stormont at the same time asking for a 'flying squad' of security forces to protect Catholics threatened or attacked in isolated rural areas.

The two reprisal killings were linked to an astonishing reign of terror involving several members of the UDR in County Londonderry, which began in the early 1970s after a premature explosion at a farm in which a man died while constructing a bomb.

The surviving activists, many of them ex-B Specials, then decided to infiltrate the UDR as a cover for their activities, which only came to light some seven years later when one of their number, having emigrated to Birmingham, experienced a religious conversion and confessed to the police.

As a result of subsequent investigations six of them went on trial in Belfast in May 1978, charged with a list of offences dating back to 1971. Two of those in the dock were members of the UDR. At the end of the trial, one of them, Robert Davis, who had been a full-time member of 5UDR, was sentenced to life imprisonment for the murder of Samuel Millar, aged 71.

In January 1976, Davis and another man went to Millar's farm to persuade him not to give evidence against them in a case arising from the earlier armed robbery of £1,400 from a post office. Davis later told the police that when the old man refused to back down he took an iron shaft from his car, used for killing foxes, and hit him over the head several times. Then he reversed his car over him, threw the body in the boot and transported it to the shores of Lough Neagh, where he dug a grave among some bushes and buried it.

Unknown to Davis, the burial was witnessed by a man sympathetic to the Provisional IRA, who informed them what he had seen. The RUC were tipped off over the Confidential Telephone.

Davis says that four days later he heard that the IRA knew about the burial so he came back with an accomplice and exhumed the body. It is said by police sources with a knowledge of the events that Davis and his accomplice, both clad in UDR uniforms, masquerading as part of the security force searching for the missing man, travelled with the body propped up between them in the front of a military Land Rover and were waved through at least one checkpoint before weighting the body with a concrete post and dropping it into a deep water-filled quarry. Army divers recovered the body in September 1977, when Davis told the police where it had been dumped.

The other UDR soldier, Ronald Nelson, was jailed for ten years for his part in the armed robbery of 220 assorted weapons, including 148 self-loading rifles, 35 Sterling sub-machine guns and a general purpose machine-gun, as well as 9,500 rounds of ammunition, eight grenades and a rocket from the armoury in the UDR base at Magherafelt at about 3 am on 16 June 1975.

The twelve-strong gang overpowered guards, knocking one unconscious, before taking the keys to the armoury and escaping with their haul in two UDR vehicles. A patrol from 5UDR recovered the entire haul the next day after 50,000 gallons of slurry was pumped from a storage tank at the farm where the weapons were found. The police think that they were quietly surrendered to take the heat off the local UDA gang, which numbered several of the local UDR soldiers among its members.

Nelson was also convicted, with others, for his part in additional sectarian crimes which included possessing firearms, car theft, armed robbery, arson and a petrol bomb attack on a Catholic draper's shop which caused £162,000 worth of damage.

In January 1979, another member of the gang, who was not a UDR soldier, was imprisoned for life after admitting that he had carried out the two reprisal killings. Another man was also given life for his part in one of them. The double-killer, Benjamin Redfern, met his own bizarre death in August 1984 when he was crushed to death in a refuse lorry after concealing himself in a dustbin while trying to escape from the Maze prison.

These events created fears about the integrity of the UDR amongst Catholics far beyond the areas in which they took place. And there was already further cause for concern.

Late in the evening of 7 May 1974, Mrs Gertrude Devlin and her 17-year-old daughter left their home on the outskirts of Dungannon, County Tyrone for what was a regular journey to collect the head of the family, James, from nearby Coalisland where he managed a public house. After picking him up, they bought fish and chips for supper and headed home.

As the car turned into the lane leading to their house, a man in a military type uniform, with his hand raised, stepped into the headlights. As Mrs Devlin slowed the car, thinking that they had encountered a military checkpoint, it was sprayed with automatic gunfire, badly wounding her.

Mr Devlin, sitting in the back of the car, said that he would go for help but as he tried to get out of the car a second burst of fire killed him and his wife, wounding their daughter in the front passenger seat who had put her hands over her face when the shooting started. Although hit in the legs and arms, she was eventually able to get out of the car and reach the house of a neighbour to raise the alarm. Police later recovered twenty-nine bullet shells from the scene and found footprints indicating that the killers had waited for their victims.

There was no motive for the shocking killing save sectarianism. The Devlins were a well known Catholic family in the area. Mr Devlin was widely recognised as a stalwart of the County Gaelic football team and his wife, a librarian, was equally popular. Both worked for and supported the Social

Democratic and Labour Party. Over 2,000 people attended their funeral where Cardinal William Conway, the head of the Catholic Church in Ireland, condemned the 'slaughter of the innocent, irrespective of religion'.

Fifteen months later, on 21 August 1975, William Leonard, aged 21, a telephone engineer from Dungannon, serving part-time as a UDR soldier, was arrested by police investigating the double murder. A day later he was charged, having admitted driving the killers to the scene on the night of the murders. When he came to trial, in December 1975, Mr Justice Kelly was told that since the incident Leonard had changed his way of life, become a Christian and took part in evangelical meetings in the Dungannon area. 'It is a pity he did not become a Christian before 7 May 1974,' the Judge commented. Leonard was sentenced to life imprisonment.

At a separate trial during the same month Leonard was further convicted, with three men, one a former UDR soldier, of a series of sectarian explosions in the Dungannon area. As the men, who were sentenced to twelve-year terms, left the dock one of them shouted: 'Up the UVF. No surrender.'

At another trial, in March 1976, Leonard was again convicted for his part in holding up a bus from the Irish Republic, robbing a passenger of £58 and then causing £12,000 worth of damage by sprinkling the bus with petrol and setting it alight. A concurrent sentence of eight years was imposed.

In another incident in 1974, a UDR soldier was involved in a sectarian reprisal. On 15 November a 30-year-old Protestant man lost a leg when a booby-trap bomb exploded as he got into his car outside his home in Larne, County Antrim. Some hours later four local members of the UVF resolved to carry out a reprisal.

That evening one of them drove a car to a point in the centre of the town and a second kept watch while the others walked into Maguire's Bar in Lower Cross Street and sprayed the premises with gunfire, seriously injuring a woman and another customer, Kevin Regan, a Catholic, who died in hospital from multiple gunshot injuries five days later. Shortly afterwards, a submachine gun, which turned out to have been stolen from the UDR in Larne, and a shotgun were recovered when the gang were apprehended in a stolen get-away car, ironically at a UDR-manned vehicle checkpoint at Glynn, a few miles away.

Four men later appeared at Belfast City Commission in connection with the incident. Three of them, one UDR Private Ronald Dempsey, aged 21, were given life sentences. During the hearing the judge was told that the death toll could have been higher but for the fact that the sub-machine gun jammed as Dempsey fired indiscriminately at the eight people in the bar.

In another case the body of Collette Brown, a separated mother of four children aged between 2 and 13, and thought to be associated with the UVF, was found dumped in a ditch beside a quarry at Killyglen, near Larne on 6 February 1975. The woman, shot twice in the head, had spent the previous day at her brother's wedding and then gone on to a party the night before her death.

Two days afterwards the RUC in Larne charged four people in connection with the killing, among them UDR Lance-Corporal Jack McAuley. In September 1975 at Belfast City Commission, Mr Justice Murray imposed life sentences on the corporal and another man after they admitted murder. 'Yours was not the finger that pulled the trigger but you drove the car which carried the unfortunate woman to her death and were there when the deed was done.'

Referring to the background to the case the judge said: 'The facts before me disclose a truly appalling state of affairs. It appears that some time before the date, the dead woman fell foul of an organisation and her death had been decreed by that organisation.'

As already described in chapter 2, two terrorists died when a bomb they had planted exploded prematurely during the attack on the Miami showband in July 1975, and three UDR soldiers were later imprisoned for life.

There was further embarrassment for the UDR later that year. In the early hours of 6 October 1975, more than 500 police backed up by 1,000 soldiers took part in Operation Jigsaw, a major RUC operation to break a UVF terrorist gang operating in East Antrim. When the case came to court in October 1977, twenty-eight men, including two members of the UDR, stood in the dock accused of a catalogue of appalling crime, including murder, attempted murder, causing explosions, possessing firearms and armed robbery. Two of their victims had been buried in a secret grave on cliffs overlooking Belfast Lough and for several summers a member of the gang had planted grass seed on the spot to prevent it from being discovered.

Much of the incriminating evidence against the gang came from a former member, identified only as Witness A, who had escaped from their clutches shortly before he would probably have been killed. In a speech from the dock, threatening reprisals, one of the terrorists accused him of 'grovelling before God and Ulster for self-preservation'.

At the end of the seventy-seven-day trial, at the time the longest and most expensive criminal case in legal history, the prisoners fought with prison officers and police guarding the court room. Lord Justice MacDermott handed down life sentences on eight men and terms totalling 700 years to another eighteen. Two were acquitted.

Among those convicted were the two UDR members, William Workman, who got five years for possessing guns and ammunition, and John Gaw, jailed for four years for giving arms instruction to other terrorists at the British Legion Hall in Carrickfergus. The judge said that he could think of nothing worse than members of the UDR training members of the UVF.

Gaw had originally been charged with the murder of Robert McCreight, in August 1975, but the charge was withdrawn for lack of evidence. McCreight had fallen foul of the gang for 'talking too much' but they feared that if they merely kneecapped him he might go to the police. So they decided to kill him and a member of the gang was instructed to lure him to a lonely farm building for the purpose.

During the trial, Gaw was recharged with the murder, after another of the defendants, Roderick Griffith, who was freed after the judge decided that he had acted under duress, gave sworn evidence that Gaw had fired the three shots which killed McCreight. Three months later, after another trial, Gaw received a life sentence with the recommendation that he serve at least twenty-five years. During the hearing Griffith testified that after the murder, Gaw remarked that he was turned on by the sight of blood.

Sectarian bigotry played a part in another murder. An off-duty UDR private, Richard William Long, shot and killed a Protestant man by mistake when he fired into the home of a Catholic at Comber, County Down, late in the evening of 2 June 1976.

Long, who was drinking in a bar in the village, rang another man to ask him to drive him to a house said to be owned by a 'Provo'. When they got there, Long fired several shots into the house, killing David Spratt, aged 23, the brother-in-law of his intended victim.

The gun used in the shooting was recovered and traced to Long, a full-time member of the UDR based at Carryduff, County Down. As soon as he was arrested and charged with murder, Long resigned from the UDR. In May 1977, after the murder charge was dropped, he admitted conspiring to murder and possessing the firearm for which he was sentenced to life imprisonment. His accomplice received a fourteen-year term.

The easy availability of a firearm led another UDR soldier to commit what a judge later described as 'an unpardonable crime'. Charles Patton, a UDR full-timer, shot the father of his estranged wife dead after a scuffle with his new girlfriend. The incident took place after a night's drinking when Patton, his girlfriend and another UDR man were eating a takeaway meal in a doorway. Andrew Armstrong, father of Patton's estranged wife, approached them, knocked the girl to the ground and kicked her in the face. The police were called but the girl refused attention and went home.

Next day, 29 October 1987, Patton went to the armoury at his base in South Belfast and drew a Browning pistol. He went first to his sister and told her he was going to shoot Armstrong. They were unable to restrain him and he ran off, went to Armstrong's house, kicked in the glass door and then shot him through the chest as he lay sleeping in a bedroom upstairs. A short time later he returned to the UDR base, handed in the gun and told the corporal in charge: 'Don't touch it. I've just shot my father-in-law.' He told the police who came to arrest him that he had not meant to kill, only scare him. 'I was in a rage and boiled over. I am sorry for what I have done.' After a murder charge was dropped, Patton pleaded guilty to manslaughter and in June 1978 was sentenced to nine years' imprisonment.

Another UDR soldier, with six months' service, used his officially issued personal protection weapon to wound two Catholic youths the day after it was issued and a short time later he shot and killed a Catholic student described as 'harmless and innocent', by the police.

The first incident took place in the aftermath of rioting on 12 July 1981 when two Catholic youths were fired on. A month later, in the early hours of 9 August, two more Catholic youths were fired on, this time one of them, Liam Canning, 19, was hit in the head and died in hospital three hours later.

Spent bullets recovered from the scene by the police were forensically tested and linked to a Walther pistol legally issued to Private Brian Roberts. When he went on trial in January 1983 he changed his plea on the second day to guilty of murder, wounding and endangering life with his pistol. He was sentenced to life imprisonment.

During seven years' full-time service in the UDR, Geoffrey Edwards saw fifteen of his closest colleagues and friends murdered by terrorists and many more injured. He formed the view that not enough was being done to combat the evils of terrorism so he decided to take the law into his own hands.

As a serving member of the security forces he was privy to the most secret suspicions of the police about those responsible for the death and destruction in the Armagh area, so he used that information to target his victims.

Between May 1982 and December 1983, when he was arrested by the RUC, Edwards was responsible for one murder and six attempted murders.

In his first attack in May, a local council labourer was shot and injured as he thumbed a lift on the city ring road on his way home from work in Armagh. Four months later, Edwards hijacked a car and late on the night of 8 September fired shots into the home of Seamus Grew, a prominent terrorist suspect in the area. (Three months later Grew and another man were shot dead by an undercover police unit, one of three 'shoot-to-kill' incidents which were controversially investigated by John Stalker, then Deputy Chief Constable of Greater Manchester.)

On 25 October, Peter Corrigan, a father of eleven, was walking to the Labour Exchange in Armagh with his brother and one of his sons, Martin, aged 17, when a car pulled alongside them. A gunman, leaning out of the front passenger-side window, fired three shots, one hitting Peter Corrigan fatally in the head. The boy later described how his father dropped to his knees and died as the car sped off.

Corrigan was no random victim. A week before his death he had represented Sinn Fein's interests at a polling station and the party described him as a 'lifelong Republican'. In the early 1970s he had been detained without trial for a period on suspicion of IRA involvement. (In April 1990, Martin Corrigan, who had witnessed the murder of his father, was shot dead by members of an army patrol when he was seen acting suspiciously at the home of a part-time policeman. Two sawn-off shotguns were recovered at the scene and the outlawed Irish People's Liberation Organisation said he was on 'active service'.)

In March 1982, Edwards struck again, this time seriously wounding a man returning to his home from the Labour Exchange. At about the same time he fixed a booby-trapped explosive device to a car belonging to a cousin of the shot man and when it went off a few days later, on 19 March, it injured the car owner, another man and a 5-year-old boy.

Several of Edwards' crimes were claimed by the 'Protestant Action Force', a badge of convenience adopted by some Loyalist terrorists. When he was being questioned about his accomplices by the police, after his arrest in December 1983, Edwards refused to name names or disclose where weapons were hidden because 'it would be more than my life's worth'.

After he was charged his lawyer said that he had acted out of 'a misplaced sense of duty' but at the conclusion of his trial in January 1985, after he admitted nineteen terrorist offences, Mr Justice Murray sentenced him to life imprisonment for murder with six concurrent terms of twenty years for attempted murder. 'It was your duty as a member (of the UDR) to protect the public from terrorism but instead you inflicted the horrors of terrorism on your fellow men.'

One evening in September 1982, two men were walking across a building site near Ballymena when one of them suddenly pulled a gun from his pocket and without warning shot the other, James Galway, dead.

The killer was Lennie Murphy, a notoriously cold-blooded sectarian assassin from Belfast, known as the Master Butcher for his leading role in the Shankill Butchers UVF gang who terrorised North and West Belfast for five years with a series of cut-throat sectarian killings.

Murphy had only just been released from prison and was once more imposing a reign of terror to win back his senior position in the UVF. (Murphy in fact died at the hands of the IRA later the same month, reputedly having been set up for them by rival Loyalists.) His partner that night, who helped bury Galway in a secret grave, was Cyril Rainey, a UDR part-timer, also leader of the UVF in Ballymena. He had long been abusing his position as a member of a UDR intelligence cell, siphoning secret material about the IRA and its sympathisers from the official files entrusted to him. Names, addresses, photographs and other information had all been leaked to the UVF unit, who frequented an Orange Hall in the Ballymena area.

In November 1983, the RUC caught up with him and under questioning he revealed the secret grave at Broughshane and the close links between the outlawed UVF and the UDR in the area.

Rainey pleaded guilty to a catalogue of terrorist crime, including the manslaughter of Galway, when he came to trial in 1987. He was sentenced to twelve years in jail. Twelve others, four of them with UDR connections, also stood in the dock charged with a variety of offences. One was given a four-year term for fire-arms offences and UVF membership, another received a suspended sentence and two were given recorded sentences. The judge said that they had disgraced themselves and discredited the Regiment.

Two ex-members of the UDR, William Orr and Stephen Watson, and Colin Doak, from Blackpool, Lancashire, a 19-year-old runaway technician from the RAF, beat a Catholic man to death in Lurgan on 3 April 1983. In the early hours of the morning, after a bout of heavy drinking, they were driving along the town's North Street 'looking for a Catholic to beat up' when they spotted their victims.

Orr, aged 21, who had left the UDR some time previously and had just returned from a spell at an Israeli kibbutz, got out of the car along with Doak and assaulted John McConville, breaking his jaw with a crash helmet he found in the car. McConville fell to the ground, inhaling blood, and died two hours later in hospital. His companion suffered bruising but was not seriously hurt.

All three assailants were charged and admitted manslaughter when they came to trial in January 1984. The third man, Stephen Watson, who was driving the car and played no part in the assault, was sentenced to seven years' imprisonment. He had resigned from full-time UDR service in 1980 on health grounds. Orr was imprisoned for ten years and Doak for five.

Heavy drinking was a factor in another murder committed by a

UDR soldier. A gas meter containing £15 cost partially disabled pensioner, Mrs Daisy Craig, aged 73, her life. She was battered and stabbed to death on the night of 5 November by two men, one of them a serving UDR soldier.

Private John Ferguson and an accomplice, who had both consumed a large amount of drink, entered the two-bedroomed house in East Belfast in search of money. All they could find was the money in the gas meter. However, they were afraid that the old lady, confined to a chair and only able to move around by holding on to the furniture, would be able to identify them, so before leaving they stabbed and killed her and set fire to the house to destroy the traces.

The post-mortem on their victim showed that she had sustained more than one hundred stab wounds to the face, neck, trunk and legs.

When Ferguson and the other culprit appeared in court two days later they broke down in tears in the dock and put their arms around each other for comfort. It was two years before they came to trial when the judge was told the motive was not sectarian or political but only money. At first they denied murder but on the second day of the case they changed their pleas and were given life sentences. Forty-eight hours later the accomplice was found hanged in his cell at Crumlin Road prison in Belfast.

What is now known as the case of the UDR Four began late in the afternoon of 8 November 1983: Adrian Carroll, an Armagh council painter, finished his day's work and set out to walk the short distance home. As he approached his house in Abbey Street, a narrow cul de sac at the edge of the town centre, a lone gunman walked up behind him and fired, wounding him in the neck, back and head. He was rushed to hospital where he died three hours later. The murder was claimed by the Protestant Action Force, a *nom de guerre* used by the Ulster Volunteer Force.

Carroll was a member of a strongly Republican family. A year earlier the dead man's younger brother had been killed by an RUC undercover unit in one of the three so-called 'shoot-to-kill' incidents. Another older brother was, at the time, serving a fifteen-year prison sentence for explosives offences.

Three weeks after the murder, the RUC began arresting UDR soldiers, based at Drumadd Barracks, Armagh, for questioning. Those held included the thirteen members of a four Land Rover patrol, commanded by a sergeant, operating in the town that day. After intensive questioning in the RUC Holding Centre at Castlereagh, Belfast, by the end of December seven of them had been charged with Carroll's murder.

In February 1984, the murder charge against Walter Roleston, the sergeant in charge of the patrol, was dropped when another of the accused, Private Noel Bell, who had implicated him in statements made to the police, signed an affidavit saying that he would not testify against him.

By the time the case came for trial at Belfast Crown Court in February 1986, the murder charge against another soldier, Private David McMullan, had been replaced by one of failing to give information about the killing.

Five of the soldiers remained charged with murder: Privates Bell, Alfred Allen, Colin Worton, Neil Latimer and Lance-Corporal James Hegan.

The case was dogged with controversy from the start. After the opening speech there was a dispute about the calling of a witness and the judge, Mr Justice Hutton, who was sitting without a jury, as in all terrorist cases, decided to dismiss himself in the interests of justice.

Opening the case again a month later, this time before Lord Justice Kelly, the Crown prosecutor, Mr Liam McCollum, QC, said that the soldiers had plotted and carried out the callous and premeditated murder of a Roman Catholic while on duty, hoping that their military tasks would provide an alibi for the killing.

During the afternoon of the killing, the judge heard, the UDR patrol was engaged in a search operation at Moy Road,

Armagh. One of the Land Rovers, driven by Worton, left the search party and drove into the town. On board were Latimer and another soldier, not before the court.

At Lonsdale Street, according to the Crown, Latimer was dropped off and while the Land Rover returned to the search operation, he went into the grounds of the Technical School where he changed into civilian clothes 'of a quite distinctive nature' – a blue duffle coat and tartan cap – and put on spectacles.

Shortly afterwards, counsel told the court, two of the UDR vehicles arrived in Lonsdale Street, where Latimer was picked up again. Allen was driving with McMullan and Bell aboard, while Latimer got into the other vehicle, driven by Hegan, with Worton as passenger.

At the Mall, in the town centre, Latimer was dropped again, from where he stalked Carroll before firing at him three times with a handgun provided by Hegan. After the shooting Latimer was again picked up by Land Rover and two men, Worton and Bell, gave cover to obscure him as he changed back into uniform while they drove to the local RUC station.

The Crown case relied on the testimony of two witnesses and the statements of admission made by the soldiers during their interrogation by the RUC, after their arrests.

The first witness, a woman, said that she was posting letters when she saw a man with a moustache, wearing a light blue duffle coat, tartan cap and glasses, take out a gun, and turn out of sight into an entry, immediately before she heard two shots. Asked to identify the killer she said that the man she saw that day was not in court. Asked if Latimer was the man she saw she replied, 'definitely not', disclosing that she knew Latimer and would have recognised him.

The evidence of the second witness was equally clouded. Originally, she had claimed to have seen Latimer, whom she knew well, in civilian clothes, being put into the Land Rover at the Technical School by the two other soldiers. After hearing a description of the killer on a news broadcast she thought it fitted the clothes Latimer had been wearing, but it was several 'sleepless nights', and some two weeks before she aired her suspicion to a priest who took a statement from her.

Doubts were cast on the reliability of her evidence, however, when the court heard she had signed blank sheets of paper for the statement to be typed on and when she gave conflicting accounts of the timing and circumstances in which she made the statement to the priest. There were also discrepancies in her evidence concerning what she had seen. She said, for instance, on one occasion that there were seven soldiers at the Technical School, on another that there were only four.

During the course of the proceedings, she contacted Bell's family and indicated that she was going to withdraw her evidence. With a reminder from the judge of the severe punishment possible for interfering with witnesses and threats of proceedings for contempt of court, the woman was recalled to the witness box, where she told the court she stood by her account of what she had seen but believed the accused were innocent and she was retracting her evidence.

When the court turned to consider the statements of admission made to the police by the accused soldiers, defence lawyers submitted that these were inadmissible because they had been obtained under duress by torture and inhuman and degrading treatment. If the defence could prove ill-treatment by the police, then the statements would have had to be ruled out under the emergency laws governing the single judge, no-jury courts, set up to deal with such terrorist cases.

Bell claimed from the witness box that RUC detectives had repeatedly punched and slapped him after his arrest at 4.15 in the morning, when he was suffering a hangover after drinking the previous evening. He claimed that he had only made the statement of admission after being repeatedly beaten and questioned continuously all day. 'I couldn't take any more of it. I had to get them off my back. I was exhausted,' he said. He admitted he had made no complaint during medical examination.

Latimer expressed similar sentiments during his evidence. 'The detectives would not shut up – they just went on and on. It got to the stage where I just went along with whatever they said to me.' After several days in Castlereagh, he said, he would have admitted to anything.

After this 'trial within a trial' about the validity of the statements, the judge ruled that Worton should be acquitted. He said that he believed the detectives questioning him had found out his vulnerable spot – his deep attachment to his girlfriend, who was now his wife. Conversations about her, the judge said, brought about feelings of jealousy and, having discovered this vulnerability, the detectives played on it. Lord Justice Kelly said they told Worton that if he did not make a statement he would go to jail for twenty years and his girlfriend would get married and have children with someone else. If he did make a statement, he was told he would get a lesser term and get out on bail to marry her. The judge said that this induced Worton to make a statement, but he stressed that he was not making any finding on the truth of the statement and his decision did not mean that he disbelieved the police evidence.

A week later, McMullan, who faced only charges of withholding information about the murder, was also freed after the Judge decided he should benefit from the principle 'enshrined in English law' that a person is not bound to incriminate himself.

The trial ended in June 1986 after sitting for sixty-one days over the previous four months. On 1 July, after delivering a reserved judgement in which he convicted them, all four were sentenced to life imprisonment by Lord Justice Kelly.

He accepted the evidence of the women witnesses as 'overwhelming' and said that the inconsistencies by one of them were 'peripheral'. The police, he decided, had not acted improperly and he said that it was incredible to think a member of the security forces would admit to taking part in a sectarian murder if he were innocent.

The judge remarked that evidence given during the trial by UDR witnesses led him to the conclusion 'that some members of the Regiment got together to distort true events and present the results in court for the sole purpose of assisting the accused'.

After a criminal trial, before a jury, any appeal must be built on legal grounds but in Northern Ireland, the emergency legislation provides for an unfettered right of appeal to three judges on legal grounds as well as fact. The appeal of the 'UDR Four' was heard over three weeks by Lord Lowry, the Lord Chief Justice and Lords O'Donnell and MacDermott, at the end of 1987 but it was almost six months later before their verdict upholding the life sentences was given on 5 May 1988.

Lord Lowry, who delivered the reasons, said that, like the trial judge, he and his colleagues would have accepted the evidence of the woman who recognised Latimer in civilian clothes being walked out to the Land Rover at the Technical School. She thought he was getting married and his comrades were 'doing him up'.

The Appeal judges did not find it surprising that for two weeks she had wrestled with the conflicting factors of linking Latimer to the killing because of the police description of the killer's clothing and her own belief that Latimer would not commit a murder. Her statement, the Lord Chief Justice said, had a devastating effect on the suspects when relayed to them by police at Castlereagh and thereupon all confessed their guilt.

The Appeal Court pointedly remarked that it was clear that someone over and above the four appellants had planned the murder and it was to be hoped that in due course such person or persons would stand trial when the necessary evidence was available.

From the outset relatives of the four convicted soldiers protested their innocence. Outside the court, after the appeal had been dismissed, they made their feelings clear. A man shouted: 'You call this British justice but it's a sham.' Turning to one of the RUC detectives involved in the case he said: 'Lying bastard. Not enough of you are blown up.'

They began campaigning for the case to be re-opened but without much support. There was, in law, no way the case could be re-opened unless significant new evidence, casting doubt on the safety of the convictions, was uncovered.

What appeared to be a significant development came on

5 February 1989, when the second of the women witnesses, whose evidence had been a vital element in securing the convictions, gave an extraordinary interview to the Irish radio service, Radio Telefis Eireann.

> I believe now that the police made a blunder. I think the police should open up and tell the truth about the events of what happened.
> I think they have tricked me. I see it as tricks . . . dirty tricks department.
> I certainly support the truth being brought out unto the open. There is a cover up here with the police and somebody's working on this . . . but there is definitely some thing . . . some reason or other that they wanted to put them men down.

However, there was insufficient substance in the remarks to fuel any demand for a new trial. The families of the men on the outside kept up their campaigning anyway and in the latter months of 1989, when the Guildford Four were released after being declared the innocent victims of a miscarriage of justice, interest in the case heightened.

Jim Hegan, one of the four convicted soldiers, wrote from prison to the influential author and broadcaster, Robert Kee, urging him to support their demand for a retrial. After studying papers on the case, Kee, who had backed the Guildford case, publicly declared his belief that the men had been wrongly convicted.

By then, several local Unionist MPs, Harold McCusker (before his death from cancer in early 1990), Ken Maginnis and Peter Robinson, had all joined the campaign to have the men freed. In the wake of the Guildford releases they extracted an undertaking from the Northern Ireland Office that, if new evidence were forthcoming, the Secretary of State would consider using his powers to refer the case back to the Court of Appeal.

The two MPs enlisted Ian Paisley, the son of their well known political colleague, to do the spade-work. Paisley Junior's ambitions to be a journalist had been thwarted by the reluctance of several editors to have such a controversial name on their pages, so he was available to help.

A transcript of the original trial and the appeal was obtained and scrutinised, as were all the relevant documents, including the statements the men made under police interrogation, which they still claimed were involuntary. The MPs and their helper walked the routes in Armagh, testing the evidence that had been given in the trial. Every line of enquiry that might help was pursued. From their point of view, the most significant breakthrough in the campaign came in the summer of 1990 when the RUC agreed to submit the police statements and notes made during the interrogations at Castlereagh to the ESDA test.

Electro-static document analysis is a new technique which was developed by accident. It was first discovered by two research scientists while working at the London College of Printing at the end of the 1970s. Since then the method has been refined to the point where it is accepted as evidence by the courts.

A fine covering of clear stretch film, like domestic cling film, is stretched over the document to be examined, which is placed on a flat metal plate and sealed to it by suction. It is then subjected to electro-static impulses, by having an electrified bar passed across it.

Carbon powder is then sprayed over the document and reacting to the electronic charge it settles, highlighting the impressions and indentations made by writing or typing on pages previously placed above the sample. The impression is finally sealed under another layer of clear film to make what is known as an 'ESDA foil' which is then used for investigative and evidential purposes. This enables the scientist to read indentations left on a page by a person writing on another page above it. More importantly, it establishes if pages have been written or typed consecutively and shows up any alterations which have been made subsequently.

When examined in conjunction with longer established tests on inks and papers and the individual characteristics of nibs and typewriter keys, scientists can establish with a high degree of certainty the authenticity of documents and whether or not they have been tampered with at any stage.

On 3 January 1991, the RUC announced that, as a result of the ESDA tests on police documents connected with the UDR Four case, the Chief Constable had appointed a detective chief superintendent to examine the results of the forensic report. 'Certain points require further clarification/investigation,' said the RUC.

The campaigners claimed that the tests had thrown up 'an abundance of irregularities'. These figured largely in an extensive dossier that had been presented to Peter Brooke, the Secretary of State for Northern Ireland, at a meeting in London a week later, to press the claim for a re-trial. The dossier listed, in some detail, all the reasons why the conviction of the four soldiers should be questioned. Apart from the doubts raised by the ESDA findings, the dossier reported that syntax analysis, another modern technique, cast doubt on the authenticity of the confessions made by the soldiers to the police.

Syntax analysis depends on the premise that everyone has a pattern of sentence construction and speech as individually distinctive as a fingerprint. By analysing disputed material and comparing it with authentic writing or speech, the authenticity can be established.

According to Andrew Morton, an expert in this field of thirty years' standing, who had been retained on behalf of the UDR Four to examine the disputed confessions of all four men: 'Not one of them is a genuine confession of the accused.'

Doubts have been cast on the reliability of the vital woman witness by claiming that she twice spent periods in a mental institution undergoing treatment for a psychopathic personality. The UDR Four campaigners claim that her credibility as a witness is compromised by this factor, which was not known to the original trial judge. They say that this compounds other flaws in her evidence and her extraordinary behaviour both during and after the trial.

Other new evidence is adduced which, the dossier states, throws further doubt on the case against the soldiers. The central thrust of this is that the real killers came from Belfast, used a stolen car which they brought with them and then abandoned in Armagh. A Cortina found later that night is connected with the case, the campaigners claim.

They have also traced several witnesses who place the UDR Land Rovers in other places at crucial times during the incident, key facts in upsetting the course of events leading up to the murder of Adrian Carroll, as outlined by the prosecution.

The dossier reiterates that the four soldiers have claimed all along that they were ill-treated and threatened by the police to such an extent that they made involuntary confessions.

Finally, the dossier highlights repeated claims from the 'Protestant Action Force' that its members were the real culprits and not the convicted soldiers. Peter Robinson says that he has been told the name of the real killer, who has been questioned by the police.

At the time of writing, the MPs and other believers in the innocence of the UDR Four continue to clamour for an urgent retrial as Mr Brooke's legal advisers study the dossier and the RUC probe the reliability (or accuracy) of the documents. All the signs are that a retrial is likely to be ordered at the conclusion of the police investigation. Whatever the strength of the other evidence adduced in the dossier, any proven irregularity in the police documents, whatever its cause, would be more than enough on its own to cast a reasonable doubt on the convictions.

On Easter Sunday, 8 April 1985, Martin Love, a 24-year-old Catholic, went to a dance at a football club in Enniskillen and then on to a local hotel. Shortly after midnight, as he was walking home, a gunman approached him, fired and hit him five times in the head, chest, stomach and thigh. Some of the shots were discharged as he lay slumped on the pavement. As the gunman ran off, people who rushed to Love's assistance heard him moan 'help me'. He was taken to hospital but died shortly afterwards.

The Ulster Freedom Fighters claimed responsibility for the shooting, saying that the victim was a member of the IRA involved in attacks on Protestants in the area. The police and his family vehemently disputed the accuracy of the claim and at his funeral, Monsignor Sean Cahill said that the dead man 'had been selected for slaughter . . . for some twisted reason in the tangled web of politics and bigotry'.

The police responded quickly to the shooting and in follow-up operations arrested two men in the town centre immediately afterwards. The tragic truth rapidly emerged. The victim had been mistaken for another man who was prominently associated with the Republican movement and was regarded as an active terrorist.

The killers were, once again, members of the security forces taking the law into their own hands. In September 1986, Belfast Crown Court heard how UDR Private Robert Kenny, aged 23, had provided a Walther pistol for Mark Trotter, aged 22, the son of a policeman, who was home on leave from the army in England.

Kenny pleaded guilty to murder, possessing the weapon, gathering information for the purposes of terrorism and an unconnected armed robbery of £4,525. Trotter, who denied the charges, claimed that he had been 'terrified' by detectives who had assaulted him and forced him to sign a confession. The judge, who heard that Trotter had taken a considerable amount of drink before shooting Love, decided that the confession was valid and convicted Trotter of 'cold blooded murder'. Both were given life sentences.

'Things got out of hand and we had to kill him,' was how one of the killers described the events in a field beside the Coleraine-Bushmills road on 10 August 1988 which culminated in the brutal murder of Samuel Patton.

Patton had driven to the field voluntarily with four other members of the UVF, not knowing he was going to be called to account for personally pocketing the proceeds of an armed robbery at a public house.

When they got there, according to one of the participants, five or six shots were suddenly fired at Patton who said: 'Don't be killing me.' As he tried to run away two of the men grabbed him and hit him with the pistol and their fists. A third then hit him on the head with a stone and jabbed at him with a knife. Patton put up strong resistance and one of them kicked him in the chest because he 'just wouldn't go down'. When he was eventually floored, he was again stabbed repeatedly.

Next morning a farmer found the body in the field. Patton had suffered severe head wounds from the beating, stab wounds, including having his throat cut, and was shot four times.

When his assailants were traced by the police, they were found to include UDR soldier Robert Douglas. Throughout the brawl in the field he had waited in a getaway car and then disposed of the gun and knife by throwing them into the River Bann.

At the conclusion of their five week trial in October 1989, Mr Justice Carswell jailed two of the UVF gang for life for what he described as an 'horrific and bestial' murder and sentenced the others to lesser terms for wounding with intent, as well as membership of an illegal organisation.

Referring to Douglas, the UDR member, the judge said that there was sufficient evidence that he had known that he was to play a part in a punishment shooting but he was not satisfied, to the required standard of proof, that he had contemplated the killing of the man. 'I have grave suspicions, however, that Douglas knew of this, but suspicion does not equate with proof,' he said.

The UDR now acknowledges that seventeen of its members have been convicted of murder and that twelve of the fifteen victims have been killed either because they were Catholics or for suspected terrorist links.

UDR involvement in murder has inevitably attracted a good deal of attention, but many more soldiers have been involved in and been convicted for a wide range of other offences. Those compiled here, mainly from contemporary newspaper accounts of court proceedings, are a representative sample by time and type. They include both terrorist related crimes, purely criminal offences and others caused by bad behaviour or heavy drinking.

In October 1970, a UDR soldier, in uniform and carrying a rifle, mingled with disorderly crowds at an election rally. When police searched him they found that he had eggs in his ammunition pouch and he was dismissed from the Regiment the next day.

A UDR soldier ended up in jail for a year after putting his gun to the temple of a young girl and threatening that 'he would blow her brains out' if she gave police the names of a crowd who had attacked a police patrol called to a dance hall brawl at Upperlands, County Londonderry in March 1973.

Three young Belfast Protestants, two of them UDR soldiers aged 19 and 20, became embittered at seeing friends and relations becoming victims of terrorism. During a drinking spree in June 1973, they resolved to bomb a pub at Crossgar, County Down which they had heard was a meeting place for Catholic terrorists. Each was jailed for nine years for causing an explosion which injured a young woman.

At Antrim County Court, in October 1975, several soldiers from the Royal Engineers and UDR were found to be involved in a racket selling army petrol to other soldiers for private use. The two Royal Engineers, a UDR sergeant-major and a former UDR soldier were fined and given suspended sentences of between six and twelve months after admitting the theft, and eight other soldiers, including three from the UDR, were fined for handling stolen goods.

A full-time UDR soldier was jailed for life after pleading guilty when a murder charge was replaced by one of conspiracy to murder. The judge said that he had 'played a significant part in the murder of a totally innocent (Catholic) man' in June 1976.

A 20-year-old UDR soldier was a member of a UDA gang who petrol bombed a number of Catholic homes and twice attacked the house of a police sergeant in the Finaghy area of Belfast throughout the summer of 1976. A year later he was jailed for three years.

In November 1976, a man who had been simultaneously a

member of the UDR and the illegal UVF was imprisoned for fifteen years by the Special Criminal Court in Dublin, after being found guilty of conspiring to cause a car bomb explosion at the border village of Pettigo on 28 September 1973.

Three UDR part-timers desecrated a Catholic church at Whitehouse, near Belfast, on 15 August 1978, after a drinking bout at their barracks. After gaining entry to the church by breaking a window, one of the men defecated near the altar and used pages torn from a missal as toilet paper. Suspending four-month prison sentences, only because they had the 'guts' to apologise to the parish priest, the magistrate also fined them £50 each and ordered them to pay compensation.

In March 1979, a UDR soldier who threatened a rival for his girlfriend with his gun was given a three-month prison sentence, suspended for two years.

A full-time UDR soldier admitted that he had joined the UVF after a van bomb caused devastation to his home town, Markethill, County Armagh in April 1979. When he was detected, six months later, he was dismissed from the Regiment and, after pleading guilty to being a member of an outlawed organisation, he was given a twelve month prison sentence, suspended for three years. It transpired that he had lent his officially issued weapon to others who used it to hijack vehicles and carry out robberies.

A 21-year-old UDR soldier was given a two-and-a-half year prison sentence for assault with intent to rape near Queens University, Belfast in October 1980.

Two members of the UDR were fined £25 each in November 1980 for painting twenty-seven feet of kerbstone red, white and blue and for daubing sectarian slogans on walls. These included 'Remember 1690' and 'Fuck the Pope'.

On 5 March 1982, a part-time UDR soldier, who was drunk, fired several shots in the air after he had been recognised and threatened while buying food in a Chinese restaurant at Strabane. Describing his behaviour as 'reckless and totally irresponsible', an 'overreaction to provocation', the magistrate imposed a three-month suspended sentence for assault, fined him £250 for illegally discharging his weapon and a further £100 for having a firearm when drunk.

A UDR soldier resorted to armed robbery because of pressing debts. He was arrested after using his service pistol to steal £500 from a post office at Derryfubble, County Tyrone on 2 November 1984 and sentenced to seven years' imprisonment.

An off-duty UDR soldier was caught up in a fracas between Catholic and Protestant youths outside a Chinese restaurant at Maghera on 3 March 1984. A police sergeant, trying to quell the trouble, later said in court that after the soldier was called a 'UDR bastard' and taunted to 'pull out your wee toy gun', he did so and fired two shots into the air. He was fined £100 for unlawfully discharging it in a public place.

In 1984, the government decided that in future the name of the Londonderry Council would be changed to the Derry City Council. The decision sparked off Loyalist protests and during one disturbance a protester convicted of throwing stones at the police, who was fined £40, was a full-time member of the UDR.

In January 1985, a UDR sergeant was convicted of making obscene telephone calls to women and fined £100.

Two members of the same UDR platoon, based at Ballymena, were convicted at Belfast Crown Court on 7 May for offences connected with the illegal UVF. One of the soldiers admitted membership, armed robbery at a filling station and other firearms offences and was jailed for five years. The other was given an eighteen months suspended sentence for possessing a firearm and ammunition.

A UDR commanding officer spotted one of his own soldiers in a police video of a riot at Portadown on 12 July 1985. When the soldier reported for duty the next day he was apprehended. The local magistrates' court was later told that he did not realise what he had done until he saw the video for himself and said it was 'just drink'. He was fined £200.

A man, discharged from the UDR after his hand was blown off in an explosion and stitched back by surgeons, became an armed robber and sex attacker after resettling in London. On 9 October 1985, he burst into a travel shop in Kent with an imitation firearm and after stealing £200 from the young female manageress, he sexually assaulted her. Later, at the Central Criminal Court in London, it was disclosed that he had previous convictions for dishonesty and violence. He was imprisoned for seven years for the travel shop robbery and other offences.

On 23 May 1986, a full-time UDR soldier was being driven by his wife through a housing estate in Antrim when a number of objects hit their car. They stopped, the UDR man got out and threw several large stones at a crowd of youths before assaulting one of them, leaving him with four teeth missing and a head wound that required seven stitches. The magistrate said that but for the provocation he had suffered, the soldier would have gone to jail. He fined him £500.

A drunken crowd who attacked the police during a disturbance at a bonfire party in Larne, County Antrim on 11 July 1986, included five men with UDR connections. All subsequently admitted a range of public order offences, including obstruction, criminal damage and assault and received a range of fines varying between £50 and £75 as well as suspended prison sentences.

In October 1986, four Catholic families, living in a housing estate in Ballymena, County Antrim, received threatening letters containing bullets, giving them a week to leave their homes. Only one family defied the threat from the UDA. The bullets had been supplied by a 23-year-old UDR soldier who was later imprisoned for two years.

A man who was a member of both the UDA and UDR at the same time in the mid 1970s pleaded guilty at Belfast Crown Court in January 1987 to keeping guns at his home. The court heard that the man joined first the UDA and then the UDR, where he served for three years, while storing at his home a revolver, four sub-machine guns and ammunition. The judge decided to record his seven year sentence for three years and bound him over to keep the peace at a surety of £1,000.

A 37-year-old father of two children, serving part-time in the UDR, abducted an 'entirely blameless' 17-year-old girl at gunpoint and then raped her in his car on 21 June 1987.

Sentencing him to five-and-a-half years in prison, the judge told him that he had brought disgrace on his Regiment and family.

A man who had served in the UDR was sentenced to twenty-years in October 1988, for what a judge described as 'chilling and appalling' sex crimes against an 8-year-old girl over a period of two years.

The UDA obtained information about private cars, owned and driven by policemen and prison officers from a 21-year-old woman member of the UDR from Dromore, County Down, who surreptitiously used a military computer to record the registration numbers. The judge said that it was difficult to conceive of a more serious breach of trust and in November 1988 she was sentenced to six months' imprisonment.

A former UDR member, described in court as 'a mere puppet' whose 'kind nature and inability to say no was taken advantage of', was imprisoned for twelve years at Belfast Crown Court after a cache of firearms, 5,500 rounds of ammunition, hand grenades and explosive material was found hidden at his home in Armagh in November 1988. The court was told that the weapons were for use in a 'doomsday situation' by the Loyalist Ulster Resistance Movement.

A similar Ulster Resistance arms cache was uncovered at the home of another UDR member at Richill, County Armagh, at the same time and he too was jailed for twelve years. This cache included five RPG rockets and a launcher as well as assault rifles, hand grenades, detonators and 4,900 bullets.

A Catholic youth was assaulted on the street and pursued into a public house, where he sought refuge, in the border village of Castlederg, County Tyrone on 25 February 1989. Among the attackers was an off-duty UDR soldier who was later sentenced to three months' imprisonment for assault and a concurrent two-month term for damaging the door of the pub. The magistrate said that this type of sectarian assault by a member of the security forces must be unreservedly condemned.

At Armagh Crown Court, in March 1989, a 34-year-old full-time UDR corporal was given two years' imprisonment for indecently assaulting two 10-year-old boys.

Public anxiety about the UDR's conduct has also been fanned by repeated arms raids and thefts of UDR weapons, frequently with the collusion and even involvement of members of the Regiment. The 1975 raid at Magherafelt by the UVF killer gang which included members of the UDR, was not an isolated occurrence. Incidents have been reported from the earliest days of the Regiment's existence.

On the night of 17 July 1972, an off-duty soldier, socialising in the UDR base at Aughnacloy, took a sub-machine gun from a sleeping colleague on standby. Next day he brought the police to a river near his home and retrieved the weapon from a polythene bag immersed in the water. When he came to trial in January 1973, charged with unlawful possession, he received a one-year suspended sentence after telling the court that he had taken the weapon for protection as he lived near the border.

In November 1972 eight armed men overpowered a watchman at a water pumping station in North Belfast and lay in wait for the UDR overnight guard force. When the soldiers arrived shortly afterwards they were overpowered. The gang took their thirteen rifles and 260 rounds of ammunition and the UDR Land Rover, which was later abandoned in the strongly Loyalist Shankill area of the city.

By the end of 1972, according to the Ministry of Defence in a parliamentary answer, 193 UDR weapons had been stolen, 130 of them in raids on armouries or points of duty. Only 76 were recovered.

A UDR armoury at Armagh was robbed on 23 October 1973. In July 1975, one of the stolen weapons, a Sterling sub-machine gun, was recovered from the home of a full-time UDR soldier in Belfast, together with 759 rounds of ammunition. At a subsequent trial, the judge accepted that he had been pressured into keeping the weapon and sentenced him to a period of Borstal training.

Late on 22 February 1987, a UDR soldier going on duty at Laurelhill base in Coleraine, County Londonderry, smuggled two members of the UDA past sentries in the boot of his car. These men eventually overpowered five other UDR soldiers, and left them handcuffed, tied and gagged in the guardroom before loading weapons from the armoury into a UDR van. One of the soldiers managed to remove his gag and radio an alert about the raid and, at about the same time, a corporal arriving for duty freed them. Some time later, a police motorway patrol became suspicious of a heavily laden, red van travelling towards Belfast. It was stopped and inside they found the weapons haul: 144 rifles, two light machine guns, 28 pistols, as well as ammunition and other military equipment.

Two members of the Regiment were later convicted for their part in the theft. A lance-corporal, who played a prominent role in the affair, was jailed for nine years, while a part-time private was given a two-year suspended sentence for passing on information and conspiring to steal the weapons. In sentencing them Mr Justice Nicholson said that the raid was mounted 'to obtain an arsenal for a private army loyal to its leaders but disloyal to the Queen' and that he was sure that if they had got away the arms would have been used in further sectarian attacks and against the security forces.

In August 1986, after a drinking bout at a boxing match in Palace Barracks, Holywood, County Down, a UDR colour sergeant with seventeen years' service, took the keys to the armoury, loaded a van with eighteen weapons and drove off, after signing the log book.

He went across the city to a UDA drinking club and there sold them the arms for £3,000. (One of them was used in the murder of Belfast solicitor Patrick Finucane in February 1989.) A few days later, police in the Irish Republic arrested him at the Imperial Hotel in the border town of Dundalk. He had already squandered £800 of the money and was charged with unlawfully possessing a firearm and fined £50. Outside the Irish court he was re-arrested and extradited to Northern Ireland, where he later pleaded guilty to the arms theft from the UDR and received a five-year sentence.

The court heard that he had 'deep-seated psychological problems' brought on by traumatic experiences, including being kidnapped and having to identify a brother blown up in a terrorist bomb attack. These were aggravated by gambling debts and excessive drinking.

In an information booklet about the UDR, published in 1990, it is stated that:

> These crimes are totally inexcusable and abhorrent to the Regiment. They may occur, in part, because soldiers of the Regiment have been under enormous strain from being continually on operations and continually at risk of murder by terrorists.
>
> During this time, they may have seen friends and relatives murdered by terrorists, who in some cases are known to the security forces but have not yet been brought to justice, owing to a lack of admissable evidence which would be sufficient to secure a conviction in a court of law.
>
> In a number of cases, no one has been brought to justice for the murder of UDR soldiers; their murderers have consequently remained at large, so far unconvicted, living in the community. In addition to these pressures, UDR soldiers can sometimes be subjected to direct pressure from extremist or paramilitary organisations which exist in the 'Loyalist' community. Nevertheless, any sectarian offence is one too many.
>
> During its existence, some 40,000 individuals have served in the UDR. In the circumstances, it is a tribute to the discipline and training of the vast majority of soldiers who have served in the UDR that they have acted with restraint, and resisted the enormous pressures to take the law into their own hands.

Ken Maginnis, the Unionist MP, who previously served in the UDR for twelve years, becoming a major, says that in all his time in the Regiment he never came across a 'bad apple, only bruised apples. There are those whose level of tolerance is breached and make a mistake and we deplore it. There is a terrible stress and strain on UDR members serving the community in the fight against terrorism.'

The true extent of subversion and criminal indiscipline within the UDR is a carefully protected official secret and ambiguity, obfuscation and, often, evasion, have habitually been deployed to conceal it, although in recent years the authorities appear to have monitored the situation more carefully and provided information, usually in response to parliamentary questions, or letters from MPs.

Ever since the formation of the UDR and the emergence of the first concerns about Loyalist infiltration, the army, the Ministry of Defence and the government itself have gone to considerable lengths to shield the Regiment from embarrassment, tactics which have only nourished the doubts about its integrity and contributed to suspicion about the failure of vetting and the true extent of the problem.

Researchers have been told that records are not kept of the number of soldiers convicted of civil or criminal offences. MPs have been told that such records could only be compiled at excessive cost, a routine ploy to avoid answering embarrassing questions tabled in parliament.

With a regularity that implies that it is standard practice, the UDR connections of accused soldiers have been suppressed in the courts and usually only emerge when a period of meritorious service with the Regiment is pleaded in mitigation.

When soldiers get into trouble they are frequently forced out of the Regiment at the earliest opportunity. Thus, if the UDR connection comes to light, the offender can be distanced as a 'former' member. In the Roberts case in October 1981, the UDR soldier was arrested by police investigating a murder. After five days of questioning, and just before he was charged with the offence, he 'resigned' from the UDR, while in custody at RUC Castlereagh. For a long time he was not included in the list of 'bad apples' acknowledged by the Regiment, an omission that has now been remedied.

The case of Edward McIlwaine, aged 25, also illustrates the practice. He was a member of the notorious 'Shankill Butchers', a UVF gang who terrorised North Belfast between 1972 and 1977, committing at least twenty-one murders, cruel, even by Belfast's brutal sectarian standards, because they usually cut the throats of their victims.

At Belfast City Commission, in February 1979, at the end of a trial, Mr Justice O'Donnell imposed forty-two life sentences and other terms totalling 906 years on eleven members of the gang. McIlwaine was sentenced to eight years after admitting charges of kidnapping and wounding.

McIlwaine was arrested by the police team dealing with the Butchers case on 13 June 1977 and charged within a week. In August 1977, after he had been charged and well before the case came to court, he was discharged from the UDR for 'poor attendance'. The Regiment insisted that the process of discharging McIlwaine was already well underway before his arrest. The UDR cover story was almost certainly disingenuous, for McIlwaine was on a police suspect list for some time before his arrest and it is inconceivable that the UDR was not aware of his wanted status, either directly from an RUC tip-off or, indirectly, from the police enquiries about him. His membership of the Regiment, lasting three years and coinciding with the activities of the gang, was not disclosed in open court and was only publicly admitted by the UDR after Michael Canavan, the SDLP law and order spokesman, sought confirmation from the Secretary of State for Northern Ireland.

The controversy over McIlwaine drew from the Regiment an admission that by March 1979, more than thirty of its members had been convicted for serious terrorist offences, the frankest count published up to that time. Five had been found guilty of murder, five of manslaughter; ten for arms and explosives offences; four for serious assault; and another nine for other terrorist type offences.

At the end of 1989, the Armed Forces minister, Archie Hamilton, told Seamus Mallon, MP, that in the previous four years seventy offenders had been dismissed or had resigned from the Regiment, sixteen voluntarily, having been involved in an offence; fifty-four being discharged after being convicted and imprisoned.

Mr Hamilton said that it was not policy to terminate a soldier's engagement before he had been tried and convicted and that members of the army were not allowed to resign voluntarily after involvement in an offence.

The minister side-stepped Mallon's attempt to explore the pre-1985 position because the information 'could only be obtained at disproportionate cost' – another parliamentary euphemism which really means that the government is not prepared to disclose the information.

These sanitised figures are not much help in measuring the actual scale of criminality and subversion in the UDR and it has to be assumed that the government's consistent refusal to publish the information, which, given the implications of the problem, is almost certainly compiled, conceals a worrying situation.

Research carried out by the Irish Information Partnership, analysing information supplied by the Northern Ireland Office, confirms convincingly that there is a serious criminal problem in the UDR, when compared with both the RUC and regular army.

Between 1985 and 1989, six policemen and eight regular soldiers were convicted of scheduled offences, compared with twenty-nine members of the UDR. In the same period 2,662 civilians were also convicted.

When these figures are extended to give the incidence of crime per 10,000 people, the UDR tops the scale decisively with a rate of 9.1 per cent compared with ratings of 5.9 per cent for the community as a whole. The police score only 0.9 per cent and the regular army 1.7 per cent. These official figures, therefore, go a long way to justifying the critics of the UDR and its record. It cannot be a matter for continued complacency or evasion by government that an arm of the security forces is significantly more lawless than the community which it is charged with protecting. By repeatedly breaching the expected standards of discipline and integrity, some members of the UDR have prejudiced the Regiment's reputation and compromised the high level of public confidence which it ought to enjoy. These 'bad apples' have also betrayed the gallantry and sacrifice of those who have served honourably in the force.

The point was made publicly by the outspoken Sir John Hermon, while Chief Constable of the RUC in May 1985. Speaking at a passing out parade at UDR Ballykinler, Sir John, said:

> It is regrettable in the extreme that over the years a small number of individuals have badly let down the overwhelming majority of soldiers who have served bravely and well in the UDR.

All of us know and accept that misconduct and criminality cannot and will not be tolerated. In all disciplined organisations such as ours there must and will be an insistence on high standards. From my contact with the UDR, I know that nowhere are the crimes of those who have dishonoured the name of the UDR more bitterly regretted than within the Regiment itself. The reputation of your Regiment lies largely in your hands.

6 1981–1991

As the UDR embarked on its second decade, its role and responsibilities were steadily increasing in line with the policy of 'Ulsterisation'. The regular army presence had been progressively reduced to about 10,000, less than half of the 1972 peak. With more than 50 per cent of the garrison committed to administrative and support tasks, at any given time of the day or night only about 2,000 regular soldiers were actually deployed on anti-terrorist work. The RUC and the UDR were carrying more and more of the workload.

The Defence White Paper for 1980 reiterated that the government's purpose was to restore normal life to the people of Northern Ireland.

> Removing the constant threat of violence is a first priority and vital to this is the work of the services – demanding, often tedious and always dangerous. Already in many areas the RUC can handle the bulk of the anti-terrorist task without military assistance. But in other areas a more active army role remains essential. Much of their work in support of the RUC is necessarily spent on patrolling, whether in city streets or open countryside, on checkpoints and on static guard and observation duties. But, since they are a prime target for terrorist attack, commanders take continual care that only necessary operations are undertaken. Great responsibility devolves upon junior NCOs and on individual soldiers. These duties, particularly searches of people and their vehicles, demand high levels of concentration, tact and sensitivity towards the community.

The paper emphasised that because of 'undramatic and painstaking gathering of evidence and the high level of cooperation between all parts of the security forces' suspect terrorists were being charged and brought before the courts for trial. 'Taking terrorists out of circulation through the processes of the law remains the security forces' chief weapon,' it said.

These comments were particularly relevant for the UDR. By the beginning of 1981 it was providing military support for the RUC in eleven out of the sixteen police divisions. Although there were still restrictions on where the Regiment could operate, its 'tactical areas of responsibility' now included some previously sensitive areas such as parts of inner-city Belfast and South Londonderry, but hardline Nationalist areas, particularly in Belfast and Londonderry, were still firmly out of bounds. Equally, there was no prospect of the UDR being deployed in plainclothes for undercover work, or assuming any capability to deal with riots – the RUC had formed teams of Divisional Mobile Support Units who were to be trained to take that task back from the regular army.

To meet its expanding workload, the UDR needed more recruits, especially for the new permanent cadre which was already sixteen platoons strong. Some extra manpower had been found by closing a small number of operational bases, such as those at Loughgall, County Armagh and Derryvolgie House at Lisburn. The soldiers freed from guard duty were therefore available for work on the streets, leaving the Regiment with thirty-six locations to protect.

While another 350 UDR members had been recruited and trained, bringing the total strength up to 7,559, including 105 officers seconded from the regular army, a recruiting campaign was begun with advertisements on local television and in newspapers.

Under close-up photographs of a 9mm Browning pistol, 7.62mm self-loading rifle and 7.62mm light machine-gun, the copy read:

> Learn how to use these and stop senseless killings. It'd be sheer lunacy to put the likes of these in the hands of anyone but a professional soldier. We don't hesitate to issue them to farmers, solicitors and factory workers. The men of the UDR. The fact that

they're part-time makes them no less professional. In their spare time they go through a training programme as tough as that of their regular counterparts. Getting fit, map reading and battle tactics are included, of course. So is a thorough grounding in the use of weapons. It's nothing if not intensive. And even when we've knocked the raw recruit out of you, we keep you up to scratch. You'll spend entire weekends on the range, mainly with self-loading rifles and light machine-guns. Some of you might even be good enough for Bisley, home of the world's most famous shooting competition. Right now, you probably couldn't hit a bull from three feet, let alone a bull's eye. Give us a few months and we'll have you pumping twenty rounds into the target from three hundred metres with deadly accuracy. To achieve that, we're asking for a few hours of your time each week. It'll be enough to make senseless killers give up for good.

Motivating sufficient people to join the Regiment was becoming increasingly difficult. Despite all the bold talk about the rates of attrition against terrorism and the inevitability of its being defeated, which emanated from Stormont and Lisburn, there was a growing sense of frustration and hopelessness among the members of the UDR. Early in 1980, it was given fresh expression at the funeral of Harry Livingstone, who had been murdered feeding cattle on his farm in Armagh close to the border, despite the fact that he had resigned from the Regiment some months earlier. The Reverend Tom Taylor, officiating at the funeral, called on the leaders of all the Protestant churches to seek an audience with the Queen to tell her of the pain and sorrow of the border communities and to ask her to intervene with the government to relieve their plight.

At about the same time, a sense of the frustration was publicly vented by two UDR battalion commanders within days of each other. Lieutenant-Colonel Gordon Duff, of 3UDR, urged the men of County Down to answer the call now as they had done when the UDR was formed in 1970. He said that part-timers were doing eight duties a month and that 300 more were needed to spread the load.

Lieutenant-Colonel Tony Ward, commanding 10UDR, addressing Rotarians in Belfast, was even more outspoken. He hit out at the well-to-do sections of the community, the business and professional men

> who had grown tired and weary and who wanted peace but not involvement. Top people have adapted to the less pleasant side of life, sit back and let others fight the vile cancer of terrorism. Every once in a while one comes across the attitude of, to hell with it anyway, things are not too bad, the family is all right, the business is all right and why should I worry?

Warning that the 'Provos' were 'no longer the bunch of cowboys of earlier days but a ruthless, highly trained, security conscious terrorist organisation', he wondered what some of the top people would say if their factories were bombed or burned out. The security forces, he claimed, could beat the IRA but only with the help of all the people, all the time and not just those in the security forces.

Referring to the 'intolerable strain' on his soldiers, on the streets and off, he revealed that some of them, working for two big international companies, had to keep their UDR membership secret. 'I often wonder if patriotism, particularly among the young, is dead.'

In being so unusually frank, the Lieutenant-Colonel shed considerable light on how the UDR perceived its task and role at that stage. What he did not refer to, however, was the widespread grumbling within the ranks about pay. Working ever more closely with the RUC, the financial gap between the two forces became ever more apparent. The RUC rank and file were entitled to overtime payment at enhanced rates for hours worked above their basic shifts. Some of them were regularly taking home pay packets twice or nearly three times their basic salary. This enabled them to buy the latest models of cars, enjoy good holiday trips abroad and equip their homes and families with virtually all they wanted.

In sharp contrast, the standard of living of UDR soldiers, who were paid on a par with the regular army and accrued no entitlement to overtime, however long they were on duty, was much lower. In the early days the differences had not been so noticeable. Many part-timers enjoyed the soldiering and the extra money often made a considerable difference to their financial position. Now, with the increase of the professional, full-time element comprising one-third of the strength, and the fact that many more UDR members were in the Regiment for financial reasons as an alternative or supplement to the dole, the rate of remuneration became more important to them. Resentment was aggravated when policemen taunted the 'County Mounties', as the UDR were disparagingly referred to, by waving their superior pay slips at them. The net result was a noticeable trend of resignations, either because the pay was considered inadequate, or because it was not enough to compensate for the risk inherent in being a member of the UDR.

In 1983, because of substantial shifts in the patterns of population and crime, the RUC implemented a major territorial reorganisation. The number of divisions was reduced from sixteen to twelve and greater local autonomy was devolved on the thirty-eight sub-divisions. These moves had implications for the UDR, who carried out their own organisational review. In order to integrate the support operations more closely with the police, it was decided to amalgamate two of the eleven battalions. Accordingly 1 and 9UDR amalgamated to form 1/9UDR in June 1984 and 7 and 10UDR merged in October the same year to form 7/10UDR. At the amalgamation parade at Palace Barracks, Holywood on Sunday 14 October, Lieutenant-General Sir Robert Richardson, the GOC Northern Ireland, congratulated the men and women involved. 'Your turnout, steadiness and bearing have been first class,' he said. 'Very well done.'

This battalion structure is still in operation. 1/9UDR is now 756-strong, and is responsible for a 700 square mile area of South and Mid-Antrim, including the 153 square miles of Lough Neagh, which terrorists often use as an alternative to the main roads across the province. With bases at Antrim, Ballymena, Larne, Carrickfergus and Newtownabbey the battalion carries out a wide range of anti-terrorist work, protecting key points and patrolling the vital road and rail links that run through their patch.

2UDR is responsible for 650 square kilometres of Armagh, the smallest but arguably one of the most violent UDR areas in Northern Ireland. Its 456 men and women include the first Greenfinch to join the Regiment, who is now a warrant officer. Based at Armagh, Newry, Lurgan and Portadown, it regularly provides units for duty along the border as well as supporting the police throughout the county.

3UDR, the first battalion to be raised in 1970, shares its headquarters with the UDR training depot at Ballykinler, County Down. In 1989 its soldiers, also based at Kilkeel and Rathfriland, put in some 900,000 man hours dealing with the terrorist threat. In a joint operation with the RUC it helped uncover a highly sophisticated factory at Ballynahinch, County Down, turning out workable, home-made sub-machine guns for a Loyalist terrorist group.

4UDR operates from the newest and best equipped UDR location, Grosvenor Barracks, Enniskillen. From there it sends patrols out night and day, usually by helicopter, to patrol the county, which is surrounded on three sides by the Irish Republic. Because of the danger of ambush, it only uses vehicles in the urban area around Enniskillen. Water-borne patrols are also deployed on Upper and Lower Lough Erne and among their duties in late 1990 was the task of patrolling the waterway alongside Enniskillen when Mrs Thatcher made her last visit to the area as prime minister, a few days before her resignation.

The largest UDR area of tactical responsibility is covered by 5UDR. 1,600 miles stretching across three police divisions and parts of two counties, Londonderry and Antrim. Based at a former RAF airfield at Ballykelly, the company headquarters at Coleraine, Ballymoney and Magherafelt, the battalion is especially proud of its champion pipers and drummers who have represented the Regiment at massed band displays on Horse Guards Parade and at the annual Royal British Legion Festival of Remembrance at the Albert Hall, in London.

6UDR, headquartered at Omagh covering a large part of County Tyrone, with companies at Castlederg and Clogher, has suffered heavily at the hands of the terrorist murder campaign, with thirty-one serving members and four ex-members killed. Most of its patrol area has to be covered cross-country, on foot, because of the risk of landmine attacks on the roads.

The Belfast battalion, 7/10UDR with 1,100 members, is the largest infantry battalion in both the UDR and the British army. Organised into seven companies, three of them full-time, it operates throughout the Greater Belfast area carrying out an extraordinary range of duties. These include searching ships at Belfast docks and sometimes at sea, securing the city centre by day and night and carrying out searches and guard duties to protect visiting dignitaries to the city. Several times a year, the part-time companies are assigned duties out of the city, in rural areas or along the border to broaden their experience.

8UDR, raised in 1971, is a pretty small unit by comparison with 7/10UDR, with under 500 soldiers. Based at Dungannon, with other companies at Cookstown and on the border at Aughnacloy, the battalion has sustained losses of thirty-two soldiers over the years. Theirs is an area fraught with terrorism and difficulty but, like the other battalions, its members pursue an active social and sporting life. Among their achievements is a third place in the army Tug-of-War championships.

11UDR, based at Portadown, with a company at Lisburn, patrols an area of 1,500 square kilometres, basically the two towns and the strategic M1 motorway corridor between them. This battalion is 772 strong.

The basic armament of the UDR is now the SA80 5.56mm rifle of which the Regiment holds 5,843. It is also equipped with 912 5.56mm Light Support Weapons and six 7.62mm machine guns. The handguns in service are the Browning gun and the Walther 9mm pistols. Of the 865 Brownings, 265 are authorised for use by soldiers off duty, for their own protection. Similarly, 1,846 of the 1,985 Walthers are in use as personal protection weapons. The Regiment also holds three shotguns and 167 L67 riot guns, used for firing plastic bullets. (Although these have not been fired in service yet, there has been controversy about the UDR being trained to use them.)

The basic patrol vehicle is the Land Rover, with 447 in service. Most are older models, protected by Makrolon, but plans are in hand to equip the UDR with new Land Rovers, fitted with the latest lightweight armour to give the soldiers better protection from gunshots and the effects of bomb blast. The Regiment also runs another 425 vehicles, ranging from unmarked vans for carrying stores and equipment between bases, to a brightly-painted recruiting trailer, which tours local agricultural shows during the summer months to show the UDR flag and encourage enlistment.

In line with standard army practice the commanders of the Regiment continued to rotate at two-year intervals. In May 1982, a high-flying brigadier, Peter Graham, aged 45, arrived at Lisburn. Of Scottish stock, he earned his military spurs in the Gordon Highlanders, rising through the ranks to command his battalion. Having served in Kenya and Borneo, as well as several other conventional British army locations, he acquired considerable first-hand knowledge of Northern Ireland during several postings in the 1970s. After his departure from the UDR in June 1984, he went on to command the Royal Military Academy at Sandhurst and later to become GOC Scotland. His place at the UDR was taken by Brigadier Roger Preston, aged 48, a Yorkshireman educated at Eton and Sandhurst. In his early career he served in Kenya, Cyprus, Germany, Malaya and Borneo, with a year at the Indian army staff college. Before taking over the Regiment, the Brigadier had served six previous tours in Ulster, with his own regiment, the Light Infantry.

In the early 1980s the restlessness within the UDR not only centred on money but also reflected the high degree of political uncertainty among the Protestant community at large. Thousands of members of the Orange Order, among them some members of the Regiment in Orange regalia, had marched through Belfast to a rally outside the City Hall on 15 March 1980. There they passed a resolution calling on the government to use to the full its military and civil powers to restore the rule of law, to protect the lives and livelihood of its citizens and to bring terrorist criminals to justice. It was a significant occasion, for the Order, the largest and most influential of Protestant groupings, had hitherto steered clear of day to day political involvement.

The immediate cause of anxiety was the ease with which the Provisional IRA was managing to carry on its campaign of violence, especially in the border areas. Many Protestants genuinely feared that the British government lacked the will to tackle the IRA and was allowing the Unionist community to be softened up in preparation for their being 'sold-out' and left at the mercy of the hated Irish Republic. These fears were enhanced at the end of 1980 when Mrs Margaret Thatcher, the prime minister, brought a high-powered team to a summit at Dublin Castle with Charles Haughey, the Irish prime minister. Both sides agreed on the formation of official working parties to examine 'the totality of relationships' between the two islands of Britain and Ireland. Given their existing fears, these words had an ominous ring to the ears of even the most liberal and pragmatic Unionists.

The IRA hunger strikes at the Maze Prison dominated the year of 1981 and when the lead hunger striker, Bobby Sands, was elected to the London parliament in an untimely by-election, the level of inter-communal tension soared. In all, ten prisoners starved themselves to death in support of the IRA's demand to be recognised as political prisoners, not common criminals. Outside the prison, the issue polarised opinion as never before and there was an accompanying upsurge in street violence and tension. The number of people killed jumped from 76 the previous year to 101, shootings increased from 642 to 1,142 and bombings from 400 to 529. During the year thirteen members of the Regiment were murdered. Major Ivan Toombs, who had survived an ambush five years earlier, was shot dead at Warrenpoint docks where he worked as a customs officer. Lance-Corporal Samuel Montgomery was killed at his work-place in Londonderry, while Private David Smith was gunned down on a Belfast street on his way to work. Lance-Corporal Richard McKee, Private Thomas Ritchie, Lance-Corporal Ronnie Graham, Private Alan Clarke and Private Mark Stockman were also all murdered off duty. A terrorist disguised as a postman murdered Sergeant Julian Connolly on his doorstep in Belfast. The names of Private Cecil Graham, Corporal Thomas Beacom and Lance-Corporal John McKeegan were also added to the UDR roll of honour that year. Among those who attended the McKeegan funeral in Strabane was the local Catholic priest, Father Anthony Mulvey. Next day, in a unique reaction, he was given a standing ovation by parishioners in his own church when he condemned the killing and called for the IRA killers to be extradited from the Irish Republic to face justice.

The growing Protestant feelings of vulnerability and anger at the continued IRA campaign spilled over after the murder in November 1981 of the outspoken Reverend Robert Bradford, the Unionist MP for South Belfast. At his funeral a couple of days later, police bodyguards had to protect the Northern Ireland Secretary, James Prior, who was hissed as he walked into the church for the service.

Over the next few months there emerged the 'Third Force', yet another shadowy Protestant paramilitary grouping which carried out road check operations in some rural areas to point up what its leaders considered to be inadequate cover provided by the legitimate security forces. In a major propaganda exercise some 15,000 masked men in paramilitary uniforms, with many carrying cudgels, paraded at Newtownards, County Down early in 1982. At their head was the figure of the Reverend Ian Paisley, whose distinctive voice had been loudest among those complaining about the lack of security. Photographs taken at the rally showed that many of the marchers were wearing berets with UDR cap badges and leaders of the 'Third Force' claimed that members of the Regiment were indeed involved.

The UDR had already issued an internal notice, through each

battalion commander, reminding soldiers that there could be no divided loyalties between the UDR and the 'Third Force'. It called on those concerned to resign forthwith if they could not give undivided loyalty to the UDR. Answering questions from concerned MPs in the House of Commons, Mr Prior vowed that private armies would not be given a free rein and allowed to usurp the duties of the security forces. Speaking on behalf of the Nationalist community, Mr Gerry Fitt, the MP for West Belfast, said that the creation of the 'Third Force' had caused real fear and concern, especially with the reports of UDR involvement. Many Catholics regarded it as the UDA story over again – with the army prepared to tolerate dual membership as a safety valve for hardline Loyalist feelings on the dubious grounds that the 'Third Force', like the UDA, had not been declared illegal. These events once more focused attention on what could only be described as the continued uneasy and often hostile relationship between the UDR and the minority community.

By now, Catholic membership of the Regiment had fallen to less than 2 per cent, a mere 160 soldiers. A handful were outstandingly brave Catholics of local origin, whose membership of the UDR required total secrecy. The bulk were, however, ex-servicemen and women with the British army from non-Irish Catholic backgrounds. A handful were ex-regulars, who described themselves as Catholics, and who had stayed on in Northern Ireland, transferring to the UDR, after marrying local girls. It has to be said that their Catholicism and the local brand of Catholic/Nationalism, had very little in common.

The army and the UDR insisted that there was a place in the Regiment for Catholics. The IRA had driven them out and, through intimidation, was keeping them out. After all, seven of the first twenty soldiers singled out for murder had been Catholics, they said. The UDR was impartial and required by law to be so, they claimed. What a pity that Catholics would not join in the drive against the IRA. These themes were repeated by successive commanders time and time again. 'It is not true,' said Brigadier Preston, at one point, 'that the Regiment acts in a sectarian manner. A terrorist is a terrorist in the eyes of my soldiers and they do not distinguish between Catholic and Protestant terrorists.' To underline his proposition, he cited the occasion when Loyalist gunmen attempted to murder the Sinn Fein leader, Gerry Adams, while his car was stopped at traffic lights in the centre of Belfast. The gunmen were promptly apprehended by an off-duty UDR soldier in plain clothes, who held them at the point of his personal protection weapon until uniformed reinforcements arrived. The soldier, a Protestant, was later threatened and forced to move from his house, in the Protestant area where he lived.

Although those who had let the Regiment down, through what was often described as 'misguided patriotism', were uncompromisingly disowned, the UDR seems never to have realised that it was these incidents, not the greater multitude of brave and positive acts carried out by the soldiers, which were setting and perpetuating its image as a sectarian, partial force. Not for the first time, and sadly, not for the last, the Regiment closed its ears and its mind to the criticisms and retreated into a hurt sulk. For whatever reason, it never seriously attempted to allay the fears of its critics. Information about action against offenders within its own ranks had to be prised out through parliamentary questions, which were usually answered as briefly as possible. The Regiment drew a cloak of secrecy and injured innocence around itself. The need to protect its 'security' became paramount and fostered an almost siege-like mentality among those in the Regiment.

This attitude aggravated one overwhelming factor. Most Catholics, especially SDLP supporters, who abhorred the IRA and deplored all it did and stood for, regarded the UDR as the other side of the same bad coin – 'Ulster's Disreputable Rogues', as one wag called them. These views persisted because the UDR never made any serious effort to change them. This was not entirely their own doing. Government approval and support would have been necessary for the sort of public relations effort necessary but, even within the resources available to them, the UDR showed neither the understanding nor the inclination to make their case for Catholic support. The deep-seated Catholic views about the position of the security forces, and their historical context, were given highly articulate expression in a paper submitted to the Secretary of State by Michael Canavan, the SDLP spokesman on law and order, in January 1980:

> From inception the boundaries of Northern Ireland were delineated specifically so that the majority tradition would always be in power, thereby frustrating democracy.
>
> The permanent exclusion of the minority tradition from authority, exacerbated by the discriminatory practices against it, placed the two traditions in positions of permanent confrontation. The conflict thus generated created permanent instability which in every generation erupted into violence, reaching a crescendo in the last decade.
>
> It is this conflict which has always posed and will continue to pose the greatest threat to peace and therefore to security in Northern Ireland first, spreading inevitably throughout the whole island. The problem cannot be solved by security measures alone, which concentrated on violence, which is the symptom not the cause of violence.
>
> Neither is it simply a matter of being either for or against the RUC, it is much more fundamental. In Britain the majority in parliament enact laws and the courts and police enforce them. But because the society is fundamentally in agreement on how it should be governed, its people accept the law, the courts and the police as 'our' law, 'our' courts and 'our' police.
>
> If you apply the system of majority rule in a divided society like ours you get a situation where the majority think of 'our' law, 'our' courts and 'our' police, but the minority think of 'their' courts, 'their' law and 'their' police. When the institutions of the state come under attack this peculiar attitude of both the majority and the minority community towards the state and the police becomes obvious. This has been the fundamental weakness of the state of Northern Ireland and subversive organisations using violence to overthrow the institutions of the state have consistently exploited it.
>
> The SDLP is committed to removing this fundamental weakness in Northern Ireland by the creation of agreed institutions of government based on partnership not confrontation between the two traditions which the whole community will commit themselves to wholeheartedly support, protect and defend.

In the field of security it is obvious that both the British and Irish governments are to a considerable extent interdependent particularly in the context of political violence accepting both.

Therefore it must also be their common concern to work together to develop the political institutions which alone can remove the basic causes of conflict and guarantee support for law and order. The emphasis on security at every summit meeting between the two governments indicates the importance of practical cooperation in ensuring that joint resources are maximised against terrorism.

In a section focused specifically on the UDR the paper said:

The UDR which in Ulsterisation becomes the RUC's back-up service has by far the worst record for serious sectarian crimes of any regiment presently in service with the British armed forces on land, sea or air.

Former members of the Regiment have been convicted in the courts of (*inter alia*) sectarian multiple murder; sectarian murder; sectarian attempted murder; sectarian pub bombing in Northern Ireland, England, the Republic of Ireland; sectarian arson; sectarian assault; sectarian intimidation; arms theft of their own weapons; murder to pervert justice; arms offences and common criminality of all kinds, including social security frauds and the robbery of post offices.

The more serious of these crimes have often been connected with loyalist paramilitary activity with which the Regiment is known to be seriously infiltrated.

My party has consistently – but in vain – campaigned for every UDR man to be security rescreened in order to root out the paramilitary elements. Until this is done the Regiment will be identified amongst the minority community more as a menace to than a support for law and order.

In addition both the RUC and the UDR are overwhelmingly (96 per cent and 98 per cent respectively) drawn from the Loyalist tradition and are therefore completely unrepresentative of the community at large. This to an extent represents Westminster's failure to convince the minority that the dispensation of justice here is evenhanded.

The exclusive pursuit of a military solution to the problems of Northern Ireland has failed to end the violence, which was its sole objective and only justification. The end result has been to brutalise the security forces, alienate large sections of the community and weaken support for law and order in a community which is now more polarised than ever.

The gulf separating the UDR and the minority community was more colourfully illustrated by an encounter at a roadblock between a patrol and John Tierney, an SDLP councillor, who was at the time the Mayor of Ulster's second city, Londonderry. 'Where are you going?' asked one of the soldiers as he is entitled to do under Northern Ireland emergency legislation. 'Home to Derry,' replied Tierney. 'There's no such place,' replied the soldier. 'Surely you mean Londonderry?' After protracted argument, Tierney, anxious to be on his way, replied: 'I've changed my mind. I'm going to Strabane.'

Many members of the Catholic community have experienced similar instances of petty sectarian harassment by members of the UDR. A Catholic businessman, who prefers to use the Irish language version of his name, says that UDR patrols invariably make him translate it. In another case in 1984, a Belfastman was actually charged with obstruction and brought to court, after giving his name and address in Irish at a UDR manned checkpoint. From time to time, UDR patrols have been seen to note the registration numbers of all vehicles parked outside Catholic churches during Sunday morning services. There have been frequent reports of priests being subjected to delay or incivility at road checkpoints. Others, such as members of the Convery family from Draperstown, County Londonderry, have fallen foul of more serious behaviour.

On Sunday 9 May 1982, Joseph Convery, accompanied by his wife and young son and his father and brother, were driving at Lisnamuck cross roads, near Maghera, when a soldier called on them to halt. As his driving licence was being checked, some members of the patrol began calling the family 'Fenian bastards'. After some delay, during which he was told that they could be detained all day if the patrol so wished, he again asked when they would be allowed to proceed. One of the soldiers then shouted that if any of the Converys moved, they would be arrested. At this point a concerted attack on the family took place. The father was struck and violently kicked while on the ground, as was the brother, who went to his aid. The driver was hit with a rifle butt and injured in the neck and shoulder by several of the soldiers while his young son screamed: 'Don't kill my daddy.' When the Converys' claim for damages came before Magherafelt County Court in October 1984, counsel for the Ministry of Defence accepted the substance of the complaint. Describing the incident as 'totally disgraceful', Judge Peter Gibson awarded Convery £2,500 damages. In separate claims his father received £2,000 and his brother another £1,250 in compensation for assault.

In another case in the same area, in August 1983, a judge awarded five men, aged between 19 and 23, £250 damages each for unlawful detention by the UDR but he dismissed claims for personal injuries because the men themselves were 'largely responsible for what happened to them'. All were sitting in a parked car at Bellaghy and refused to open the doors when approached by a UDR patrol. Two of the soldiers then smashed the car windows with their rifle butts and dragged the occupants out. Dismissing claims that they had been subjected to sectarian remarks, the judge ruled that the patrol had exercised their lawful right to enter the vehicle as it had been observed acting suspiciously in an area where there had been terrorist activity and that the patrol had used necessary force. However, he decided that removing the men to the local police station in the UDR vehicles, from where they were later released without charge, constituted unlawful detention.

In fairness to the UDR, who make many such checks during their operations, they encounter hostility from some Nationalists as soon as they realise, usually by the local accent, that they have been stopped by the UDR and not the regular army. Without any provocation whatever on the part of the soldiers, unpleasantness therefore often develops. Sometimes there are good security reasons for what the UDR does, which are misconstrued by critics of the Regiment, often deliberately discrediting it through propaganda. One agent provocateur received his just desserts, however. Halted at a UDR checkpoint late at night, he refused to get out of his car and, through a narrow gap in the window, intimated that he would only deal with the RUC. The assistance of a police constable was summoned by radio and when he arrived, the man in the car was promptly arrested on suspicion of drunken driving, breathalysed and subsequently convicted.

An indication of just how prickly Nationalist opinion was about the UDR came in the early part of 1984, soon after the murder of Adrian Carroll, which gave rise to the case of the 'UDR Four'. (See chapter 5.) During a Christmas trip to Northern Ireland, Margaret Thatcher, the prime minister, visited Drummadd Barracks, Armagh where the UDR soldiers had been based. In a subsequent interview on Irish radio, Cardinal Tomas O'Fiaich, the Catholic primate of all-Ireland, said that the visit had been 'a very insulting thing to do as far as the Catholics of Armagh were concerned'. John Hume, the leader of the Nationalist party, the SDLP, raised the visit with the prime minister during Question Time in the House of Commons a few days later, when he said that it had aroused 'deep feelings of outrage' in the Catholic community'. The prime minister replied that she had been visiting the Grenadier Guards, who were also based at the barracks. 'I am entitled to do that. There were of course some members of the UDR there, and the UDR, if I may say so, does a superlative job.'

The ripples from this episode had hardly been calmed when, on 3 February, the Duke of Edinburgh, Colonel of the Grenadier Guards, flew into Drummadd for a private visit to the Guards, which did not include any contact with the UDR. Seamus Mallon, the deputy leader of the SDLP, described the visit as a 'calculated insult'. In Dublin, Charles Haughey, the former prime minister who was to come to power again, actually called for the Regiment to be disbanded. 'I know enough about the North to know that a force like the UDR only heightens community tension and is counter-productive to security. I had personal experience of the B Specials and I do not see any difference in the present situation.' At government level in Dublin, the British ambassador, Sir Alan Goodison, was called in by the Minister for Foreign Affairs, Peter Barry, who had made an informal diplomatic protest about the prime minister's earlier visit. This time his protest was formal.

At the same time, Dublin's concern about the UDR was being more forcefully pursued through another channel. After the ending of the IRA hunger strikes, the Irish government, at the suggestion of John Hume, established the New Ireland Forum, to conceive new ways to break down the divisions between the people of Ireland.

The Forum got underway in May 1983 and lasted for a year, holding a series of public hearings in Dublin Castle, once the seat of British power in Ireland. Its members were drawn from all the main political parties in the Irish Republic and the SDLP from Northern Ireland. Sinn Fein were excluded because of their support for IRA violence. Efforts to include the Unionists from the North came to nothing, although some individual Unionists and several Protestant churchmen were among those who made both written and oral submissions to the Forum.

The final report, published in May 1984, was certainly the most searching study and analysis of the Irish problem ever made. Research papers on transport, energy, agriculture, the legal systems, the cost of violence and the economic implications of partition provided a comprehensive picture for the political leaders to consider. Their report on the political framework for a new Ireland identified three equal options for consideration: the unitary state, with both parts of the island being ruled from Dublin; a federal or confederal state, which would provide for local rule with a joint national policy on certain matters; and, finally, joint authority, with Britain and the Irish Republic sharing responsibility for governing Northern Ireland.

The report provided the basis for an Irish approach to Britain to take a major political initiative on Northern Ireland. The Irish were concerned that the rise of Provisional Sinn Fein as a political force, in the aftermath of the hunger strikes, had the potential to undermine democracy throughout the island. The prime minister, Dr Garrett FitzGerald, spoke of the IRA as the 'common enemy' of Britain and Ireland. James Prior, the Northern Ireland Secretary, undoubtedly shared the Irish concerns. He even said that if Sinn Fein were ever to take over, Ireland could become a European Cuba.

The need for a major political initiative was quickly grasped by some of the most senior officials in the Thatcher administration but the prime minister, a Unionist by instinct who had once said that Ulster was as British as Finchley, her own North London constituency, was harder to convince. Dr FitzGerald pressed his case at successive summit meetings but in the end it was President Ronald Reagan who applied the decisive pressure.

Irish diplomatic lobbying in Washington has long been regarded on Capitol Hill as second only in its effectiveness to that of Israel. Any Senator or Congressman with Irish roots or an Irish vote in his neighbourhood was identified and marshalled into the promotion or protection of Irish issues and interests. Reagan, whose family roots had been traced to the tiny Tipperary village of Ballyporeen, was more than happy to acknowledge his Irish ancestry and visit the Irish embassy on St Patrick's day to receive a Waterford glass bowl of shamrock, specially flown across the Atlantic. So during a visit to Washington by Mrs Thatcher, during 1984, it was none too difficult for the Irish to persuade Reagan to push her into giving appropriate attention to the Ulster issue.

The thrust of the British/Irish inter-governmental negotiations which followed was about creating new political arrangements to put their common Northern Ireland problem on a new footing. The talks addressed every issue that contributed to the alienation of the substantial Catholic minority from the Northern Ireland state. High on this agenda was the future role and, indeed, the very existence of the UDR.

Irish attitudes on these questions had been very heavily influenced by the 1980 Canavan/SDLP paper and subsequent developments. Reflecting their lack of confidence in the mechanisms to make the security forces accountable, the SDLP and other northern Catholics had increasingly been using the Irish government as a vehicle to press their discontent on the British. So, through the Anglo-Irish section at the Department of Foreign Affairs in Dublin, there passed a series of cases, some complaints, some reports, which built up a picture of affairs in Northern Ireland, as seen by those on the receiving end of security policy. Individual complaints were pursued at diplomatic level through the British Embassy in Dublin, or sometimes at ministerial level through the Foreign Office in London.

An indication of just how seriously the Irish government viewed the UDR came from the prime minister, Dr Garrett FitzGerald, during a visit to the United States in May 1985, when he said that they were 'a dangerous force whose loyalty does not lie with the British Crown'. Back in Ireland he returned to the subject a few days later.

> What I was saying was what is the Nationalist view of the UDR and so long as you don't make radical changes in the present structure and method of working of the security forces you won't end the alienation and you keep the IRA alive and prevent peace coming to this island.

Accepting fully the IRA threat to the Regiment, he said:

> Nonetheless the force in its present form, in its composition, its discipline and in its performance, is a force which Nationalists must and do fear. There have been just too many people murdered by the UDR, either on duty or off duty. In a number of cases they have been found guilty. Others have not yet been brought to justice, and some have been acquitted in particular circumstances. But for a peace-keeping force, their record is one which I don't think any government should be satisfied with.

But it was not only at the inter-governmental talks that the UDR's future was being considered. At the same time, senior officers in the RUC, prompted by the Chief Constable, Sir John Hermon, had been carrying out their own appraisal of the Regiment. Ever since the policy of 'Ulsterisation' had been implemented, reservations about the expanded role for the UDR had been firmly entrenched in the highest echelons of the RUC. They knew, from Special Branch vetting of applicants and their own work, that there were some soldiers with questionable records in the Regiment. Although only 56 per cent of those who applied to join were accepted into the UDR, RUC officers were regularly astounded to come upon people who had actually been recruited after being given an adverse vetting report.

RUC objections to the UDR were also founded on more practical grounds. With the high level of IRA threat to members of the Regiment, their homes and workplaces had to be carefully watched by security patrols. In some extreme cases, especially in isolated rural areas, special arrangements had to be made to escort UDR soldiers to and from their homes. This frequently tied down three or four other members of the security forces, calling into question the cost-effectiveness of the membership of soldiers. 'Red hot targets are being advised that it would be in their best interests and ours if they did not join up,' one senior police officer disclosed.

The police were also keen to 'get khaki off the streets' as a further sign that they could cope with their responsibility to maintain law and order and that the tide of terrorism was being well and truly reversed. The army in general, and the UDR in particular, was regarded as being a blunt instrument to use in a delicate and sensitive situation. What the police wanted was a gradual rundown of the UDR and a transfer of their duties to an expanded RUC. They calculated that it would need another 4,000 full-time police officers to replace the 7,000 UDR soldiers, bringing the strength of the RUC up to some 12,000. The RUC argued that their proposal was not only politically astute but cost-effective. Statistically it required the support of only half a police officer to put one officer on the streets, compared with a back-up of five soldiers to deploy one for duty.

These RUC views were soon endorsed by an unofficial but highly influential committee, chaired by Lord Kilbrandon, the distinguished peer who had earlier headed the Royal Commission on the British constitution. He had accepted a mandate from the British-Irish Association to formulate a non-Irish response to the New Ireland Forum report. The British-Irish Association, founded in 1972, provided a private platform for public figures from the two countries to exchange views. Although it was often written off as 'toffs against terror', because its annual conferences normally alternated between

Oxbridge colleges, it had long played an important mediating role. Consequently, when the Kilbrandon report, prepared by a team of ten which included David Howell, a former Northern Ireland minister, called for the UDR to be gradually disbanded and merged into an expanded RUC, it was noted by those in both governments concerned with the problem.

Also noted was perhaps the most telling denunciation of the Regiment, from Lord Hunt, its progenitor. As a member of the Liberal-SDP Alliance, he served on a commission appointed by the party leaders to review the security situation in Northern Ireland. After consulting widely, including conversations with Sir Kenneth Newman, the former chief constable, and Field Marshall Sir Edwin Bramall, past chief of the defence staff, the Alliance commission concluded that the UDR should be phased out.

Writing in the London *Independent* on 22 February 1990, Lord Hunt explained the reasoning behind the conclusion.

> I reluctantly agreed with my colleagues that the UDR should be phased out. The hopes I had entertained fifteen years earlier, that the encouraging indications of a proportionate Catholic recruitment to the Regiment would continue, had not been realised. The distrust of the minority population in the B Specials had been inherited by its successor. Serious crimes, attributed mainly to the part-time members of the UDR, had tended to discredit the whole Regiment –however unfairly. It was arguable that, in this respect, the position had reverted to that which obtained in 1969. In the changed constitutional situation of the mid-Eighties, we recommended that the duties of the UDR should be taken over by the RUC, appropriately strengthened with full-time personnel, given that the RUC is under direct rule, directly accountable to the British government.

The SDLP's longstanding opposition to the UDR had reached a new point when, in January 1985, the party unanimously passed a resolution at its annual conference calling for the UDR to be disbanded. Seamus Mallon, the deputy leader of the party, said that the UDR

> would always be seen as the armed wing of that brand of Unionism which has always sought to impose its will on the Nationalist

community. Let them be in no doubt about the strength of feeling in this party and among the Nationalist community that the only answer to the problem is the disbandment of this Regiment as a matter of immediate importance.

This sustained criticism of the UDR provoked a predictable and angry reaction from the Unionist community. Ken Maginnis, the Ulster Unionist MP, said that disbanding the UDR was a recipe for civil war. 'If it was wound up, the vacuum would be filled by a collection of groups and we would soon have warring militias fighting for territory on a scale similar to the Lebanon.'

Peter Robinson, the Democratic Unionist MP, said that

the pronouncements from Seamus Mallon and the Roman Catholic Church about the UDR, illustrate the hypocrisy of those in the Roman Catholic community who cry crocodile tears when a UDR man is killed by their co-religionists yet, at the first opportunity, put the boot into these men who are facing danger twenty-four hours a day.

His party colleague, Sammy Wilson, later to be Lord Mayor of Belfast, said: 'The proposal to run down the UDR is in essence laying the foundation for leaving us defenceless. We are being exhorted to run down the UDR so that Republicans can overrun Northern Ireland.'

The Ulster Unionist leader, James Molyneaux, said that 'nothing could bring greater joy to terrorism than to see another element in the battle against it, taken out'. As a sign of support for the Regiment, many Unionist and Loyalist supporters began wearing the Regiment's golden harp insignia, as a badge in their buttonholes. The Reverend Ian Paisley drew a parallel with what he said was 'the campaign of vilification' which had undermined the B Specials before their disbandment.

First James Prior, then Douglas Hurd, who replaced him at Stormont Castle, moved to reassure Protestant opinion. Hurd described the Regiment as a non-sectarian, highly disciplined force, which Catholics should be encouraged to join. He said that it made 'occasional mistakes'. Despite this public position, throughout the summer of 1985 as the Anglo-Irish talks moved to their conclusion, it is now clear that the future role of the

Regiment and its very existence were one of the major issues in the negotiations.

These inter-governmental talks culminated in the Anglo-Irish Agreement, signed at Hillsborough Castle on 15 November 1985, which, for the first time, gave the Irish government the right to be consulted about a whole range of issues, including security, thus affecting the way Northern Ireland was governed. Despite the hopes of 'peace, stability and reconciliation' which it was designed to foster, it ushered in a period of unprecedented Protestant disaffection and disorder. The new Anglo-Irish secretariat, established at Maryfield, outside Belfast, where British and Irish civil servants worked side by side to implement the Agreement, became a focus for protest. Within days of the signing the scale of Protestant opposition became clear when some 300,000 gathered at Belfast City Hall to protest. Over the next few weeks as red, white and blue posters, bearing the legend 'Ulster Says No', were plastered all over the province, the Unionists withdrew from the district councils, boycotted public bodies and severed all contacts with government ministers. In one ugly incident at Belfast City Hall, Tom King, who had replaced Hurd shortly before the signing of the Agreement, was attacked by a mob. It was to be more than five years before a minister visited the building again.

During 1982 seven UDR soldiers, all off duty, were murdered: Private Steven Carleton, Lieutenant James Hamilton, Private Lexie Cummings, Lance-Corporal Frederick Williamson, Sergeant Thomas Cochrane, who was first kidnapped and held for several days, Corporal Charles Spence and Corporal Austin Smith, a Catholic, gunned down on the doorstep of his Armagh home. Another ten UDR members died in 1983. Lance-Corporal Cecil McNeill was shot, Private Andrew Stinson died instantly in an explosion. In July, the Regiment suffered its worst single tragedy to date when four soldiers perished in an explosion as they travelled along the main Belfast-Omagh road. They were Corporal Thomas Harron and Privates Ronald

Alexander, Oswald Neely and John Roxborough. The other fatalities that year were Corporal Ronald Finlay, Private Thomas Campbell, Major Charles Armstrong, who was also a Unionist Councillor and Lance-Corporal Brown McKeown. There were also ten victims in 1984: Private Robert Elliott, Lance-Corporal Thomas Loughlin, Private David Montgomery, Colour-Sergeant Ivan Hillen, Private Robert Bennett and Private Jim Johnston. At the latter's funeral in Pomeroy, children from two Catholic schools jeered abuse and shouted pro-IRA slogans. In the worse incident of the year, Private Norman McKinley and Corporal Heather Kerrigan, the fourth Greenfinch to give her life, were murdered when a 200lb bomb exploded. Four more names were added to the Roll of Honour in 1984: Privates James Graham and Trevor Harkness, Sergeant Robert Boyd and Captain Gordon Hanna.

The reaction to events within the UDR mirrored that in the community. There was at least one well-founded report of Tom King being snubbed during an unannounced visit to a military base at Dungannon where several UDR patrols refused to come back until he had left. Feelings were in fact running so high in the community that the prospect of a mutiny by either the RUC or UDR was seriously raised by security advisers. At least one Unionist politician had come close to being guilty of incitement. Towards the end of 1984, the Reverend Ivan Foster, a Free Presbyterian minister and member of Paisley's Democratic Unionist party, had said he would 'love to see rebellion in the RUC and UDR against the present (security) policy'. In December 1985, he said: 'No Loyalist should resign from the UDR but rather sit tight. There is a day coming when Ulster will need their services to a greater degree than ever before.' Such sentiments prompted a special assessment of the morale of the police and UDR and the likelihood of mutiny, but military security chiefs and the Inspectorate of Constabulary both calculated that neither force would rebel. UDR officers, like their police counterparts, did, however, have to embark on a programme of lectures to their troops reassuring them that the vast majority of the rumours circulating about the future of the UDR were both wild and unfounded.

The Agreement conferred on the Irish the right to consultation on a wide range of issues concerning Catholics in Northern Ireland, including security policy. Increasingly, Irish reservations were to focus on the UDR and its interest in the Regiment's activities was to be a dominant feature of Anglo-Irish intercourse over the next six years.

Britain had resisted the Irish pressure for root and branch UDR reform and reorganisation during the Anglo-Irish negotiations but had made two important concessions. Although they were not contained in the Agreement, the accompanying communiqué bound the British to two undertakings to improve relations between the security forces and the community.

The first was to secure 'the application of the principle that the armed forces (which include the Ulster Defence Regiment) operate only in support of the civil power, with the particular objective of ensuring as rapidly as possible that, save in the most exceptional circumstances, there is a police presence in all operations which involve direct contact with the community.'

The second undertaking was to find 'ways of underlining the policy of the Royal Ulster Constabulary and the armed forces in Northern Ireland that they discharge their duties even-handedly and with equal respect for the Unionist and Nationalist identities and traditions'.

These provisions opened the way for continued Irish government pressure on the British government about the way the UDR was being operated. Dublin's attitude to the RUC had changed markedly. It was increasingly seen as impartial and professional and the way it confronted Loyalist violence arising from protests about the Agreement persuaded the Irish of this still further. Ministers and officials from Dublin, confronted with the blunt Sir John Hermon at the regular meetings arising from the Agreement, soon held him in high respect and some awe as he grappled with the implications of the new accord, despite the fact that he made plain his opposition to the police providing an escort for each UDR patrol. Once he had been appraised of this government commitment, he immediately made it clear that he had neither the funds nor the manpower to fulfill it and he said that such accompaniment could only take place where there was local available manpower. Hermon had a folder prepared, with index tabs outlining the implications of the security section of the accord, and he quickly became articulate and expert on the minute details. Peter Barry the Irish Foreign minister and Tom King regularly clashed on the UDR issue. One British official said it was like 'two pieces of sandpaper grating against each other' at the ensuing Anglo-Irish Conference meetings when the UDR came up for discussion.

The gulf between the two governments over the issue has been a theme of Anglo-Irish relations since then, causing intermittent crises, and has yet to be satisfactorily resolved. The width of the gulf between the differing positions became apparent in March 1986 from a confidential briefing paper provided by the Ministry of Defence to a House of Commons committee in which the record and behaviour of the Regiment was stoutly defended.

> The government rejects any suggestion that the UDR operates in a sectarian manner. It is a regrettable fact that the UDR is mistakenly seen by many in the minority community as a sectarian body. It is not, and this was well demonstrated by its record during the 1977 Ulster Workers Strike, when it continued to play a full part at a time when the government was under pressure from Protestant extremists. However, it is undoubtedly the case that, except for brief periods, the predominant threat has come from terrorists claiming to represent the Nationalist community and, for the most part, terrorist activity has tended to be concentrated in Nationalist areas. This has inevitably meant that the operations of all the security forces, including the UDR, have had a greater impact on the normal life of the minority community. This problem was recognised in the Anglo-Irish Agreement and one of the objectives of the inter-governmental conference is to identify ways of improving relations between the security forces generally and the minority community. The government continues to encourage Roman Catholics to join the UDR so that the Regiment can once again

become more fully representative of both communities, as this would be the best way of demonstrating its impartiality.

There was more robust support, in similar terms, for the Regiment in the 1986 White Paper on Defence which also contained a notable rebuke for Catholic opponents of the UDR, but at the same time a series of fundamental reforms to improve the calibre and professionalism of the Regiment was put in train. The man charged with carrying them through was Brigadier Michael Bray, certainly the most outspoken and radical commander ever to head the Regiment. Bray, the son of a general, educated at Wellington College and Sandhurst, came from a family whose successive generations had given the army some three hundred years' unbroken service. After being commissioned into the Duke of Wellington's Regiment in 1957, he served for two years at Palace Barracks, Holywood, a period he regards as memorable for his failing to marry an Irish girl. Clearly a high flyer, Bray served in Aden, Arabia, East Africa, Cyprus, British Honduras, Germany, Canada, Norway and England as well as several stints with NATO in Brussells. In 1983/84 he undertook a Master of Philosophy degree at Downing College, Cambridge, reading International Relations and writing a thesis on the relations between the government and the media. He took command of the UDR in June 1986.

The thrust of the Bray plan was to make the UDR more professional and to integrate it more intimately into the British army infrastructure. 'Without the nine battalions of the UDR, the British army could not cope with its commitment to Northern Ireland. Their contribution is vital to security policy,' he said. Basic training for the part-timers was increased from nine to fourteen days, all to be completed within the first three months of service. An extra regular army training officer was attached to each of the battalions while another regular officer, this time a Lieutenant-Colonel, was drafted in to fill a liaison post designed to draw the RUC more fully into the training of UDR soldiers. As part of a conscious move to develop a UDR officers corps, intensive six-month courses at the Royal Military Academy Sandhurst were made available. As a contributory part of this strategy young sixth-formers were also targeted in Northern Ireland schools in a bid to entice them into a long-term career as an officer with the UDR. 'Twelve months at Sandhurst will prepare you for a cold night in Tyrone,' said the recruiting advertisements. Existing UDR officers were also to be encouraged to go for tours of voluntary attachments to other British army units to widen their military experience and give them the feel of soldiering away from the narrow confines of Northern Ireland.

A little later, Bray pioneered the 'Break' programme which gave each of the permanent cadre soldiers a one-week assignment away from Northern Ireland to broaden their skills and training. Utilising the worldwide resources of the army, this enabled the Ulster-based soldiers to undergo adventure training or live with other units as far apart as Wales and Belize. Bray's philosophy recognised the need for an element of unwinding from the constant strains at home. 'Hills by day and pubs by night,' he instructed the departing soldiers.

Compared with virtually all of his predecessors, Bray maintained a high public profile, regularly stretching the content of his public pronouncements to breaking point and even beyond the bounds defined by his more discreet military and political superiors. In August 1988, in a typical outburst, he stated that the IRA would be defeated.

> We are going to win this campaign not by military means alone but by a combination of social, political, economic and security measures. It is going to take a long time but time is on our side and I will tell you why I believe that we are going to win. Sinn Fein and the IRA have no credible policy to offer the people of Ulster. Violence is extremely unattractive to the vast majority of decent people and the vast majority of people in Ulster are very decent.

When any criticism of the Regiment was aired he would fire off letters to the newspaper concerned and frequently contact the complainant direct to clear the air, as he saw it. He was particularly exasperated by the attitude of the SDLP towards the UDR. Indeed he actually believed that the SDLP exploited every opportunity to worsen the UDR relationship with the

Catholic community. In 1989, Seamus Mallon complained to the Ministry of Defence about a UDR briefing given to a visiting all-party group of MPs. One of them, a Labour member, also complained that during a slide presentation, one of the illustrations showed a boy with a football talking to a soldier and the critical commentary asserted that the SDLP had used the UDR as a 'political football'. Mr Archie Hamilton, the Armed Forces Minister, later conceded that the briefing had been revised and the UDR hierarchy reminded of the need for balance in such presentations.

To his credit, Bray, with the support of Lieutenant-General Sir Robert Pascoe, the GOC Northern Ireland at the time, made some genuine efforts to clarify the long-blurred line between the UDR and the world of Loyalist paramilitaries. In a speech to recruits in May 1988, Pascoe told the Regiment that it must 'exercise self-control and self-discipline, not over-react or take the law into its own hands'.

Bray took the view that the UDR provided a way for people concerned about terrorism and disorder to do something positive about it. 'The only legal, military way that a citizen can support government policy is to join the UDR. It meets a requirement in the democratic framework that government ignores at its peril. Without the UDR, the government is inviting people to take the law into their own hands,' he said.

During his command, a six-month monitoring programme of all 6,500 UDR soldiers was introduced to ensure that they had no links with paramilitary organisations. In addition an out-of-bounds list was compiled and circulated throughout the Regiment. This detailed premises, notably notorious Loyalist drinking clubs in Belfast, and UDR members were warned by Bray that they would be 'severely disciplined and likely sacked' if they were found to have breached the order. Bray believed that the prime responsibility for detecting the 'rotten apples' had to be borne by the officers of the UDR, using the chain of command to keep tabs on those lower down. He was particularly concerned about 'tribal loyalty' among colleagues, leading to suspicious activity not being reported and the dangers of the confused political situation in which the UDR had to operate, putting soldiers unwittingly at risk from association with relatives or acquaintances whose own activities were questionable.

At about the same time a formal code of practice, similar to one applicable to the RUC, was drawn up and introduced. It was designed to lay down standards of behaviour expected of UDR soldiers, both on and off duty. In April 1988, Bray expressed himself satisfied with the results of the first six-monthly monitoring process.

> In consultation with every commanding officer of each battalion, I go through his list of soldiers to see there are no areas of concern. As a result of doing this for the first time last autumn, I was satisfied that we do not have a problem of association with paramilitary organisations.

When Bray left Northern Ireland in October 1988, he could point to considerable progress. He felt that the balance of half full-time and half part-time soldiers was about right and that the UDR was leaner and fitter with only about a quarter of those applying to join meeting the standards required in the selection and training process. But his dangerously precise assurance about paramilitary links was already discredited, for events were underway within the Regiment which would prove Bray wrong and lead the UDR into further serious embarrassment and disrepute.

Eight members of the Regiment were killed in 1986, three by gunshot wounds, five in explosions. Private Victor Foster, aged 18, died and his girlfriend, also 18, survived, although she lost the sight of her right eye, when an under-car booby-trap blew his vehicle apart outside his home. The other victims were Private John Farly, Private Thomas Irwin, Private William Pollock, Corporal David Brown (see chapter 4), Private Robert Hill and Private Martin Blaney. In August, Sergeant David Taggart became the first of three UDR soldiers to die by the same gun, when he was killed outside his home in the Shankill area of Belfast. In the city, in June 1987, the other two victims, Private Joseph McIlwaine and Private John Tracey, were murdered within fourteen days of each other. They were among another eight UDR casualties in 1987. The others were: Major George Shaw, Corporal Thomas Oldman, Private William Graham, Captain Ivan Anderson and Privates Stephen Megrath and William Megrath, who died two months apart and were not related.

The first of the twelve UDR victims of 1988 was Captain David Armstrong, who was shot while walking with his girlfriend on a Belfast street by Loyalist gunmen who thought he was a Catholic. The next victims were Private William Stewart and Corporal Alan Johnston (see chapter 4). Privates James Cummings and Frederick Starrett died together when their Land Rover was caught in a massive explosion at security gates in the centre of Belfast. Starrett was a lay preacher in the Free Presbyterian Church and is commemorated by a bible study scholarship in his name. Others killed were: Corporal William Burleigh, Private Edward Gibson, Lance-Corporal Michael Darcy and Lance-Corporal Roy Butler. (The gun used to kill him was taken from one of the two British army corporals, Derek Howes and David Wood, who were attacked by a mob, beaten and shot after straying into the path of an IRA funeral in Andersonstown, Belfast, earlier in the year.) Private Raymond McNicol, killed on his way to work, was buried at Desertcreat, near Cookstown and three times over the next two years his grave was to be desecrated. Private Stephen McKinney was next to die, on 25 September, shot on his way home after completing his last spell of duty, on a three-year engagement with the Regiment. The final casualty of the year was Private John Moreland, a coalman murdered while out on his delivery round.

Scarcely a month after Bray's statement, a Catholic man, Terence McDaid, was shot dead outside his home in North Belfast on 10 May 1988. According to a reliable security source, when news of the shooting and the identity of the victim reached the UDR base at Girdwood Barracks, not far away, a young woman UDR part-timer exclaimed: 'Oh, they've got the wrong man.' Her remark caused concern to some of those who heard it and the woman, Joanne Garvin, aged 21, was quietly put under investigation. Within two weeks she was in the dock at Belfast Magistrates Court, charged jointly with Corporal Cameron Hastie, aged 22, of the 1st Battalion the Royal Scots, with supplying information belonging to the army which was likely to be of use to terrorists. Both later pleaded guilty and were given eighteen-month suspended sentences. Thus the full details of their treachery were not revealed in open court.

What had happened began in Belfast taxis ferrying Garvin between her barracks and home. Some of the drivers had links with the illegal UVF and, when they got to know Garvin, asked her to check out car numbers and provide them with other information. After the murder of a UDR colleague by the IRA, Garvin became deeply embittered and willingly cooperated with the UVF. Her treachery was compounded by Hastie, one of a number of Scottish soldiers, who allegedly provided security material about Republican suspects for the UDA and UVF at the end of a tour of duty in Belfast in April 1988. Hastie gave Garvin some photographs and documents to be delivered through the taxi drivers and these were used to target the man, McDaid, murdered soon afterwards. He was in fact shot in mistake for his brother, who was well known to the security forces and had a terrorist record and convictions for IRA offences. The Garvin affair exposed a web of overlap and cooperation between some UDR members in Belfast and both the UVF and UDA. A major political row ensued some time later when more details of the case emerged and it was discovered that Hastie had not been discharged from his regiment. But by then the case had been overshadowed by much more sinister happenings.

In the early hours of Friday 25 August 1989, Laughlin 'Locky' Maginn, aged 28, was sitting watching television with his wife, Maureen, in the downstairs front room of their house at Lissize

Avenue, Rathfriland, a small County Down market town, Their four children aged from 11 months to 10 years, were all asleep upstairs. Just after 1 am, the glass in the window was suddenly broken, and a burst of shots was directed into the room.

As Maginn, already wounded, ran for the stairs, the gunmen threw a piece of carpet over shards of glass left in the window frame, climbed in and pursued him. Slowed by his injuries, he was cornered on the landing and shot in the hand, arm and chest. As the gunmen escaped in a stolen car, later found burned out a mile away, a neighbour reached Maginn, who was covered in blood and choking. With his wife and children screaming in terror, he died a few minutes later.

During the night a member of the outlawed 'Ulster Freedom Fighters', a *nom de guerre* frequently employed by the UDA, telephoned a Belfast newsroom and said that Maginn had been killed because he was a 'liaison officer' for the Provisional IRA.

It is highly probable that matters could have rested there. Maginn, the 2,754th victim of the Troubles, would merely have joined the long list of sectarian murder casualties, forgotten by all but his family and close friends. Sooner or later, the RUC might have picked up somebody involved in the murder, and in due course secured a scarcely noticed conviction. The question of his supposed IRA activity may never have been satisfactorily resolved.

This time, however, in a propaganda stunt of pyrrhic proportions, the UFF decided to confront its critics, including Protestant politicians and churchmen, who said that it merely killed Catholics at random for reasons of pure bigotry. In attempting to justify the Maginn murder, however, the UFF triggered off a series of far-reaching events that have loosened the hold of the UDA in its Shankill and East Belfast heartlands and, much more significantly, could yet prove to be the very death-knell of the UDR.

Over the weekend after the shooting, Chris Moore, an energetic young reporter with the BBC in Belfast, received a phonecall from a contact within the UFF. On the Sunday night, when he turned up at the rendezvous in a car park, he says that he was taken at gunpoint by masked men to a house near Ballynahinch, Count Down. There he was given a photocopy of an intelligence document and shown others, as well as a video tape, apparently shot inside a security base. All the material, compiled by the security forces and classified as 'confidential' or 'restricted', related to the identities and movements of alleged IRA suspects. Among them was Locky Maginn – 'heavily traced as an IRA suspect', according to the document.

The Maginn family, through their solicitor, Rory McShane, had already vigorously denied the UFF claim. Moreover, in the aftermath of Moore's report, broadcast on 29 August, they now revealed that Locky had been systematically harassed by the security forces and had even been threatened. At police headquarters in Knock and nearby at Stormont Castle, where these facts were well established, the alarm bells were ringing loudly. The Irish authorities were also interested. For months they had been pressing their concern about the harassment of suspects by the security forces. Over a hundred specific complaints had been made, ranging from petty taunting at road checks or during house searches to serious threats against individuals or their families. After the SAS killing of three IRA terrorists planning an atrocity in Gibraltar, there were reports of security force personnel shouting, 'SAS – 3, Provos – nil' in the streets. Now, minority confidence in the police and army was further threatened by these serious disclosures, which appeared to confirm allegations of collusion with the Loyalist murder gangs.

Mistakenly, as events turned out, the culprits at first appeared to be from the RUC. The document, which identified Maginn as an IRA suspect, was said to have been circulated to some three or four hundred police, operating in the South Down area. Finding the paper which had gone astray was considered to be a tall order. What had not been publicly disclosed at that time, but was known to police chiefs and ministers, was that a display cabinet inside the RUC station at Dunmurry, on the outskirts of Belfast, had been forced open earlier in August and other documents, relating to twenty-nine IRA suspects, were also missing.

Hugh Annesley, facing the first real test of his mettle since becoming Chief Constable a few months earlier, decided to be open about the problem and to demonstrate that the RUC would not tolerate such behaviour. He therefore decided to bring in a senior police officer, from another British force, to lead the investigation. On the surface it was a straightforward option. The principle of an apparently independent officer coming in to sort out wrongdoing in another force was well-established within the British police service, but the RUC still had open wounds as a result of a recent outside investigation. John Stalker, then the Deputy Chief Constable of Greater Manchester, had been appointed in 1984 to look into the background of three cases where an RUC anti-terrorist unit had shot six men dead in three incidents. Two years later he was controversially removed from the investigation, alleging that he had been obstructed by the RUC at the same time as allegations, which turned out to be unfounded, were made about his relationship with criminals in Manchester, known as the 'Quality Street Gang'. The RUC have always denied obstructing Stalker and say that his removal was not connected with his investigation.

The legacy of the Stalker affair was therefore a major factor in choosing which outside officer would be brought in this time. The issue struck right at the heart of public confidence in police discretion and confidentiality and the RUC's critics had to be convinced that the investigation would not be a cover-up, but meticulous and thorough.

A quick trawl was carried out through the ranks of Britain's most senior and experienced policemen, those above the rank of assistant chief constable. Most of the high-flyers were rejected outright, for the Ulster job needed a man who had extensive experience as a detective. One who fitted the bill, was John Stevens, the recently appointed Deputy Chief Constable of the Cambridgeshire force, based at Huntingdon, who had come up through the ranks of the Metropolitan Police in London, including a spell with the legendary Flying Squad. After consultation between Annesley and the Chief Constable of Cambridgeshire, Ian Kane, Stevens was appointed. He had a reputation as a shrewd, unflappable and tough detective, precisely the qualities needed for what was going to be a demanding assignment which, if it went wrong, could well ruin his reputation and even end his police career.

So, having recruited his own CID chief, Detective Superintendent Laurence Sherwood, also ex-Flying Squad, as the first member of his team and leaving his wife to cope alone with the bare floorboards and the carpet fitters in his new home, Stevens flew into Belfast for the first time on the evening of Friday 15 September. Over a late supper in RUC headquarters at Knock, on the eastern outskirts of Belfast, the Chief Constable, Hugh Annesley, and other RUC officers, briefed the two English detectives about their task well into the early hours of Saturday morning.

Stevens had quickly grasped the political essentials of his brief, and during a lunchtime photocall at the RUC's front gate, he pledged a thorough and independent investigation. Fears that his work would degenerate into another war of nerves and obstruction between outside investigators and the RUC were quickly dispelled. The Police Federation and the Superintendents Association, who between them represented virtually the entire force, said that their members would be giving full cooperation to the Stevens team.

Annesley underlined the point in a tough statement shortly afterwards.

> The RUC will not tolerate wrong-doing should it be uncovered within its own ranks or flinch from tackling it in any other branch of the security forces or elsewhere in society. Criminality will be dealt with without fear or favour, as has been evidenced by the bringing to justice of a substantial number of both Loyalist and Republican terrorists over many years.

To ensure that his message would reach the widest possible audience, it was published as a sizeable paid-for advertisement in the Belfast newspapers on 21 September. Significantly it was also inserted in the Dublin published *Irish Times*.

Over the next few days, installed in offices on new police premises at Carrickfergus, which once served as a cigarette factory, Stevens set about building his team. At its peak it numbered twenty-two, detectives of all ranks, handpicked from four forces: Cambridgeshire, Surrey, Hampshire and the Metropolitan police. Two were women. Later, a member of the Royal Military Police Special Investigation Branch joined them. Within a short time they had established a computerised incident room at Carrickfergus and another at Huntingdon. Both were fully computerised and linked by secure data transmission lines, utilising HOLMES, the Home Office Linked Major Enquiry System, state-of-the-art software developed to meet police needs in major criminal investigations as a result of serious shortcomings identified during the Yorkshire Ripper case some years earlier. Security at both locations was paramount. Access to the incident rooms was confined to the members of the Stevens team and entry to the computer system was only possible through the use of special passwords. By the time the team started work they had been given three major lines of enquiry to follow: the leak of the security documents identifying Maginn; the theft of other material from the police station at Dunmurry; and the disappearance of a further document from the 3UDR base at Ballykinler.

But over the next month they were engulfed and sidelined by an avalanche of further leaks. Classified security documents were scattered like confetti as widely as the *Sun* newspaper, the *Darlington Northern Echo* and the *Daily Record* in Scotland. Seamus Mallon, the SDLP MP, also produced some. Altogether details and photographs of almost 1,000 male and female terrorist suspects surfaced. These were known officially as 'terrorist recognition aids' – usually photo-montages containing mug-shots of terrorist suspects and a brief description about them or why they were wanted. The documents, usually of the lowest 'Restricted' security classification under the Official Secrets Act, had been passed out in their thousands over the years of the Troubles to police and soldiers operating on the streets. They were sometimes known as 'bingo lists' and the people featured were often called 'players'. Without such documents there would have been little point in deploying patrols and carrying out checks for terrorist suspects, as the security forces would have had no idea for whom they were looking. However, instead of the documents being handed back, as they should have been, some were kept for undoubtedly sinister purposes, but most were retained as no more than souvenirs by soldiers at the end of tours of service in Northern Ireland. In this regard the Stevens team scored an early success. The document published in the *Sun* on 21 September was seized by the police and subjected to forensic examination. Indentations and other marks on it enabled them to trace the origin of the document and its distribution. Within a week, a 21-year-old private, Shaun Cunliffe, serving with the Royal Artillery in West Germany, had been questioned, arrested and brought back to Northern Ireland where, later in March 1990, he was fined £500 for leaking the montages to the *Sun*.

In a bid to stem the rising tide of montage leaks, some 153,000 members of the army, Royal Navy and Royal Air Force, were given a short amnesty, until the end of October 1989, to hand in any unauthorised documents in their possession. From that date a new disciplinary offence of obtaining or having unauthorised possession of security documents, was introduced. The amnesty did not apply to the RUC, whose regulations already covered the situation.

With the heat now firmly on them, Loyalists made two distinct efforts to lay confusing trails for the Stevens investigators and to discredit the RUC, who had carried out a two-hour search of the UDA headquarters in East Belfast on 3 September and removed videos and other documents for examination.

In the first attempt, photo-montages of some twenty-five suspects, provided to the RUC by the Irish police, the Garda Siochana, were pushed through the letterbox at the Belfast home of David McKittrick, the correspondent for the London *Independent*. This was a deliberate attempt to embarrass the Irish authorities, but Dublin did not rise to the bait and said that it would not be allowed to prejudice cross-border security cooperation.

The second episode was a much more elaborate plot. Terry McLaughlin of the *Irish News*, the Belfast morning newspaper mainly read by Catholics, was lured to a city hotel. There he was shown, but not given, sixty-four 'documents' containing the names of 233 people, said to be Republican activists living across the border in Bundoran, Dundalk and Drogheda. McLaughlin was told that the material had been compiled by the 'Inner Circle', a clandestine group extensively organised within the RUC with the twin aims of 'eradicating Republican terrorism' and 'doing all in its power to bring down the Anglo-Irish Agreement'. The spokesman said that there was no way the Stevens enquiry would stop the flow of information to which they had access. The paper devoted the top half of its front page to the hoax on 2 October, creating further controversy and concern.

The RUC sent detectives to interview McLaughlin officially, but the Chief Constable had been assured from the outset by the Special Branch that the claims were groundless and the very next day he publicly and unambiguously dismissed them as 'arrant nonsense'. He was able to do so with such confidence thanks to the work of a secret counter-intelligence unit within the RUC. It had been set up by Sir John Hermon in 1981 after the Central Committee of the Northern Ireland Police Federation had discussed reforming the B Specials and failed to pass a confidence motion in his leadership by one vote. Since then the 'watchers' had become a permanent team who monitored the behaviour of any police officers suspected of being security risks or Loyalist sympathisers.

At a later stage of the investigation, in January 1990, a fire seriously damaged the office complex at Carrickfergus, being used by the team. At first there were fears that the blaze was an arson attack, another attempt to discredit or disrupt the investigation. The Irish Foreign Minister even supported this version of events. It seems, however, that a member of the team had caused the fire by carelessly stubbing out a cigarette in the wastebin close by a desk. The RUC said that forensic tests had clearly established an accidental cause of the fire. When an embarrassed Stevens failed to endorse this, the conspiracy theorists enjoyed a field day. RUC officers were said to have worn out a juke-box playing the Billy Joel song, 'We didn't start the fire', in the presence of members of the Stevens team sharing secure RUC living accommodation while they were working in Northern Ireland.

These other matters, as they were clearly designed to do, succeeded in diverting attention from by far the most sinister events to be examined: those surrounding the Maginn murder. Even before the Stevens team had been formed, the RUC had made some progress with the murder investigation. They had established that some weeks before the killing, a man on a motorcycle had been in the locality asking neighbours about Maginn's movements. From their own intelligence, gained through effective penetration of Loyalist groupings, the RUC had already picked up whispers of a UDR link to the case. Indeed the Special Branch were already following up reports of rogue UDR members residing in the Lisburn area. On 8 September a number of suspects from there were arrested and taken to Gough Barracks, Armagh for questioning. Among them were two UDR soldiers, Privates Andrew Smith and Andrew Brown. On 10 September both were charged with murdering Maginn and remanded in custody. (At the time of writing, the soldiers and a number of other men, are still in custody awaiting trial.)

Even in death Maginn had not been allowed to rest in peace. On 21 November 1989, his grave was dug up and the coffin damaged. The name plate was ripped off as well as a crucifix and efforts had been made to smash it and prise off the lid, probably with spades.

Maginn worked with his father, running a poultry business, and travelled extensively through South Down and Armagh every day delivering chickens to shops and restaurants. According to those who knew him, he was 'a big, strong, strapping country fella'. They say he was straight talking, head-strong, undiplomatic and not easily cowed. He was more than prepared to defend his corner. These friends deny he was involved with the IRA but say that, because of some of the company he kept, they can well understand why the police should think he was.

According to his mother, speaking on the BBC *Panorama* programme in February 1990, the cycle of harassment which culminated in Locky Maginn's death began when he was arrested in September 1981, aged 20. After his release, she said:

> He was very pale and very quiet and I asked him what was the matter. He told me that the police had blackmailed him – what they called blackmailed – offered him money, for him to infiltrate, to get into the IRA and become an informer. He was very, very frightened, very frightened, scared, very scared.

In fact Maginn made his wife write down his account of what the police said to him.

> If I did not do it [become an informer] they said that the UDR and police would harass me all the time. They said that they would put the word around that I was in the IRA. They said that there are plenty of good Loyalist Protestants who would like to take a shot at me if they thought I was involved in the IRA.

Events in the last two years of his life seem to sustain Maginn's version of the threats that were made against him. According to the record kept by Rory McShane, Maginn was constantly being stopped and prosecuted for a variety of offences. On 20 May 1986 he was stopped at Rostrevor and subsequently prosecuted for having no Public Service Vehicle certificate and failing to produce his driving licence and insurance certificate.

The next month he was in trouble again, this time for failing to notify the change of ownership of a car. In May 1987, after he disturbed three men interfering with his car outside his house, a row developed. Maginn was eventually charged and the men were produced as crown witnesses against him. The list continues with a series of traffic offences. Often he was prosecuted for failing to report to the police station with his documents after being stopped at checkpoints or booked for having no road tax. He stopped going to the station because he was only delayed or further harassed when he did so, said McShane. More than once they made him empty the contents of his vehicle, including his poultry, and then left him standing by the side of the road to reload as they drove away. Once, in June 1987, he was even stopped and searched three times in the length of three hundred yards, by two patrols of Royal Marines. In August 1989, two days before his death, he was disqualified from driving for three years after being convicted of further offences, including failure to produce his driving licence and insurance certificate. Only a few days earlier, on the way back from a day out to Butlins holiday camp with the children, his wife had finally persuaded him to move over the border to the South and settle there, to get away from the mounting trouble he faced in the North.

During all of this time, and before, he was never questioned, charged or convicted in connection with any terrorist-type offence. Only once, in August 1988, had he been taken into custody. Held at Gough Barracks, Armagh for two days, his clothes were taken away for examination but he was released without charge and they were later returned.

It was a few months after this that the incident took place which frightened Maginn the most. On 9 November at about 1.30 pm, he was stopped by a UDR patrol at the Cove Bar, between Hilltown and Newry. During the encounter, one of the soldiers said to him: 'I have a wee word of warning. I will stiff you when I get the chance.' In the argot of the Northern Ireland Troubles, the word 'stiff' had become a verb, meaning to kill.

McShane recalls that the incident caused Maginn great

concern and distress. 'He was very nervous, very agitated, very concerned and he asked us to write in specific terms outlining the exact words of the threat that had been made against him.' So on 14 November, five days after the incident, McShane wrote a formal letter of complaint to the UDR, drawing attention to the incident and the unwarranted frequency with which his client was being stopped and checked by the Regiment. The UDR replied on 18 January 1989 admitting that Maginn had indeed been stopped, that he was searched and had his identity checked. They denied that he was threatened and said that he had been treated courteously at all times.

The Stevens team set about tracing the official record of how Maginn had been treated. The papers concerning the prosecutions yielded some details of the dates, times and locations where he had been stopped. Patrol records and reports provided further information. Most detailed of all were the print-outs from 'Vengeful', the sophisticated computer system, used to monitor the movements of suspect and stolen vehicles, which contains the registrations of every vehicle in Northern Ireland. Within seven seconds a security patrol anywhere in Ulster can verify any vehicle. The computer also records details of each time any vehicle passes through certain fixed points like Belfast airport and the permanent border checkpoints, or is stopped and checked by a patrol.

While this work was going on, another section of the Stevens team was following up the Dunmurry police station thefts. It had been established that the two display cabinets in the station had been forced open and the montages removed between 11 and 14 August 1989. This period coincided with the twentieth anniversary of the British army being deployed to help keep the peace in Northern Ireland. Accordingly, with many demonstrations planned and the threat of a major IRA atrocity to mark the anniversary, the security forces were on full alert. Dunmurry, located on the fringe of the IRA's West Belfast heartland, provided an ideal location to hold reserve units. So, during the days in question, far more than the usual number of personnel had been in the station, making it highly difficult for the Stevens team to narrow the scope of their suspect list. Undeterred, they traced the identities of detachments of police present during the period and began the arduous process of interviewing each one. Several hundred RUC officers were involved and every statement was filed in the Holmes system and cross-referenced.

Before long, the Stevens collators recognised a clear pattern developing in their investigation. The Ballykinler document incident was soon seen to be an isolated red herring – it had been removed from a drawer to get a soldier into trouble. To their surprise, however, the lines of enquiry from both the Maginn and Dunmurry investigations had begun to converge and point in the same direction, towards one company of 7/10UDR, based at Palace Barracks, Holywood, just outside Belfast.

At first the Stevens team were suspicious and feared that they were being sidetracked deliberately, just like they had been over the 'Inner Circle'. At that time, it was still the conventional wisdom that rogue policemen rather than UDR soldiers were to blame for the most sinister leaks. Every shred of evidence was therefore re-examined and re-evaluated, but the more the work progressed the more positive were the grounds for suspicion of the UDR.

The RUC Special Branch already harboured their own suspicions about 7/10UDR, the same unit from which a colour-sergeant, John Fletcher, had absconded and sold eighteen weapons to the UDA in August 1986 (see chapter 5). Accordingly, the decision was taken that every soldier currently in it would be subjected to intensive vetting. What was turned up was later described by one senior police officer as 'a can of worms'.

As a result of the screening of the soldiers, an arrest list was drawn up. The Stevens team had no powers of arrest in Northern Ireland, so a major swoop was planned with the RUC to carry it out. Some sources say that the team wanted to lift a hundred UDR soldiers, the entire company concerned, and were pressed to scale it down. In the event, in the early hours of

8 October, the top secret swoops took place. Twenty-eight UDR soldiers were taken into custody and their homes were searched. John Cope, the Northern Ireland Security Minister, later estimated, in a parliamentary answer, that the operation, involving 334 RUC officers, had cost £45,000.

The operation provoked strong anger from Unionist politicians. Ken Maginnis, once again the champion of the UDR, criticised the way in which the personal security of the officers had been compromised. Until the swoops, even their neighbours did not know that some of the men were in the UDR. As a result of their exposure, ten of them, who were released without charge after being questioned, subsequently moved home, with financial help from the funds provided by the government to assist members of the security forces compromised by the terrorist threat.

There was criticism, too, of the apparently trivial extent of UDR wrongdoing exposed by the Stevens investigation as a result of their comprehensive operation. Of the twenty-eight suspects, eight were released without charge; a further nine, reported to the Director of Public Prosecutions for a variety of firearms and ammunition irregularities, had no further action taken against them; three other soldiers were found guilty of similar offences and given absolute discharges; four more were fined £50 and another £100 for breaches of the Firearms (Northern Ireland) Order, 1981, while only three faced serious charges and were imprisoned. Stephen Harris and Wallace Andrews were each given twelve months for the theft of the montages from RUC Dunmurry. In the most serious case, Edward Stewart was given ten years. He turned out to be an armourer, supplying and servicing weapons for the UDA.

The Stevens team shrugged off the criticism and, in so doing, were vigorously supported by the RUC. There was no way in which they could achieve the necessary element of surprise by giving any warning of their intentions of inviting the soldiers to attend for interview. Even if they had been apprehended, coming or going for duty, to protect their security as the critics suggested, it would still have been necessary to search their homes. Despite the recriminations of some UDR people, the RUC has not demurred in its support for the operation. Indeed, the army itself recognised that if there was a UDR boil, the sooner it was lanced the better. For that reason, there was no criticism from the headquarters at Lisburn, who cooperated thoroughly as the saga unfolded.

Eight months after beginning work, the Stevens team finally submitted their report to Annesley. Alongside the results of their criminal investigation, the weighty volume contained eighty-three specific recommendations, some general, some applying to the RUC, others to the army and a number exclusively to the UDR. The full worrying report was not published, but in May 1990, a security-sanitised summary was. Reading between the lines it paints a far from flattering picture of the conduct and accountability of the UDR, clearly reflecting what Stevens judged to be a highly unsatisfactory state of affairs. The authorities have so far managed to conceal the extent of the scandalous irregularities exposed by Stevens. The implications of his hard-hitting report have also been seriously underestimated, for they impose a large question mark over the effectiveness of the UDR's structure and management in the past. It also raises doubts about the future role and existence of the Regiment. Fundamental organisational recommendations included the need to ensure that UDR duty rosters were accurate, that unofficial notebooks should be banned and that official notebooks, to be retained for a specified period, should be introduced. He also called for a review of personal protection weapon training and security, a series of measures made necessary by the difficulties which the Stevens team had encountered in the Maginn and Dunmurry enquiries and the lesson which they drew from the big swoop they had made.

Twenty years exactly from the raising of the Regiment, and many controversies on, Stevens finally confronted the long-standing ambiguity governing the UDR and Loyalist paramilitarism. The UDR should agree on the definition of a paramilitary organisation, he said. Soldiers should be required to make a declaration that they would not be members of such organisations and they should also compulsorily disclose any family membership.

Other recommendations were designed to improve the calibre of soldier being accepted into the Regiment. The report said that the vetting and screening system employed to monitor UDR membership was deficient and under-staffed and called for higher recruitment and monitoring standards for the UDR, comparable with those applying to the RUC. It suggested that there should also be far greater police involvement in the process.

In particular, Stevens said that there needed to be a review of the screening and vetting specifications and for senior police and army officers to discuss cases where adverse police vetting reports are received about UDR members and recruits. Referees nominated by applicants were to be interviewed, while all applicants should be subjected to a security interview. While the army would have the final say on who was recruited into the UDR, the RUC was to be more fully and formally integrated into the selection process.

Extending beyond that part of the report which focused exclusively on the UDR, its most important recommendation was that, in future, all intelligence material relating to terrorist suspects should be subject to rigorous audit and accountability. Its most startling admission was that applicants for the Ulster Defence Regiment who had received adverse police vetting reports, were nevertheless recruited into the Regiment and went on to commit terrorist-related and criminal offences while in service.

The report also confirmed that some members of the security forces did pass classified intelligence information to Loyalists and criticised the serious lack of controls and adequate accounting procedures to protect sensitive documents. However, Stevens reported that while there was a degree of collusion, 'it is restricted to a small number of individuals, who have gravely abused their positions of trust' and he stressed that the abuse was 'not widespread or institutionalised'. Stevens defined the dilemma for the security forces as finding a way for them to be properly informed and operationally effective without compromising restricted information. 'It must be acknowledged in the present climate that leakages of information from the security forces may never be completely eliminated,' he said. 'However, if the measures recommended in respect of the police, the army and other organisations are introduced, then there is every hope that future collusion between the security forces and paramilitary groups will be eradicated.'

The Stevens enquiry took written statements from 1,900 witnesses, followed 2,000 lines of investigation and expended 2,000 man hours interviewing detained persons. They recovered 2,600 documents, most of them having originated in the security forces. 'A complex network of intelligence of all types was uncovered, involving the supply and exchange of information between Loyalist paramilitary groups, with the Ulster Defence Association at the centre,' the report said. The security force documents were all of the lowest security classification, 'Restricted', and dated from the 1970s. The most recent document recovered was prepared in June 1988. All the material gathered during the enquiry and recorded by HOLMES totalled 96,000 cross-referenced entries.

During its course, the report said, ninety-four people were arrested, with fifty-nine subsequently being charged with offences under the Prevention of Terrorism, Official Secrets and Firearms Acts. No RUC officers were charged but a report concerning two of them was submitted to the DPP, who decided that no further action should be taken.

One of Stevens's main suggestions affecting the RUC, the formation of a special Anti-Terrorist detective unit, was quickly discounted by Annesley, who said that this was impracticable in the Northern Ireland context. He pointed out that in 1989, on the British mainland, there had been twenty-three terrorist incidents requiring detailed scenes of crime examination lasting from three days to three weeks. In the same period in Ulster there were 1,655 similar terrorist incidents. Mr Annesley said that in terms of logistics, personnel and containment, the same approach was not viable for the RUC. However, another Stevens suggestion to set up a Serious Crimes Unit for the RUC, pulling together the range of scientific support services, fingerprints, forensic science and photography into a single expert unit, was already under way. A major shake-up of the RUC's fingerprint bureau was also foreshadowed with more staff, better, modern equipment and advanced training.

Stevens called for better accounting and supervision of intelligence systems and new procedures to restrict the production of intelligence documentation. He also suggested that there should be strict controls over the dissemination and handling of documents, recommendations which would ensure that those responsible for passing confidential information could easily be traced and held criminally responsible. He was highly critical of the ease with which a small number of individuals were able to avoid discovery while illegally trafficking security force documents because of inadequate security procedures.

Annesley revealed that all intelligence documents are now numbered so that they can be readily checked and accounted for. He also demonstrated how police collators' bulletins, containing information about terrorist suspects to brief police and troops on security duties, are now printed on sensitised paper which produces only a black sheet if it is photocopied.

Tighter controls over the use of photocopiers, access to computer systems, especially the central vehicle index, and more secure storage methods for sensitive documents were put in hand as a result of the report and have since been introduced. Intelligence bulletins were also given more limited circulation within the security forces with nominated officers being made responsible for keeping records safe.

Annesley reacted strongly to criticism that the Stevens investigation was flawed because it had not uncovered evidence of wrongdoing within the RUC itself. Describing that as a 'regretful and unjustified innuendo', Annesley said that 'the RUC is entitled to the same standard of justice as anyone else. Unless there is evidence, as opposed to speculation, of wrongdoing, then my officers are entitled to the virtue of innocence'.

The Chief Constable also paid tribute to the UDR who, he said,

> have been subjected to a level of wholesale denigration that is simply not justified. I think the UDR does an exceptional job in this province and the RUC simply could not operate effectively without them. It is, I think, particularly poignant that whilst the whole Regiment is being criticised in a catch-all way, their members, like my own officers, are being murdered by terrorists as they perform their duty on behalf of the whole population of Northern Ireland.

During the course of the investigation a number of soldiers were dismissed from the Regiment as security risks. The army would not reveal exactly how many, saying only that the number was 'small'. The Labour spokesman on Northern Ireland, Kevin McNamara, pursued this issue with Archie Hamilton, the Minister of State for the Armed Forces. His reply, in August 1990, provided little specific information other than to say the 'small number' of people concerned, who had civil convictions (motoring offences and the like) or tenuous connections with others believed to be associated with extremist organisations, would not be allowed into the Regiment under the new, more stringent guidelines now in force. Hamilton admitted that in six cases, which he did not identify in detail, soldiers subject to adverse police vetting reports, had gone on to commit criminal offences, including the theft of documents, assault and possession of firearms. The minister said that 'nothing has come to light which alters our judgement that the UDR is fundamentally sound'. The dismissals were, however, some evidence of a crackdown on those who act with what is called 'misguided patriotism', sometimes members of the UDR who live in areas where it is hard to avoid association with members of Loyalist groups, or are pressurised through money trouble, sex or drinking problems into passing information.

All 6,300 members of the Regiment are still subject to six-monthly screening by their battalion commanding officer. One of his staff is specifically charged with looking for danger signals among the soldiers, money worries, family problems, signs of stress, which might indicate trouble. The Regiment is also stepping up its welfare activities to help soldiers with personal problems, whether or not there is a security dimension to them.

The army says that unlike the police, it does not always rule out recruiting those with criminal records. Sometimes the offence is a minor one, or happened when the person was a juvenile, or the army decides that the applicant has rehabilitated himself. They say that two-thirds of those adversely vetted by the police are in fact rejected.

UDR sources say that the Regiment is more offended than outsiders when it finds members who transgress and bring it into disrepute. They insist that the commitment to cleaning up the UDR is stronger inside the Regiment than among even its most critical opponents outside.

The UDR and the implications of the Stevens Report for the Regiment still figure on the Anglo-Irish Conference agenda and Dublin still believes that all UDR patrols should be accompanied by members of the RUC and that there should be a fundamental review of the UDR role leading to disbandment.

The British government is prepared to clean up the UDR, as suggested by Stevens, but that is as far as it will go. Peter Brooke, the Northern Ireland Secretary, has made it clear that he does not share the 'whole barrel is rotten' position of Collins, the Irish Foreign Minister. He believes there may be some rotten apples to be removed from the barrel. Army and police commanders share this view.

Meanwhile, through the spring and summer of 1991, the last acts of the Stevens enquiry are still being played out in the courts of Northern Ireland. Those awaiting trial include several prominent members of the UDA in Belfast and Londonderry as well as a man feared to be an ex-informer, who, it is feared, may expose the inner secrets of the Loyalist paramilitaries.

Stevens was forced to defend his team against 'unjustified and unwarranted comments' about his work in Northern Ireland after the withdrawal of charges against five prominent Loyalists at Belfast Magistrates Court in October 1990. He said that it would be improper for him to enter into public discussion of these matters. 'I hope the public will understand that I am restricted in what I may say because many matters which are the subject of my investigation are still to be decided by the courts.' The measured tone of the statement concealed a fair degree of resentment, not only by Stevens, but in the RUC as well, at the storm of criticism that broke around them after five men, leading members of the Ulster Defence Association, were released when charges concerned with the illegal possession of confidential police documents were withdrawn.

The row reflected the core problem in fighting terrorism in Northern Ireland, which is that the police all too often cannot substantiate charges brought against suspects because of insufficient evidence. Police say that in many cases witnesses are threatened, corroborative evidence is rarely available, suspects refuse to make statements and forensic evidence is often inconclusive or inadequate to secure conviction.

Stevens was forced to learn, like the unfortunate John Stalker before him, that it is the supreme test of the professionalism of any mainland police officer to work in Northern Ireland and emerge unscathed from the all-engulfing maelstrom of political controversy.

Nevertheless, Stevens has emerged with his reputation not only intact, but enhanced, and the RUC has shown that it too is the enemy of all those who break the law. The report stands as a telling indictment of the UDR and the way in which it has been run for many years. Despite all that has happened to the Regiment during that time, and the repeated assurances from government and commanders about its accountability and integrity, Stevens has exposed alarming complacency and shown that the problem has merely been tinkered with.

7 The Future: An Instrument of Peace?

The Protestant majority in Ulster have watched these developments with mounting concern. Ken Maginnis fears that the Regiment is being subjected to a 'well orchestrated and cleverly coordinated campaign of vilification and complaints'. He is not alone in drawing a parallel with the last days of the B Specials. Back in October 1989, as the Irish government began pressing their campaign for UDR reform, the Reverend Ian Paisley and some of his closest supporters made a midnight journey to Dublin to paste 'Hands off the UDR' posters on the pillars of the General Post Office in O'Connell Street, Dublin, scene of the 1916 Rising. A few days later, Paisley met John Cope, the Northern Ireland Security Minister, on the same shuttle flight from London to Belfast. 'I told him in no uncertain terms that if the UDR was sacrificed he would be dragged to the nearest lamp post with a rope.'

In November 1990, a team of researchers from the Centre for the Study of Conflict, at the University of Ulster, published the results of a comprehensive two-year research project on the impact of political violence on three representative communities in Northern Ireland. The areas were given the fictional names of Ballygelvin, Daviestown and Glenbarr and they were chosen by religious make up and urban/rural locations to provide an accurate cross-section of Northern Ireland attitudes and opinion. The researchers' findings did not make encouraging reading for the UDR, for they showed that even in the opinion of some Protestants the Regiment was regarded as being biased against Catholics.

Of the Catholics questioned during the survey, only 16 per

cent thought that the UDR treated Catholics and Protestants equally. According to 38.9 per cent, the RUC was even handed, and so too was the army, said 67 per cent. The UDR was in fact regarded as very biased against Catholics by 36.2 per cent of the sample, while another 29.8 per cent believed that they were a bit biased.

In Glenbarr, for example, while half of the Catholics predictably thought that the UDR was very biased against them, it was highly surprising to find that 42.5 per cent of the Protestants also believed that the Regiment was either a bit or very biased against the Catholics. In Daviestown, 15.3 per cent of the Protestant sample believed that the UDR showed anti-Catholic bias.

The survey produced further anecdotal evidence of the way in which the Regiment is seen by the two communities. Protestants in Daviestown thought that the UDR often gave local Catholics 'a lot of trouble' and were prepared to excuse any subsequent shortcomings in the behaviour of the Catholics. Catholics reported feeling insulted when neighbours on UDR duty, for instance at roadblocks, refused to acknowledge that they were known to them. This was seen to be cutting across traditional rural relationships and setting neighbour against neighbour. Generally, the survey confirmed the overwhelming and usually uncritical support for the UDR among Protestants and the deep-seated mistrust and suspicion with which Catholics regard it.

A BBC *Panorama* programme on 19 February 1990 contributed more doubts about the internal culture of the UDR and both its willingness and ability to meet the standards of behaviour and impartiality which it publicly proclaimed for itself. The reporter, John Ware, uncovered the case of a soldier who had three times assaulted Catholics with his rifle and boot, causing the Ministry of Defence to pay out £1,300 in damages. None of the incidents was recorded on the man's service record and he remained a member of the Regiment. (A short time after the transmission of the programme, he was badly injured when a booby-trap bomb exploded under his car.)

In another case, soldiers harassed the key witness to an assault on a Catholic at a checkpoint before the case came to court, although, in this instance, the soldier was dismissed from the Regiment after being convicted.

Ware also obtained a notebook used by a soldier which contained the names and details of 281 terrorist suspects, all Republicans. Brigadier Charles Ritchie, a Royal Scot who had once been ADC to the Governor of Victoria in Australia and had taken over command of the Regiment from Bray in October 1988, gave an unimpressive performance defending the Regiment, on the *Panorama* programme. He admitted that UDR soldiers were not given extensive briefings on Protestant suspects. 'The difference being that the RUC are happy to deal with Protestant extremist terrorism.'

The programme again highlighted the rift between the British and Irish governments over the future of the Regiment. The Irish Foreign Minister accused Britain of a breach of faith over the 1985 undertaking to have every UDR patrol accompanied by a policeman. Throughout the early part of 1991, in the aftermath of the Stevens Report, the *Panorama* programme and the passage through the courts of cases arising from Stevens, the Dublin government has been gathering its evidence for a major push to secure fundamental reform, if not the disbandment of, the UDR. The SDLP, if anything, has adopted a tougher posture: 'Let the government face up to the fact that there is not going to be a solution to the Northern Ireland problem of which the UDR forms a part,' said the Newry and Armagh MP, Seamus Mallon.

Lord Hunt joined in the controversy after the *Panorama* programme, again repeating the view that the UDR had failed to meet the objectives set for it and should now be disbanded.

In the early months of 1991, Northern Ireland was once more approaching a political watershed. After fifteen months of 'talks about talks', Peter Brooke, the diligent and persevering Northern Ireland Secretary since July 1989, persuaded the political parties to participate in a new round of negotiations.

This time the ambitious plan was to address not only the creation of a political institution to provide better government for Northern Ireland, but also to build a formal mechanism for cross-border political cooperation with the Irish Republic. A third strand to the talks between the British and Irish governments, was designed to create a Mark Two Anglo-Irish Agreement to underpin the new arrangements. Without underestimating the historical and fundamental political obstacles which have to be overcome, the omens for success are better than they have been for many years. As Dr Cahal Daly said at Armagh in December 1990, during his enthronement as the Catholic primate of all-Ireland: 'There is a sense of newness in the air in our country at this time. There is an intimation of a new future, of new possibilities and of new beginnings.'

At the same time, there was growing evidence of a fundamental rethink of security policy inside Stormont Castle. For the first time, a detailed 'Statement of Security Policy' was published in November 1990 (see Appendix). This laid out a framework of objectives, procedures and values which promised, with elaboration and implementation, to lay a solid foundation for a new era of confident relations between the security forces and the entire community. Dr Brian Mawhinney, the Minister of State at the Northern Ireland Office, a blunt Ulsterman with a finely tuned appreciation of local sensitivities, had also launched a drive to improve community relations. He knew that the effects of security activity heavily influenced the prospects for political progress and better community relations and, with the support of Brooke, he was in the forefront of a policy to inject new thinking into the making and implementing of law-and-order policy consistent with the new guidelines.

The early signs were encouraging. After the introduction of the 'human bomb' attacks by the IRA in late 1990, which involved victims, tied into a vehicle carrying a bomb, being forced to drive it into a security post while members of their family were held hostage, tactics were reviewed. In particular, the safety of and need for the sixteen permanent checkpoints along the border was rethought. Increasingly, operational strategy was taking account of the need to avoid risking police and military lives in all but the most pressing circumstances. As a result two of the most vulnerable checkpoints on the border were closed in 1991 and the future of others was uncertain.

The government was simultaneously pushing a new Emergency Provisions Act through Parliament. Here too there was evidence of new thinking. Tough, by their own admission, draconian powers were taken to help deal with the growing problem of racketeering and extortion being used to finance terrorism. But the bill also included new arrangements to introduce, for the first time, an element of independent supervision of the way complaints from the public about the conduct of the army, including the UDR, were investigated and resolved. But in the aftermath of the Stevens Report and with the UDR topping the Irish agenda in the inter-governmental relationship, the Regiment remains the fundamental security issue. What then is its future?

There is little public sign that despite the controversy in which it is now permanently shrouded, the UDR is in any official disfavour. Peter Brooke has several times paid fulsome tribute to its bravery and fortitude. During the summer of 1991, the UDR is set to receive the distinction of the award of Queen's and Regimental colours, with ceremonies planned for the first four of the UDR battalions to receive them. The practice goes back to the days of early man, who fixed his family badge to a pole and held it aloft in battle for the dual purpose of indicating his position and acting as a rallying point should the need arise. Medieval chivalry followed the same idea when armorial bearings were placed on their banners so that these could be seen well above the mêlée. When armies began to adopt a system of regimentation at the beginning of the seventeenth century, each company was allotted a colour, a custom which has persisted. The first battalions to receive colours will be 1/9 and 2UDR, and London embroiderers have been commissioned to produce the intricate banners which feature the Regimental harp and crown crest.

In considering the future of the Regiment, from the outset it has to be understood that the Regiment presently provides a cost-effective and vital component of the shield against terrorism in Northern Ireland. During each of recent years, the Permanent Cadre soldiers of the UDR have put in some nine million man hours. Guidelines laid down by the GOC say that they should work a sixty-hour week and spend no more then one night in four out of bed. In fact they are regularly clocking-up working weeks in excess of seventy hours and missing one night's sleep in every three. The part-timers show equal dedication. They have accumulated some four million man hours, twice the total laid down if they were only to complete minimum duties. In fact the Regimental organisation heavily depends on the willingness of many part-timers to put in the equivalent of a full working week. Thus the Regiment can field 1,000 patrols a week in support of the RUC. From the government's point of view the UDR is good value for money. It costs just over £1m a week to run it. By contrast the RUC now costs almost £1.5m a day.

However, getting the troops off the streets in Northern Ireland would be the biggest contribution to making the place appear a 'normal' community again. In this day and age, particularly in Northern Ireland, even armed police are more acceptable than soldiers. Apart from helicopter provision and bomb disposal, the range of military tasks performed by the army and UDR could be readily taken over by the RUC, suitably expanded and with adequate resources. Government should therefore be prepared to define this as a public policy objective with private goals and timetables. These should be flexible and attainable within the dictates of the security situation on the ground and remain private to avoid setting targets for terrorists to aim at and dislodge. The speed with which the RUC could recruit, train and deploy sufficient officers would also be a factor in the equation. But as long as such a policy remains a vague sentiment rather than a defined objective, there is no incentive to make progress.

Finding an alternative role for the regulars is no problem. They can be redeployed to the British army of the Rhine or garrisons in Britain, training in readiness for the next outbreak of international disorder. Given that the UDR is by law and training only for use in Northern Ireland, it would seem that the only practical option is disbandment. Those who meet the rigorous conditions and are suitable in all respects, should be given encouragement to join the RUC and RUC Reserve. There are many fine people in the UDR who could play an equally, if not more, fulfilling role in protecting and serving the community as police officers. Their military skills would be no disadvantage. The army might find places for some, especially the young officers of the UDR, who would prefer a military career. Others might find an outlet in the territorial army and the UDR name might even be continued by converting it into a home defence role within the overall army organisation.

None of this could happen overnight. It takes a year to recruit and train a police officer. The RUC badly needs improved and expanded training facilities. There would need to be a high degree of reassurance for the Protestant community that they were not being left defenceless or being politically betrayed. What then could be done in the short term?

The key issue is to increase confidence in the UDR by making it more accountable and more sensitive to the community, especially the minority. There are a number of practical steps which could be taken.

The army throws a protective arm around the beseiged UDR and seeks to avoid it being singled out. Such an attitude is counter-productive. The UDR is a special case and unique within the army. It should be accepted that it may be treated differently for its own good.

Since the formation of the UDR, the GOC has appointed a six-strong UDR Advisory Council, three Catholics and three Protestants. This body has been virtually invisible and, for understandable reasons, the Catholics who have bravely served on it, have been anxious to keep it that way. There is a parallel with the Police Authority, whose membership prefers to remain anonymous. However, at this particular point, like those actually in the Regiment, Northern Ireland needs people to stand up and be counted. The UDR Advisory Council should be given a new, public lease of life to campaign for the reputation of the Regiment and liaise with its critics. Its members should speak out and, where necessary, criticise constructively, and the UDR itself should take note and act.

The role of the Independent Commission for Police Complaints should be widened so that any complaint against any arm of the security forces would be handled by one body and the investigation supervised. The Commission should also have the power to instigate investigations, in the public interest, or at the request of the Chief Constable or GOC. This would go a long way to creating in the community a feeling that the great security monolith is accountable and that there is some redress available.

UDR soldiers should wear numbers, clearly and prominently, like the police. This would not compromise their personal security, and would help prevent frivolous or vexatious complaints as well as making the Regiment more accountable. The army have long rejected this move but it is absolutely vital to improving relations between members of the Regiment and the public.

The UDR Code of Practice, like the RUC Code of Conduct, should be published and the Regiment should publish an annual report, like the police, providing the same range of information about the policy and performance of the UDR during the year under review.

Where possible the RUC should accompany UDR patrols and reduce the public's contact with them to a minimum, especially in those traditional and easily identified flashpoint areas.

Training within the Regiment, even more than it does already, should include 'human awareness' lectures and role-playing exercises to increase the confidence of the soldiers and teach them how to interact with the public more effectively.

None of these suggestions will magically transform either the reputation of the Regiment or the ingrained attitudes towards it. Pending a strategic solution to the question of its future role, they would, however, improve its tactical image.

The continued toll of casualties again underlines the price the community still asks the UDR to pay.

The Regiment suffered its lowest casualty rate in 1989 with only two victims: Private Thomas Hardy and Lance-Corporal David Halligan. The killing resumed in 1990 with eight casualties: Private Olven Kilpatrick, Sergeant Thomas Jamison, Private Colin McCullough, shot dead while sitting in his car with his girlfriend, and Colour-Sergeant Albert Cooper. Four died in a single incident when a 1,000 lb landmine was exploded in the path of a Land Rover at Downpatrick, County Down. They were Lance-Corporal John Bradley and Privates Steven Smart, John Birch and Michael Adams. A member of another vehicle, which missed the full force of the explosion later told the coroner that he had been so sickened at the sight of the bodies of his comrades that he had since been receiving psychiatric help. In March 1991, two UDR soldiers died when a propelled mortar devastated their Land Rover while it was stopped at traffic lights on the outskirts of Armagh. Private Paul Sutcliffe, who had joined the UDR to stay in Northern Ireland after serving with the regular army, died instantly. Private Roger Love died in hospital later and his kidneys were used to save the life of a child. The ashes of the other soldier, at his request, were scattered in the Mourne Mountains.

These deaths, like all those before, also emphasise the futility of violence as a way to solve the problems of Northern Ireland. In a message to the Regiment on the twenty-first anniversary of its formation, when about 190 serving members and forty-five ex-soldiers had been killed, the present commander, Brigadier Angus Ramsay, who joined the UDR in December 1990 after a tour of duty at the cabinet office in London, said:

> The great strength of the Ulster Regiment still stems from its members: ordinary, decent, caring citizens, who see what terrorism does to the country and who decide to play a part in its defeat. After

twenty-one years, many murders and injuries and much intimidation, that spirit of serving the country remains constant in members from all sections of the community; living and working under constant threat, they perform their duties with courage and steadfastness and deserve the support of every decent citizen of Northern Ireland. For Roman Catholic recruits especially, there is always a warm and admiring welcome in the Ulster Defence Regiment.

The Brigadier's anniversary statement coincided with a call from Dr Cahal Daly, the Catholic primate of all Ireland, for the security chiefs to rethink the policy of deploying the UDR in Catholic areas. Pointing out that the Regiment was drawn almost exclusively from the Unionist and Loyalist community, the Archbishop said: 'As a result, their encounter in a security role with a Nationalist community is seen and cannot but be seen as pitting one community against the other.' Dr Daly said that, 'for peaceful, Nationalist civilians it is humiliating, it is vexatious, it is provocative, to be repeatedly delayed, kept late for appointments, sometimes verbally or even physically abused by part-time soldiers'. Calling again for the IRA to abandon its campaign of violence and pursue its aims through the political process, the Archbishop stressed that there would be no need for military patrols, checkpoints, interrogation of civilians or house searches, if it were not for their violent activities.

These conflicting views of security, and the UDR provide yet another reminder that the rosy picture promoted by the British government and the military authorities is a long way from reality and that, despite the dedication, bravery and sacrifice of its soldiers, they still face a major task in demonstrating convincingly that the UDR is, as Roy Hattersley promised on its formation, an instrument for peace in Northern Ireland.

Appendix The Government's

Security Policy in Northern

Ireland – November 1990

Constitutional Position

1.   Northern Ireland is part of the United Kingdom because
that is the will of the majority of people who live there. It will
not cease to be a part of the UK unless that situation changes.
Majority desire for a change in status clearly does not exist at
present. There is no reason to expect this to alter in the
foreseeable future.

Aims and Objectives

2.   The government's aims are:
   a.   to maintain the rule of law
   b.   to ensure that all the people of Northern Ireland are
        free to express their political opinions without inhibi-
        tion, fear of discrimination or reprisal
   c.   to defend the democratically expressed wishes of the
        people of Northern Ireland against those who try to
        promote political objectives, including a change in the
        status of Northern Ireland, by violence or the threat of
        violence
   d.   to create in Northern Ireland the condition for a just,
        peaceful and prosperous society in which local people
        can exercise greater control over their own affairs.

3.   So that these aims can be achieved, it is the first priority of
the government in Northern Ireland to eradicate terrorism,
from whichever section of the community it comes. There is no

acceptable level of violence and, for so long as violence continues, it will be met with a firm and resolute response.

Strategy

4. To this end, the government will:
   a. ensure that the police, supported by the armed forces, have the resources they need to undertake their difficult and dangerous work on behalf of the whole community
   b. provide a legal framework within which the security forces can act to defeat terrorism
   c. cooperate closely on security with the government of the Republic of Ireland
   d. seek to isolate the terrorists from the communities within which they operate.

5. The government will implement this strategy with total commitment until terrorism has been defeated in Northern Ireland and the rest of the United Kingdom.

6. In parallel, the government will implement effective measures in the political, social and economic fields, designed to promote equality of treatment, economic well-being and stable democratic institutions. These measures will help create a climate in Northern Ireland in which peaceful political development can take place, thereby complementing and reinforcing the government's security strategy.

7. In accordance with this strategy, which is endorsed by the Chief Constable of the Royal Ulster Constabulary and the General Officer Commanding the Armed Forces in Northern Ireland:
   a. the government is determined that terrorism will be defeated through the evenhanded and energetic enforcement of the criminal law.
   b. the police will continue to take primary responsibility for the prevention, investigation and securing evidence

for the prosecution of crime, including terrorist crime. The armed forces will act in support of the police, but only where and when the security situation makes it necessary.

c.   wherever and whenever possible, the police will operate without military support, in accordance with the goal of restoring normality, and with the ultimate aim that all military support to the police should be dispensed with when the security situation permits.

d.   anti-terrorist legislation will be kept under review, to ensure that it is appropriate to the prevailing security threat. It will continue to strike a balance between providing the RUC and armed forces with the legal means they need in order to protect the community effectively, and at the same time providing appropriate safeguards for individuals. When the need for a particular provision no longer exists, it will be repealed or allowed to lapse, as a step towards greater reliance on the ordinary criminal law.

e.   the police and armed forces will continue to be governed by the legal principle of using only such force as is reasonable in the circumstances in preventing crime and arresting offenders.

f.   members of the police and armed forces, like all other citizens, will continue to be subject to the law. If members of the security forces break the law, they will themselves be liable to prosecution.

g.   the public have a right to expect the highest standards of behaviour from police officers and members of HM forces. Activity or actions falling short of those standards will never be condoned. The government hopes that anyone who believes that they have a genuine cause for complaint about the conduct of a police officer or member of the armed forces will use the procedures which exist for the investigation of such complaints.

8.   The government recognises that, to be fully effective, the actions of the police and armed forces against terrorism in Northern Ireland require the support of all sides of the community. The actions of the security forces must, therefore, at all times be such as to create and maintain confidence in their integrity and professionalism, as well as in their operational effectiveness.

9.   The government calls on men and women of goodwill from both traditions in Northern Ireland to cooperate with the security forces as they carry out their duty to protect the community. Such cooperation may include accepting the inconvenience which may result from security force operations against terrorists and reporting crime, including terrorist crime, to the police.

10.   The government believes that confidence between the community and the police and armed forces can best be achieved if both traditions are properly represented in the locally recruited forces. Hence the government believes that all those who recognise the importance of building and retaining that confidence have a duty to encourage members of both traditions to cooperate with and to join those forces.

Index